KU-329-482

The Partnership Principle

New Forms of Governance in the 21st Century

Alfred Herrhausen Society
for International Dialogue

Editors: Susan Stern
Elisabeth Seligmann

Archetype
Publications

London

First published 2004 by Archetype Publications Ltd.

Published and distributed by:
Archetype Publications Ltd.
6 Fitzroy Square
London W1T 5HJ

www.archetype.co.uk

Tel: (+44 207) 380 08 00
Fax: (+44 207) 380 05 00

Alfred Herrhausen Society for International Dialogue
A Deutsche Bank Forum
www.alfred-herrhausen-society.org

Editors: Susan Stern, Elisabeth Seligmann

Coordination: Maike Tippmann, Christiane Girg

Translation: Kathleen Cross

The Alfred Herrhausen Society is grateful to Thorsten Benner,
Lyn Corson and Igor Reichlin for their editorial support.

ISBN 1-873132-84-0

British Library Cataloguing in Publication Data
A catalogue record for this book is available
from the British Library

© Alfred Herrhausen Society for International Dialogue
Cover: Schaper Kommunikation, Bad Nauheim

All rights reserved. No part of this publication may be reproduced,
stored in a retrieval system, or transmitted in any form
or by any means, electronic, mechanical, photocopying, recording,
or otherwise, without the prior permission of the publishers.

Printed in Germany

Table of Contents

Table of Contents

The Art of Tackling Issues: Pooling Know-how

Table of Contents

Josef Ackermann

The Partnership Principle

The 21st century opens in twilight and obscurity
Eric Hobsbawm

At the end of his book *Die Geschichte der Staatsgewalt* (The History of State Power), Wolfgang Reinhardt comes to the conclusion that the classic European nation-state has become too small to cope with the problems facing the world today. He speaks of an unfinished phase of transition full of dynamic potential, the outcome of which will be characterised by stability, even if nobody can precisely predict what it will be.

Whatever strategies individual states undertake – be it implementing measures at national level or cutting themselves off from the outside world – they cannot protect themselves from the economic crises that are often sparked by new viral diseases, terrorism or confrontation between different religious or cultural groups, exported to many countries in the wake of migratory movements. As a result, it is becoming increasingly difficult for people in a particular country to identify where responsibility for these problems lies – all they can see is a state devoid of any capacity to exercise authority.

Which new forms of governance are emerging in the twilight era of nation-state sovereignty? This is the question the Alfred Herrhausen Society seeks to address this year. How can society regain control over circumstances that no longer lie within the influence of states acting in isolation, and which, as a host of disasters indicates, seem to be slipping out of their grasp?

One way in which states are attempting to regain sovereign control over such circumstances is by voluntarily renouncing their own sovereignty and delegating authority to suprastate institutions. With the support of representatives from international civil society, they are forming partnerships based on shared responsibility – 'temporary alliances' – within international organisations; in this way, it is no longer the sovereign state but rather a broader alliance that is seen to be responsible for addressing the problems at hand. People now know where responsibility lies and from whom they can expect appropriate action. Ordinary citizens can influence indirectly how this responsibility is carried out, either through their government or through an NGO. The global media are also taking on an increasingly important monitoring role.

With its failure to agree on a first draft of a constitution, the European Union has learned through bitter experience that partnerships based on shared responsibility amount to more than merely getting the best deal for individual countries. Focusing only one's own concerns to the exclusion of others' interests is no way to bring about partnership based on shared sovereignty.

The same experience applies equally to large companies, which have long since crossed the boundaries of the nation-state and, like the latter, have become exposed to problems on a global scale. Corporations operate in economic zones that are larger than nation-states – larger even, indeed, than state confederations. This inevitably entails an encounter with different values in those places where businesses have their operations, something that can only be turned into a positive factor if the corporation concerned is prepared to learn from different societies and to mediate between them. Being capable of learning and mediating in global contexts constitutes a core competency and a prerequisite – not only for corporations – for establishing new forms of governance in the 21st century. These two elements give rise to understanding and mutual tolerance.

However, partnerships based on shared responsibility acquire legitimacy only if they are able to make a perceptible contribution towards improving the lives of large numbers of people. Legitimacy does not grow out of the power to obstruct, something on which many NGOs pride themselves.

Partnerships based on shared responsibility have proved to be particularly successful – in combating diseases, for example – when they have involved the participation of states, international organisations, companies and representatives of civil society. Indeed, they *have* to be successful, and not only in combating disease. If they are not, the world will fall back into a myriad factions all pursuing their own special interests. And what we observe today of 'failing states' could, in some parts of the world, turn into 'failing continents'. Millions of people would feel completely powerless as a result, and this certainly does not offer fertile ground for modern governance. The emergence of modern states that are capable of forming alliances depends on the existence of mature citizens rather than powerless subjects.

Such potential partnerships may be unconventional and many are certainly yet to be discovered, but any dividend earned from their success will be manifested in improvements to the economic, cultural and social situation of many countries. Economic growth can only occur in stable political and cultural conditions. These in turn cannot be achieved without a minimum of economic prosperity.

Any society going through a period of transition in which the old is no longer relevant and the new is only dimly perceived will not emerge from it without experiencing political conflict. But the populist temptation to flee to safety from developments taking place outside our own country, to allow transformation to drift past us, merely serves to slow down the changes that are necessary if we are to remain in control of the conditions in which we live. Only when societies participate in shaping the changes that are occurring are they in a position to enable others to do the same.

Recognising that such a period of transition now exists, the Alfred Herrhausen Society has chosen to take up the topic of partnerships based on shared responsibility, attempting to help shape the process of international debate about new forms of governance in a world filled with different values. We may not yet be able to come up with any definite answers, but perhaps we will be able to find some new pieces of the puzzle – through our conferences, the annual colloquium and the present volume – so that the obscure and in part still unfamiliar picture of a new form of governance can take shape more quickly.

Josef Ackermann

Josef Ackermann was born in Switzerland in 1948. Spokesman for the Board and Chairman of the Group Executive Committee of Deutsche Bank AG, Frankfurt am Main since 2002. Board Member of Deutsche Bank AG since 1996. Member of the Crédit Suisse Executive Board from 1990, President of the same from 1993.

The Art of Governancing: Becoming Pragmatic Bedfellows

Good governance requires a pooling of skills and capacities from a range of social sectors to create public value. Convincing people with different and often seemingly opposed interests that they should cooperate to create such public value is a mammoth task. And yet, there are many actors from different sectors around the globe practising the fine art of governancing and driven by an enlightened self-interest, persuading their fellows that timely and focused cooperation is necessary for survival in a global era. To create public value, however, partners must learn to trust each other; they must be accountable, legitimate and transparent. A tall order in this complex world!

The Global View

John Ruggie

Marriages of Convenience – But Marriages Nonetheless

An Interview

Partnerships for the future. How is the world going to be governable and how can people come together to make it work?

We are living through one of those moments that macro-historians describe as conjunctural, meaning a time when various large social forces intersect and produce discontinuities at different levels of social organization. It's hard to disentangle those moments when you're living through them – it's much easier in retrospect: 'Oh yes, of course, this was caused by A, that by B and so on.'

One obvious conjunctural force with which we've experienced some difficulty in the last year is the extraordinary accumulation of power in one country, the United States – not only military but also economic, social, and cultural power. By definition, that sort of asymmetry is bound to ripple throughout the system and create friction. Secondly, we're faced with the realization that we've created a system of global economic exchange, global communication and increasingly integrated transaction-flows on the one hand, and yet on the other hand, we have a highly fragmented global political structure. As a result, I think we are beginning to experience at the global level what we in the industrialized countries experienced in the early part of the 20th century: namely, that a radical disjuncture between economic forces and political forces can be very destabilizing.

Thirdly, there are some fundamental normative changes taking place in the world today. The impact of certain universal values in the realm of human rights, for example, has been much more pronounced than anyone would have thought 10 to 15 years ago.

To what extent is this due to the activities of NGOs and civil society?

I would trace it back to the Nuremberg Trials. They forced an awareness of individual responsibility and culpability that helped to give rise to the human rights movement. That agenda was pushed by the US – even as the US Congress continually sought to exempt the US for reasons of domestic racial practices from international human rights instruments. But it has put down much deeper roots. When I joined the UN, people beyond Mary Robinson's shop were still feeling apologetic about making universal arguments. Three years later that was conventional wisdom.

A fourth area of fundamental change is the discovery that it is increasingly beyond the capacity of any single sector of society to respond effectively to the magnitude and complexity of today's challenges. So today, governance cannot simply mean that which governments do. Increasingly, governance involves drawing on the skills and capacities of different social sectors and actors, and getting them to pull in the same direction for the sake of creating public value.

So there are at least four or five of these major historical changes that all happen to be bumping into each other at the same time, causing us academics grief because we can't keep up with them. At the moment, a great deal of the creativity lies with the practitioners on the ground.

Who are the practitioners on the ground?

That depends on the area you're talking about. Take the example of health. I've been directing a project this past year with colleagues in the Harvard Public Health School and the Business School on HIV/AIDS in heavily impacted countries. We've focused on how to make multi-sectoral partnerships work. In this case, the practitioners are the senior health officials of Anglo-American Mining Company, a third of whose work force is infected, and they can't wait for the state to act. The practitioners are Deutsche Gesellschaft für Technische Zusammenarbeit (GTZ) people in Germany, who saw a need to help establish and facilitate partnerships between NGOs, local business and German companies in South Africa, for example. You find practitioners in civil society organizations on the ground, who have the vision and the commitment but not the resources to make things work. And, of course, you have players at the various levels of governments and the international sphere: UNAIDS, the Global Fund, the Global Business Coalition, and so on. We rolled out a set of partnership guidelines at the World Economic Forum in Davos this January. They are particularly useful for the second and third movers but less so for the first movers because they are the ones who invented the practice. They identify good practices and then pass that information on to others trying to grapple with the challenges. I think that model is increasingly true of think tanks and academics in a number of these areas, not just HIV/AIDS: work with the first movers and then disseminate what works, while avoiding what doesn't. Obviously, academics contribute to the solutions, but by and large reality is being created on the ground.

17

Who are the first movers, the people who start the ball rolling? What motivates them?

Well, the first movers often have diverse motives. Let's stay with the HIV/AIDS example. For Anglo-American, it was a no-brainer. Because a third of its heavily migrant workforce was infected, they had to do something. But they didn't necessarily have to go as far as they're going – moving right into community-based treatment programs. Something happened along the way. A commitment developed that was no longer purely instrumental – or at least their concept of self-interest became defined in a longer-term, more enlightened fashion than it might have been at the beginning. There is no question, however, that it began through instrumental logic. Another example is Coca-Cola, which is now engaged in providing HIV/AIDS treatment to the employees of its bottling plants in Africa. Their initial motivation was to protect their brand after being seriously embarrassed by activists. It was a question of brand management, reputation management. But neither motivation was true of DaimlerChrysler: only nine percent of their workforce in South Africa was infected versus nearly 30 percent in the case of Anglo-American, and the activists left them alone. And it wasn't true of Heineken either. In both cases, it was the leadership of the companies who decided it was the right thing to do – senior executives had served in Africa at one point or another and knew how much social degradation this disease could, and was likely, to cause.

After the first movers you get various patterns. Let's take climate change. You have the BPs and the Shells going in one direction and becoming strongly supportive of a climate change policy, and in another direction ExxonMobil is fighting against greenhouse gas emission controls. At a certain point, when there's a severe polarization of leaders and laggards, fundamentally there is only one response that will work: the state has to do what the state is there to do, i.e. it has to provide a relatively level playing field and get involved in more traditional regulatory action.

But what if the state is unwilling to step in? I'm thinking of the United States and Kyoto.

Then you get to a second level of the game. President Bush nixed Kyoto, and somehow believed that that would put an end to the discussion. Let me mention just a few of the things that happened in the US within a year or so of his saying 'No': first, a number of oil companies lobbied Congress for voluntary controls because they had so much invested in an effective treaty. They had made long-term investments in alternative technologies, and they feared those investments would go down the drain. Secondly, we have a federal system in this country, and environmental activists started working at the level of individual states. Nearly half of all the states have now passed so-called 'Sons of Kyoto' legislation aimed at establishing state-based regulatory frameworks. This will drive industry crazy because they could end up with 50 individual regulatory standards. If movement in that direction were to succeed, they would start to agitate for uniform federal standards – which, of course, are precisely what environmental groups want. The insurance industry has gotten into the picture, led not by an American but a Swiss company. Out of the blue, Swiss Re caught everybody's attention by sending out notices to firms for which it provides liability coverage for officers and board members saying, essentially: We're increasingly concerned about how effectively you as a company are managing your climate change exposure risk, so we want to know what your policies are for mitigating those financial risks. If you have no such policies, we may have to reconsider premium rates and perhaps even coverage.

Pension funds are increasingly becoming involved. Recently, treasurers of individual US states and municipalities – in all about 30 worth about a trillion dollars in pension funds – met at the UN to discuss climate change and how it might affect the pension holdings of the City of New York, the State of New York, and the State of California. Some of their money is invested in energy-intensive companies, and those funds might be subject to considerable risk if some of the more negative consequences of climate change were to occur.

An example that kept cropping up during the discussion was that of asbestos: pension funds with investments in companies associated with asbestos lost their shirts. And asbestos lawsuits are nothing compared to the possible magnitude in the area of climate change. So you've got directly affected oil companies; you've got insurance companies; you've got pension funds – and individual states are getting in on the act. On top of that, the northeastern states are suing the federal government. In short, the battle didn't end when President Bush said no to Kyoto; it escalated.

Sooner or later, the balance of power and the incentive structure are going to shift considerably for any administration. This is politics of a sort that we are used to in our country. It's a multilevel game because of the federal system. But increasingly, these processes are becoming transnationalized. The environmental movements are transnationalized – Swiss Re is a Swiss company, but it insures American firms. Increasingly, you have global platforms and transnational networks through which pressure is applied. So the Bush administration, in the end, will look like the little Dutch boy and the dykes – shove your finger in one hole and water comes out another. Borders are so porous these days that even the most powerful country in the history of the universe can't pretend it's going to stop social responses to climate change.

How will all this play out in Asia – in China, for example?

It's different there, of course. Recently, I had a really interesting conversation on HIV/AIDS with a senior Chinese official in Beijing. In the past, the Chinese didn't like to talk about this subject, particularly with foreigners. The meeting was part of a series of workshops we were holding in Asia on our HIV/AIDS-partnership guidelines during which the senior official presented statistics that were much more accurate than those that had been made public. The Chinese announced to us what they then made public a week later, namely that they were going to start treatment programs for the very poor who couldn't afford it themselves. We persuaded them to agree to issue a statement encouraging the private sector to get involved. But then we ran into a couple of roadblocks, one of them being the issue of condom distribution, particularly to prostitutes. The senior official said: 'Well, you know, prostitution is illegal. If the state distributes condoms to prostitutes, it is endorsing an illegal activity.' And I said: 'Well, you've got two problems. One, AIDS is a sexually transmitted disease, and if you can't come to grips with that fact, you're going to have a hard time coping with the epidemic. But secondly, you have a problem because of your exclusive reliance on the state. In the US prostitution is also illegal, and the state does not distribute condoms. But we have civil society organizations that do. So it would be in your interests to allow for the flourishing of certain kinds of civil society activity precisely to help resolve these kinds of moral dilemmas, where the state cannot do the "wrong" thing'. This led to a very interesting discussion. It all comes down to the trade-offs you have to make if you're committed to coming to grips with some of these issues.

The foreign corporate sector in China is becoming increasingly involved with AIDS because they are being pressured from elsewhere. They've seen what has happened in South Africa, they've learned from Thailand. They want the Chinese state to tell them they can get involved in China. The Chinese firms are not engaged yet, and that's the next challenge for these multi-sectoral initiatives. The long and the short of it is that the situation is different in China because

21

China has such a different political system. But to switch back to the pollution issue: Beijing is horribly polluted, and the Chinese are fully aware of it. They recently announced that they were adopting fuel efficiency standards, or emission standards, that are on a par with Western standards; we'll see. The Chinese have also developed sophisticated models of how regional and global climatic phenomena interact with each other; they are beginning to understand what could happen to China – and they don't like it. Although China may not be moving as fast as ideally we would want it to, there's a lot happening. Once the Chinese put their minds to something, they can usually figure out a way to get it done.

So is Asia a concern? Of course it's a concern. But it isn't as though nothing is happening, and again transnational networks have a role to play. Foreign firms are very important. Linkages with foreign science academies are important. Obviously, the character of trisectoral partnerships has to differ, depending on local circumstances – there's no cookie-cutter formula that can be applied. But increasingly the phenomenon is a general one because of the pressures of real life unless, of course, you have a government that is so corrupt that it doesn't care at all. There are no such partnerships in Zimbabwe for obvious reasons – or in Burma.

Would you say a few words about the Global Compact? Is it attempting to set standards for companies to live up to?

The Global Compact is based on a set of universal principles derived from UN conventions or declarations in the area of labor standards, human rights and the environment. Translating those principles into certifiable standards has never been the ambition of the Global Compact. It was never intended as a regulatory arrangement. It's a platform for engagement and for dialogue, and it's an increasingly effective bridge between corporate social responsibility activities and development. Half of the 1200 companies currently in the Compact are in developing countries. And the Global Compact has had country rollouts in nearly 50 countries, many of them in the developing world. The appeal there is not so much to adopt standards – every country has its labor laws. The challenge is to try to figure out ways of bridging the three sectors in a principled way, around the nine principles of the Compact. Setting standards is easy. It's developing the capacity to move in the right direction, or the willingness to move in the right direction that is difficult; getting companies to understand that social expectations about the precise role of a company are changing. Society and government look increasingly to business to work in partnership to solve large-scale social problems. But at the end of the day, there is no substitute for effective governance.

Thank you.

The conversation was conducted by Susan Stern

John Ruggie
John Ruggie was born in Graz, Austria, in 1944. Director of the Center for Business and Government at the Kennedy School of Government at Harvard University; former Assistant Secretary-General of the United Nations; principal architect of the Global Compact. Recently appointed as Kofi Annan's special advisor on the Global Compact.

Anne-Marie Slaughter

The Power and Legitimacy of Government Networks

Global governance is here, but it is more than most people think it is. It is governance through a collection of nation-states that communicate via presidents, prime ministers, foreign ministers, and the United Nations. Non-governmental organizations (NGOs) and corporations also participate in various ways. But a core part of the infrastructure of global governance – typically overlooked or ignored – is a complex global web of 'government networks'.

The European Union has pioneered this new form of 'transgovernmental' governance, creating networks of ministers, judges, and legislators to govern the EU polity and economy. On the global stage, however, it is the United States that has more frequently advocated regulation of areas such as competition policy or the securities industry through networks of national officials rather than through more traditional forms of international organization. Europeans may simply not recognize what they have created, or they may mistrust its wider application without the deeper treaty-based commitments that bind EU members. Alternatively, many EU citizens may be far more inclined to see the flaws in their own institutions – the widely proclaimed 'democracy deficit' – than the virtues.

Regardless, governance by government network has gone global. Government networks are often still fledgling in many areas. They span the globe or particular regions of the globe, but do not include all countries. Their effectiveness is more asserted than demonstrated; their legitimacy is often questioned. Their potential uses have only begun to be exploited. But they are a powerful tool for addressing global problems without the political or logistical nightmares of global government.

What are government networks?

Government networks are networks of national government officials who come together on a regular basis to exchange information, coordinate activity, and adopt policies to address common problems on a global scale. In the global economy, networks of finance ministers and central bankers have been critical players in responding to national and regional financial crises. The G8 is as much a network of finance ministers as of heads of state; it is the finance ministers who take key decisions on how to respond to calls for debt relief for the most highly indebted countries. The finance ministers and central bankers hold separate news conferences to announce policy responses to crises such as the East Asian financial crisis in 1997 and the Russian crisis in 1998. The G20, a network specifically created to help prevent future crises, is composed of the finance ministers of 20 developed and developing countries. More broadly, the International Organization of Securities Commissions (IOSCO), emerged in 1984. It was followed in the 1990s by the creation of the International Association of Insurance Supervisors and a network of national and international officials responsible for financial stability around the world called the Financial Stability Forum.

Government networks have also been at the forefront of efforts to assure global security. In the wake of September 11th, public attention has focused primarily on the military campaigns initiated by the US in a self-proclaimed war on terrorism, but networks of financial regulators working to identify and freeze terrorist assets, of law enforcement officials sharing vital information on terrorist suspects, and of

25

intelligence operatives working to preempt the next attack have been equally important. Indeed, the leading expert in the 'new security' of borders and container bombs (Stephen Flynn) insists that the domestic agencies responsible for customs, food safety, and regulation of all kinds must extend their reach abroad through reorganization and much closer cooperation with their foreign counterparts. And after the US concluded that it did not have authority under international law to interdict a shipment of missiles from North Korea to Yemen, it turned to national law enforcement authorities to coordinate the extraterritorial enforcement of their national criminal laws.

Beyond economic and security affairs, networks of national officials are working to improve environmental policy across borders. Within the North American Free Trade Agreement (NAFTA), US, Mexican, and Canadian environmental agencies have created an environmental enforcement network which has enhanced the effectiveness of environmental regulation in all three states, particularly in Mexico. Globally, the Environmental Protection Agency (EPA) and its Dutch equivalent have founded the International Network for Environmental Compliance and Enforcement, which offers technical assistance to environmental agencies around the world, holds global conferences for environmental regulators to learn and exchange information, and sponsors a website with training videos and other information.

These networks are most concentrated among regulators, but government officials from other branches of national governments are also joining in. National judges are exchanging decisions with one another through conferences, judicial organizations, and the Internet. Constitutional judges increasingly cite one another's decisions on issues from free speech to privacy rights. Bankruptcy judges in different countries negotiate mini-treaties to resolve complicated international cases; judges in transnational commercial disputes have begun to see themselves as part of a global judicial system. National judges are also interacting directly with their supranational counterparts on trade and human rights issues.

Finally, even legislators, the most naturally parochial government officials due to their direct ties to territorially rooted constituents, are reaching across borders. International parliamentary organizations have been traditionally well meaning but ineffective. But today national parliamentarians are meeting to adopt and publicize common positions on the death penalty, human rights, and environmental issues. They support one another in legislative initiatives and offer training programs and technical assistance.

All these networks are 'horizontal' in the sense that they link national government officials across national borders. But increasingly close ties also exist between supranational officials – judges, regulators, legislators – and their domestic government counterparts. These are vertical government networks. Whereas the traditional model of international law and international courts assumed that a tribunal such as the International Court of Justice (ICJ) in the Hague would hand down a judgment applicable to 'states', and up to 'states' to enforce or ignore, the EU legal system devolves primary responsibility for enforcing European Court of Justice (ECJ) judgments not onto EU 'member states', per se, but on the national judges of those states. Another version of a vertical judicial network, operating on a global scale, is the jurisdictional provisions of the statute establishing an International Criminal Court (ICC). Under this system, national courts exercise primary jurisdiction over cases involving genocide, war crimes and crimes against humanity, but must cede power to the ICC if they prove unable or unwilling to carry out a particular prosecution. Beyond judges, the EU is also pioneering a vertical administrative network between the antitrust authority of the European Commission and national antitrust regulators that will allow the Commission to charge national authorities with implementing EU rules in accordance with their particular national traditions. **27**

These vertical networks are enforcement networks. But they can also operate as harmonization networks by bringing national rules and supranational rules closer together. Still other vertical networks are principally information networks. The environmental ministers of the NAFTA countries, for instance, benefit by working with the Commission on Environmental Cooperation (CEC), a NAFTA supranational institution charged with gathering information on environmental enforcement policies and compiling an informational record of complaints of non-enforcement by private actors. This is an attempt to enhance enforcement through the provision of information. Similarly, the EU is beginning to create Europe-level 'information agencies', designed to collect and disseminate information needed by networks of national regulators. Such agencies can also provide benchmarks of progress for their national counterparts against agreed global or regional standards.

Are they effective?

It is one thing to identify the existence of government networks; it is another to demonstrate their actual contribution to the ill-defined but essential business of global governance. What do these networks actually do? Can they actually change outcomes? Solve disputes? Facilitate cooperation? Identify and implement solutions to common problems?

There is no single answer to these questions. Each of these networks has specific aims and activities depending on its subject area, membership, and history. Legions of studies and dissertations will be required to examine the impact of specific government networks of specific types of government officials (regulators, judges or legislators) on specific problems or governance issues. Yet it is possible to identify different types and modes of activity and common functions.

Government networks expand regulatory reach, allowing national government officials to keep up with corporations, civic organizations, and criminals. They build trust and establish relationships among their participants that then create incentives to establish a good reputation and avoid a bad one. These are the conditions essential for long-term cooperation. They exchange regular information about their own activities and develop databases of best practices, or, in the judicial case, different approaches to common legal issues. They offer technical assistance and professional socialization to members from less developed nations – whether regulators, judges or legislators.

Government networks lead to the 'regulatory export' (Kal Raustiala) of rules and practices from one country to another. The result can be sufficient policy convergence to make it possible over the longer term to conclude a more formal international agreement setting forth a common regulatory regime. Soft law codes of conduct issued by transgovernmental regulatory organizations, as well as the simple dissemination of credible and authoritative information also promotes convergence. Promoting convergence, however, can also give rise to informed divergence, where a national governmental institution or the government as a whole acknowledges a prevailing standard or trend and deliberately chooses to diverge from it for reasons of national history, culture or politics.

Government networks also improve compliance with international treaties and customary law. Vertical enforcement networks do this explicitly and directly by providing a supranational court or regulatory authority with a direct link to a national government institution that can exercise actual coercive authority on its behalf. Equally important, however, are the ways in which technical assistance flowing through horizontal networks can build regulatory or judicial capacity in states where the spirit is willing to enforce international legal obligations but the infrastructure is weak.

Finally, government networks can enhance existing international cooperation by providing the mechanisms for transferring regulatory approaches that are proving increasingly successful domestically to the international arena. Most important is regulation by information, which allows regulators to move away from traditional command and control methods and instead provide individuals and corporations with the information and ideas they need to figure out how to improve their own performance against benchmarked standards. This approach is gaining popularity in the US, is increasingly prevalent in the EU, and is being tried at the UN. Government networks create regional and even global transmission belts for information that can readily expand to include as many nations as can usefully participate. Moreover, government networks are the ideal mechanism of international cooperation on international problems that have domestic roots, as they directly engage the participation and the credibility of the individuals who must ultimately be responsible for addressing those problems.

These different functions can be independently assessed and evaluated in terms of their contributions to specific outcomes. What we find may tell us as much about the nature of contemporary problems and the changing organization of society in many parts of the world as it will about government networks. The extraordinary complexity and uncertainty of many of the problems we face, combined with possibilities for rapid regional and even global communications, may mean that the things networks are good at – exchanging information, collective brainstorming, experimentation in different contexts – is exactly what is needed. That does not mean that government networks are effective at addressing global problems of all kinds at all times. It is far more likely that they will often be most effective when combined with more traditional types of international and national institutions. But we should ultimately be able to make far more nuanced judgments about what institutional mechanisms are most effective for addressing what kinds of problems.

Are they legitimate?

The legitimacy of government networks is deeply intertwined with the question of effectiveness. First, the more effective these networks are at delivering satisfactory outcomes to the greatest number of people, the more legitimate they are (outcome legitimacy). However, dissatisfied customers will raise issues of accountability and transparency (process legitimacy). Indeed, such concerns are already on the table.

Some observers see government networks as promoting global technocracy – secret governance by un-elected regulators and judges. Others fear that the informality and flexibility of networks is a deliberate device to end-run the formal constraints imposed on global governance by traditional international organizations with representation rules, voting rules, and elaborate negotiating procedures. Without these constraints, critics charge, powerful nations run roughshod over weaker ones. Still others worry more that weak nations will be excluded altogether from powerful government networks. At the domestic level, critics charge harmonization networks with distorting domestic political processes and judicial networks with polluting or diluting national legal traditions. Still others picture government networks as vehicles for special interests – shadowy decision-making forums to which only those who are 'connected' or 'in the know' have access.

In response to these criticisms, I propose a set of potential solutions:

1. Recognize all government officials as performing both a domestic and an international function. Such recognition would mean that national constituents would automati-

cally hold them accountable for their activities both within and across borders.

2. Make government networks as visible as possible. Creating a common website and linking the individual websites of participants in a government network will have the paradoxical effect of making a government network real by making it virtual.

3. Increase the number and activities of legislative networks, both to monitor the activity of regulatory networks and to launch initiatives of their own.

4. Use government networks as the spine of broader policy networks including international organizations, NGOs, corporations, and other interested actors, thereby guaranteeing wider participation in government network activities but also retaining an accountable core of government officials.

5. Promote a menu of domestic political measures designed to enhance the accountability of government networks, depending on the extent to which a particular polity perceives a problem and what it decides to do about it.

Harnessing the potential of government networks

In addition to such measures, the ultimate legitimacy of government networks is likely to depend far less on their present incarnation than on the ways in which the hypothetical architects of world order (in reality, a vast complex of politicians, experts, lobbyists, scholars, and activists) choose to design and use them. We have only begun to tap the potential uses of government networks. New uses, of course, are likely to generate new problems. Nevertheless, if these networks are to be a significant component of the infrastructure of global governance, we must be imaginative about what they could do.

For instance, we could harness the capacity of government networks for self-regulation, drawing on the examples of private commercial networks which succeed in enforcing 'network norms' against cheating or other undesirable behavior. If government networks existed not only to address specific regulatory, judicial and legislative problems but also as self-consciously constituted professional associations of regulators, judges, and legislators, they should be able to develop and enforce global standards of honesty, integrity, competence, and independence in performing the various functions that constitute a government.

Government networks could socialize their members in a variety of ways that would create a perceived cost in deviating from these standards. But they could also bolster their members by enhancing the prestige of membership in a particular government network enough to give government officials who want to adhere to high professional standards ammunition against countervailing domestic forces. Just as international organizations from the EU to the Community of Democracies have done, government networks could condition admission on meeting specified criteria designed to reinforce network norms. A particular advantage of selective strengthening of individual government institutions this way is that it avoids the pernicious problem of labeling an entire state as bad or good, liberal or illiberal, tyrannical or democratic. It focuses instead on performance at a much more micro-level, recognizing that in any country and in any government different forces will be contending for power and privilege. It is critical to support those who are willing to practice what they preach in both their own laws and their obligations under international law.

At the same time, these networks could be empowered to provide much more technical assistance of the kind needed to build governance capacity in many countries around the world. They could be tasked with everything from developing codes of conduct to tackling specific policy problems.

They could be designated interlocutors for the multitudes of non-governmental actors who must be engaged in global governance as they are in domestic governance. Vertical government networks could similarly be designed to implement international rules and strengthen domestic institutions in any number of ways. How well will they do? We cannot know until we try.

Finally, self-consciously constituted government networks could acknowledge the power of discussion and argument in helping to generate high-quality solutions to complex problems. For certain types of problems, vigorous discussion and debate is likely to produce the most creative and legitimate alternatives. In addition, government networks constituted this way could harness the positive power of conflict as the foundation of lasting political and social relationships. This understanding of conflict is familiar within democratic societies; it is only within the world of diplomacy, where conflict can escalate to fatal dimensions that conflict per se is a danger if not an evil. Among disaggregated government institutions, national and supranational, conflict should be resolved, but not necessarily avoided. It is likely to be the long-term engine of trust.

Robert Keohane has argued that globalization creates potential gains from cooperation if institutions can be created to harness those gains. However, as he points out, institutions themselves are potentially oppressive and tyrannical. The challenge facing political scientists and policymakers at the dawn of the 21st century is to discover how well-structured institutions 'could enable the world to have a "new birth of freedom"' (Keohane). In this context, a world order based on government networks, working alongside and even in place of more traditional international institutions, holds great potential. It is up to us to ensure both effectiveness and legitimacy.

For more detail, see: Anne-Marie Slaughter, A New World Order *(Princeton University Press, 2004).*

Anne-Marie Slaughter

Anne-Marie Slaughter was born in 1958. Dean of the Woodrow Wilson School of Public and International Affairs. Degrees from Princeton University (BA), Oxford (M.Phil. and D.Phil.) and Harvard Law School. President of the American Society of International Law; frequent commentator on international affairs and legal issues. Most recent book is *A New World Order.*

Thorsten Benner and
Jan Martin Witte

Everybody's Business: Accountability, Partnerships, and the Future of Global Governance

Governance has gone global – and so have questions of legitimacy and accountability. The old 'club model' of international politics as a closed shop involving just governments is defunct. International organisations, non-governmental organisations (NGOs), transnational companies – all play vital roles alongside national officials in global policy-making.

Companies and NGOs increasingly work with governments and international organisations in cross-sectoral networks and partnerships that have emerged as key institutional innovations in the expanding global governance toolbox. From protecting the environment, fighting diseases such as malaria and HIV/AIDS to combating corruption: partnerships can work as coalitions for change, bridging the gap between policymakers, citizens, entrepreneurs and activists seeking to demonstrate that successful collective action is possible in an ever more complex and interdependent world. Yet, such new forms of governance raise many questions regarding their legitimacy and accountability.

With the ranting and raving about the 'democratic deficit' in global governance so often heard in recent years, many partnerships have also come under attack. The Global Compact, for example, initiated by UN Secretary-General Kofi Annan in 1999, is regularly challenged not only by NGOs but also by many governments (particularly from the South) who complain that it does not have any traditional accountability structure or monitoring system in place. Critics assert that the Global Compact amounts to no more than corporate white-washing. Similarly, the many public–private partnerships that were initiated as a result of the World Summit on Sustainable Development in Johannesburg in 2002 have also been criticised for the lack of a rules-based framework or monitoring system. Such partnerships, critics assert, will simply open Pandora's box, providing endorsement for corporations by the UN without accountability. Sceptics argue that it is questionable whether cooperation between what they regard as 'essentially unrepresentative organisations – international organisations, unaccountable NGOs and large transnational corporations' (Marina Ottaway) will contribute to promoting effective and legitimate global governance.

The challenge is clear: partnerships are bound to fail if policy-makers do not find new approaches that address the pressing issues of accountability and legitimacy. Yet, this challenge presents an opportunity. Like a microcosm, partnerships illustrate many of the complex problems of accountability in global governance. They highlight the fact that we need to address the accountability not just of the actors involved in global policy-making processes – it is crucial that the account-ability of policy-making processes is also put to the test. For an effective system of accountability to emerge, we need to develop new approaches to address the dual challenges of actor and process accountability in global governance.

Rethinking accountability in global governance

Standard approaches to accountability do not offer any satis-factory answers to the above challenge.

Traditionalists argue that there is no real problem with accountability in global governance. Actual decision-making capacity, they maintain, continues to rest exclusively with public officials delegated by national governments. To use their preferred idiom, the 'chain of legitimacy' may be stretched, but it is not broken.

Cosmopolitans, in contrast, argue that the current practice of global governance results in the disenfranchisement of citizens as decision-making capacity is effectively transferred to unaccountable international forums. For cosmopolitans, the only solution to this predicament is a thorough democratisation of global policy-making, either through the installation of a world parliament (presumably incorporated in the UN system) or by means of the extension of new forms of direct deliberative democracy that empower the individual citizen to make his or her voice heard in a new order of cosmopolitan democracy.

The *new sovereignists* also regard global governance as a threat to traditional notions of sovereignty and democracy. They advocate a 'putting back into the box' of globalisation that puts a premium on minimising international entanglements.

All three positions are short-sighted: traditionalists hide behind their claim that nothing has changed while the day-to-day reality of global policy-making tells a different story. The cosmopolitan answers to the problem of legitimacy and accountability lack political feasibility and practicality, while the new sovereignists offer little more than a defence of their absolutist views of national sovereignty.

There is a need for 'more imagination in conceptualizing, and more emphasis on operationalizing, different types of accountability' (Robert O. Keohane/Joseph Nye). What does this mean for taking the concept of accountability to the global level? In many respects, partnerships escape traditional mechanisms and conceptions of accountability. They are diffuse, complex and weakly institutionalised collaborative systems that are neither directly accountable to an electoral base nor do they exhibit clear principal-agent relationships.

Devising a pluralistic system of accountability with a multitude of often competing actors, relationships and mechanisms is far more challenging than relying on simple hierarchical command and control conceptions of accountability that used to inform policy-making in a simple state-centric model.

A pluralistic system of accountability needs to rely on checks and balances between different actors and different mechanisms of accountability. We need to complement individual actor accountability of the participants with mechanisms of 'collective accountability'. Robert O. Keohane has pointed out the general problems of devising systems of collective accountability in partnerships: the politics of 'blame avoidance' and the difficulties of assigning responsibilities for failure.

A pluralistic system of accountability

What then are appropriate accountability mechanisms for partnerships? Partnerships can only be as legitimate as the actors involved. For that reason, mechanisms need to be devised that can be used to hold the individual actors in global governance – governments, international organisations, companies, NGOs, etc. – to account.

Reputational accountability is of prime importance for guaranteeing the accountability in and of partnerships. Naming and shaming is a key strategy in this context – one that often works well if the credibility of a company, a brand, a government, an individual or a civil society organisation is on the line. Since not only information but also sanctions have to be part of our understanding of accountability, the loss of credibility is one of the most effective negative sanctioning mechanisms to further accountability in and of partnerships.

Peer accountability is also a crucial component of the accountability puzzle. Partners from a similar sector (e.g.

39

experts, NGOs, business, governments) might be subject to peer accountability by other experts, NGOs, members of the business community, or government representatives.

Finally, partnerships and their participants also have to account for the use of funds for their activities. Mechanisms of *financial accountability* therefore matter a great deal.

How can we put these mechanisms to work? Transparency is the key here. Internal procedures and governance structures have to be open to public scrutiny. This applies to government agencies, international organisations, corporations and foundations as well as NGOs. Information on the internal division of responsibilities, voting rules and procedures – and most of all on funding (sources and spending patterns) – is crucial in this context. The Internet offers a powerful medium with which such information can be made widely available, thereby enhancing the ability to identify inappropriate behaviour.

Often NGOs themselves form advocacy coalitions and networks that in turn participate in partnerships. Whereas some NGO networks regularly question the legitimacy of global policy processes and the actors involved, their own accountability has come under attack. These new demands for transparency about legitimacy and representation are emerging from within NGO networks – and most prominently from NGO critics. Many civil society organisations still do not provide sufficient information about their operations, funding sources and expenditures. Given the rise of gongos, bongos and dongos (NGOs organised by governments, business and donors), financial accountability is a particularly important element.

Certification, self-regulation and codes of conduct will also ensure greater transparency. A good approach might be to use the model of the Global Reporting Initiative (GRI) (which seeks to provide a common umbrella for different approaches of social and environmental reporting of companies) and extend it to NGO certification. Social and environmental reporting mechanisms themselves are important additional sources for information on businesses.

A broad number of codes of conduct, social and environmental reporting mechanisms have sprung up in recent years. These are attempting to establish benchmarks for good corporate citizenship and seek to enhance the accountability of firms not only vis-à-vis their customers but also vis-à-vis the public at large. These reporting requirements and the voluntary implementation of codes of conduct considerably strengthen the accountability of companies. Only the future will show whether the consolidation of reporting criteria and codes of conduct will help to create a more level playing field and improved reporting.

Finally, accountability is required just as much from states as it is from NGOs, companies and international organisations. All too often, some of the greatest impediments to successful partnership are found in inefficient, un-transparent or outright corrupt state institutions and actors.

Process accountability

The accountability of the individual actors involved in a partnership is important; but so is the accountability of the governance process of partnerships if they are to be perceived as legitimate by outside observers and the public at large.

A number of partnerships have made attempts to make sure their work conforms to widely accepted accountability standards, and a first review of the experience to date suggests that the following dimensions of process accountability are important.

Open governance structures
Partnerships require careful design of internal management and governance structures to ensure accountability – to insiders as well as outsiders. The World Commission on Dams

(WCD), for example, established a forum that brought together stakeholders who were not direct participants in the WCD process. The WCD forum served as an institutionalised mechanism to receive feedback and input from these stakeholders who otherwise may have felt shut out of the process. Of course, when such opportunities for participation are established, it is also important to find ways and means to actually respond to and work with the input that is provided. That seems to have been a challenge for the WCD, at least in the early phase of its existence.

Selection of participants

Many initiatives start out by welcoming all those who express an interest in the stated objectives of an initiative. While such an open approach should be encouraged, there are limits as to how many actors can sit at the table. Selection is therefore key. However, these partnership selection processes must be transparent and individual actors need to live up to high standards of transparency and accountability. The criteria for identifying and selecting participants (e.g. competence, representation) should be openly communicated and applied consistently. The WCD, for example, instituted a very elaborate system of participant selection that delegated decision-making to the individual sectors (public, private, and not-for-profit); forums were created in which they negotiated who would (and would not) sit at the table.

Clear terms of engagement

Common goals and guidelines for cooperation, as well as clear timetables and decision-making procedures are not only important for the effectiveness of new forms of networked governance; they are also absolutely critical for their accountability. Many partnerships fail to address these issues in the early phases of their existence. Partnership brokers have proved useful in putting collaborative ventures on the right track, sorting out objectives and the basic rules of the game.

Broad sourcing of knowledge and positions

The inclusion of actors in the core of a network or partnership must of necessity be limited, but additional broad consultations with a variety of stakeholders will ensure a wider sourcing of openness about consultations and debates in collaborative ventures. The GRI, a multi-stakeholder process whose mission is to develop and disseminate globally applicable sustainability reporting guidelines, has convened a variety of open forums during the development phase of its guidelines in order to provide all interested parties with a chance to comment and offer input.

Transparency about sources and uses of funding

Sources and uses of funding in partnerships need to be clearly documented and available to the public. The Forest Stewardship Council, for example, provides very detailed documentation of its internal decision-making structures and work programmes through its website; it fails, however, to provide any details on its financing and use of funds. If public money is being poured into a partnership, it is of particular importance to give the broader public sufficient access to such information.

Performance accountability

Partnerships should also introduce systems for performance-based evaluations. Currently, we often lack even a basic accounting let alone a thorough evaluation of what partnerships do and to what extent they live up to their self-proclaimed goals. Given the development of increasingly sophisticated evaluation tools, it seems reasonable to use them as key references in assessing a partnership's performance.

The drive towards greater accountability in partnerships is met with some resistance from all sides. The private sector, for example, fears overregulation and the imposition of bureaucratic structures on new collaborative ventures. Björn

43

Stigson, the Executive Director of the World Council on Sustainable Development, argues for example that 'Partnerships are voluntary; we go into partnerships because we want to achieve certain objectives – we don't need bureaucratic burdens or monitoring by the UN or otherwise.'

Improving accountability is neither easy nor without trade-offs. For many partnerships, such concerns over accountability crowd an already full agenda. Individual actors have their hands full simply getting the process off the ground and ensuring that it produces tangible results. Accountability is costly – both in political as well as financial terms. At the same time, we need to be acutely aware of the limitations of accountability. A pluralistic system of accountability will not single-handedly resolve the democratic deficit in global policy-making. It can only work if there is an adequate control of the decision-makers at the local and national level. And that, for example, also means a greater involvement of parliaments that are often sidelined by the executive branch.

What can be done?

At this point, it seems clear that any further delay in addressing the pressing issues related to partnerships will inevitably result in a sustained political backlash. NGOs will campaign against what they perceive to be predominantly an effort by governments to abdicate their responsibilities and a shrewd strategy of multinationals to whitewash their reputation. Governments will come under pressure not to participate in any more partnerships. And businesses will go on the defensive, trying to fend off any possible attempts at what they perceive to be a possible overregulation or bureaucratisation of partnerships. Therefore it is all the more important to swiftly develop and implement the 'rules of the game' and evaluation mechanisms for partnerships that will not let governments and international organisations off the hook, that will prevent companies from simply 'free-riding' and also hold NGOs accountable for their contributions.

One way to make the most of these new forms of governance is to create a 'learning forum' to link the work being carried out in cross-sectoral partnerships in think tanks, NGOs, companies, international organisations and public-sector agencies. By bringing together the rigour of academic research and the wealth of experience of practitioners, the learning forum could help to devise ways to scale up partnerships' experience, increase their resources and evaluate their work. It could also provide training services for partnerships supporting social and political entrepreneurs.

Why bother with partnerships? A more appropriate question should be: What other useful mechanisms are available? Traditional intergovernmental diplomacy *alone* has failed to provide solutions to the most pressing problems. Partnerships are certainly no panacea for the world's problems; but neither are they useless or necessarily dangerous. Many partnerships have found innovative ways of dealing with today's governance challenges. Yet we are only at the very early stages of a long experimentation and learning process to better understand what partnerships can and cannot achieve. Currently, the rhetoric surrounding partnerships too often presents a skewed picture: both expectations and criticisms are far ahead of reality. We need a politically astute and empirically informed view of partnerships. Partnerships are about enlightened self-interest, not about charity. Successful partnerships rely on the *different skills, resources, opinions and expertise* of their participants: NGOs do *not* turn into profit centres and companies do *not* become charities.

Our prime concern should be to ensure that partnerships do not degenerate into the equivalent of diplomatic declarations without results. As Jeffrey Sachs reminds us, the key question is whether there is 'real finance behind these goals, behind these high aspirations. If there isn't real financial help

45

and new financial help from the rich countries, these problems are not going to be solved in the poorest of the poor countries, no matter what partnerships are signed.' We need to make sure that action on the ground lives up to the grandiose rhetoric that often emanates from the corridors of power and the major institutions. We need to take G8 countries, the leaders of the World Bank, the UN as well as representatives of multinational companies at their word. Taking the G8 pledge to 'promote innovative solutions based on a broad partnership with civil society and the private sector' seriously means investing *real* resources in new forms of governance to scale up their ability to tackle the most pressing challenges – from security to health and the environment – in an efficient and accountable manner.

If executed appropriately, partnerships can be the wave of the future in global governance. The loss of this timely and useful device for international problem-solving could take us further away from success in tackling the world's pressing problems. Our task is to transform partnership approaches to global governance from a necessary evil to a virtuous institutional innovation. This can be done only if there is political will and dedication on all sides. If we want to improve global governance, accountability is everybody's business. At the same time, global governance is bound to fail without strong societal backing and involvement. All too often in political debates on global issues, oversimplification and parochial notions of the 'national interest' remain unquestioned. In order to move beyond the parochialism of many policy debates we need an active public involved in global public policy-making, holding policymakers to account.

This chapter is part of an ongoing research project 'Exploring and Analyzing the Role of Accountability in Global Governance'.

Thorsten Benner
Thorsten Benner was born in Freudenberg, Germany, in 1973. Associate Director of the Global Public Policy Institute, Berlin; McCloy Scholar at the Kennedy School of Government, Harvard University (2001–03). Has held positions with the United Nations Development Programme (UNDP) and the German Council of Foreign Relations (DGAP).

Jan Martin Witte
Jan Martin Witte was born in Bünde, Germany, in 1974. Associate Director of the Global Public Policy Institute, Berlin; PhD Candidate at Johns Hopkins University's School of Advanced International Studies, Washington DC. Assignments at the Brookings Institution, the World Bank and the United Nations Development Programme (UNDP). Numerous publications on issues of global governance and transatlantic relations.

Michael Ignatieff

New Frontiers in Partnerships

An Interview

What partners does the United States need in the rebuilding of Iraq?

The partner that the United States most needs for nation-building in Iraq is neither Europe nor the UN but the Iraqi people. Moreover, it can't handpick the Iraqis, nor can it rely on Westernized exiles. It has to acknowledge the difficult reality that Saddam Hussein was a nation-builder who used the force of terror. The structure of national identity that he created was maintained through the Baath Party. The pulverization of that nation-building project has left Iraq in smithereens, and the partners who are now available are all very difficult for the US. To start with, the Shia – not just because they are the Shia, but because their political organization is the mosque, the ayatollahs and the imams. Then the Kurds, who were gassed in the previous nation-building project and who are in no mood to settle for anything less than substantial control of their own affairs. Finally, the Sunnis, the former nation-builders, who now feel caught between the other two and are fighting for their political lives. So America has to find a combination of the three, and partnership comes at a lethal cost for these players. You can be killed for supporting the American nation-building project. As a result, until you can guarantee security for your partners, you haven't got a partnership.

Then again, partnership depends on legitimacy. America will have to genuinely transfer power to its partners, and in a time frame that is rapid, but not so rapid that the transfer comes before security is stabilized. So for nation-building to work, it will depend on a partnership between the external nation-builder and the internal ones.

The Europeans see things differently. They believe you can't succeed at nation-building unless the external partners have legitimacy through the UN, and that's true enough; but we need to draw a lesson from the death of Sergio de Mello. For more than a decade, the UN was associated with a sanctions regime seen by many Iraqis under the grip of Saddam to be an instrument of American power and supported by the Europeans. The sanctions policy was a much bigger disaster than we realized. It eroded the legitimacy of the UN. It meant that when people loaded bombs into a truck and drove it towards a UN symbol, there just weren't enough outraged Iraqis to stop them. That bomb attack would never have succeeded had the UN's legitimacy not already been compromised by sanctions. So I tend to be more skeptical than most Europeans about whether the partnership we need has to be authorized by the UN in order for it to be both externally and internally legitimate. I think the real dynamic is straight politics between the people in the green zone in Baghdad, the American occupiers and the Iraqis. That dynamic is crucial. As for the Europeans, what partnership role do they have? I think there's still a strong temptation in Europe to run their politics in Iraq either on the principle of *Schadenfreude,* 'I told you so', or on *ressentiment* towards American power. I don't think politics can be based on either – it has to be based on long-term interests and these must lie in a stable, peaceful and self-governing Iraq, free from American domination, a genuinely free state. Down the road, once Iraq has recovered self-determination sometime in 2005, there will be all kinds of partnerships that Europe can get involved in. In the energy sector, in the security sector, in the rule of law sector – what I see possibilities for standard, technical bilateral partnerships. What I don't see is a partnership in which the fraud called 'the international community' presides over

49

Iraq, and the French and the Germans have an effective say over what happens.

This leads me to a wider issue: the language of partnership in international affairs is mostly described through the language of the international community, and I'm tremendously skeptical of that as a framework. The language completely confuses the normative and the descriptive. Everybody wants an 'international community'. I want one as much as any European, but I very much doubt that such a thing actually exists. It exists issue by issue, problem by problem, but it also shatters problem by problem. The European model of partnership goes as follows: there is something called international law, we all subscribe to it, therefore we're all oriented within the same normative framework. This view doesn't describe the world we live in. In fact we live in a world that Bismarck would still recognize in which nation-states pursue their interests, constrained by international law – to a greater degree than in Bismarck's time, but much less than ideologists of the 'international community' suppose. Moreover, there are international institutions like the UN which coordinate our efforts. Well, you might as well bring back Bismarck, because we're describing a world in which nation-states pursue their interests in ways that I can rationally understand. But the language of partnership purports to build something called an 'international community', which to begin with excludes most of the southern world. What's more, let's face it, the driving impetus behind multilateral internationalism has mostly been the US, and wherever the US doesn't drive multilateral partnerships, they generally don't work. I wish this were otherwise. I wish that the reality were different. But it's not. I am not defending the status quo, I don't like the world being dominated by one power, but I equally don't like a world in which the normative and descriptive are confused and people talk about the 'international community' when it's essentially a cover for a coalition of great power interests.

Where does the private sector – business, civil society – come in?

I invoked Bismarck earlier, but there's something else which makes this a very different world than the world of Bismarck: there's an emerging set of moral universals incarnated in things like human rights, in principles like social responsibility, which you see in the business world and which are related to the emergence of NGOs, the emergence not of a global civil society ('global civil society' is as fuzzy as 'international community') but of a lot of very powerful, well-funded civil society organizations that have power in the international sphere. They have power derived from two sources. First, they are funded by historically unique wealth in the middle classes of the north Atlantic world, so that you have organizations like Amnesty and Human Rights Watch which are multi-million dollar organizations. Highly professional, highly dissident, very effective, very well managed. They are major players and they're here to stay. In the areas of the environment, human rights, humanitarian aid – there's a large constellation of these organizations in the civil society sphere and they are putting unprecedented constraint on states. They are also partnering with states, for example, in the case of the Landmines Treaty, of the Kyoto protocol, of the International Criminal Court – none of these initiatives would exist without the organized moral entrepreneurship of these new players. Neither this internationalized civil society nor formalized moral universals like human rights existed in Bismarck's time.

How does this affect business? It changes the entire framework of global business because if states are the first player, civil society is the second, the corporate sector is the third, and business is under the same dual pressure as are states from the civil society NGOs on the one hand, and the set of ratified moral universals on the other. In the business world, the universals are less ratified and less clear. The International

51

Labour Organization (ILO), labor standards, international conventions on union rights – the moral universals have less structure and traction, but they still have great influence. No big corporation going into employing labor or extracting resources these days can enter these environments believing that their actions are not subject to scrutiny. Every employer and extractor of resources is subject to forms of scrutiny that didn't exist 60 years ago. It's a comparative, not an absolute point; there may be companies that can still get away with quite a lot.

To illustrate what I'm taking about: Unocal in Burma. Unocal tries to build a pipeline and it allies itself with a coercive state. There are issues of forced labor, issues of destruction of the environment, issues of collusive support by a big corporation for a rights-violating regime. It simply blew up in Unocal's face. And what caused it to blow up? Shareholder activism, NGO activism, the modern alliance between the NGOs and the press. It's a matter of attempting to internationalize citizenship, to internationalize scrutiny, to make sure that corporations that are tightly bound by regulations in their domestic environment should constrain their behavior internationally. If you look in the human rights field, the action, the really exciting stuff, is the increasing role of complex new partnerships that are partly adversarial, partly collaborative between big corporations, the NGOs who watch them and the states who want the corporations and their business. A classic example is the Kimberley Process and the monitoring of the conflict diamond trade. De Beers is an international corporation with a semi-monopoly on this commodity – a commodity that has a lot of reputational exposure. That is to say, customers don't need to buy a diamond, they can switch to gold or platinum. So if someone starts hitting your reputation and calling your diamonds dirty, your market can collapse. This kind of power has given NGOs enormous leverage over the years. Companies understand that it is unwise to enter into an adversarial relationship with the NGOs that are subjecting them to scrutiny, that it is much wiser to have a collaborative one. This is more likely to lead to a win–win situation. In the case of De Beers, it proved best to work with Kimberley and come up with a voluntary code for the regulation of conflict diamonds. Some antagonism remains – the new form of partnership is partly antagonistic, partly collaborative. In it, NGOs become loyal oppositions – loyal in the sense that they play by certain rules, but oppositional in the sense that they continually hold these corporations up to scrutiny.

Another example: Angola. Ten percent of the US oil supply either already comes from or will come from Angola. Supplying Angolan oil entails deep-sea oil exploration off the coast, in one of the most wretchedly poor and misgoverned countries in Africa. One of the reasons it's misgoverned is that the revenue stream comes onshore and the Angolan government pipes it directly into Swiss bank accounts. It spends nothing on its own people. A small NGO in London, Global Witness, begins to look through the deals that oil companies do with the Angolan government and discovers there's a tremendous amount of corruption and very little oversight. They get the World Bank involved, they get the international press involved and suddenly all the oil companies in the consortium to develop Angola are under pressure to at least make sure that the revenue stream is transparently disclosed so that all the money they send ashore actually arrives ashore. So here you have an adversarial relationship: Global Witness against the oil companies. They effectively joined together to put pressure on the Angolan government, using the World Bank and other international organizations, to force it to behave. The goal of these adversarial partnerships involving NGOs, corporations and states is transparency, better governance, and investment in the poor of the country. This would never come about in a traditional state-to-state paradigm. States tend to cozy up to their large companies – the French government to Total, the Italian government to ENI/AGIP, **53** the American government to ExxonMobil. But once you put an NGO in there, an NGO which actually has the goods on all of them, it creates a different dynamic.

These partnerships for the future are immensely productive; they're the most exciting partnerships in human rights and development, because if they're sustained, if they're institutionalized, there's less risk of collusion. To prevent collusion in these partnerships between business, government and NGOs, you've got to have loyal oppositions. When the NGO is loyal, it doesn't go around spreading half-truths about the corporation; the corporation doesn't spread half-truths either. They enter into a dialogue and fix their problems. One problem in partnership with business that needs to be frankly acknowledged is that many corporations are very wary about getting involved in loyal opposition relations with NGOs because the NGOs keep raising the bar on reforms. Whatever the companies do is not enough. Deutsche Bank goes through a process of disclosure on Jewish assets. They clear one bar, and then suddenly they find the bar raised.

Oil companies are in the same situation – the bar is always being raised on them. One way to get a partnership to work is to create clear standards of performance from both sides, create a playing field in which when you ask me to deliver, I deliver, it's a deal, it stays a deal and then, as you consolidate that particular deal, you raise the bar together. It's when companies feel that they've had a confidential dialogue with an NGO, a human rights NGO, or an environmental NGO, only to have those NGOs rush to the media and complain about them that they become unhappy. They feel they get no reputational benefit from doing the right thing, only more criticism. Both sides in this dialogue have to be honest and transparent, and prepared to enter into confidential relations that are not collusive or complicit. This is obviously not easy to do, but I do think it's the new frontier. For if corporations wonder why they should talk to a tiny NGO, just two people with a computer in a room in North London, they don't know what's going to hit them.

The Swiss didn't know what hit them on the Jewish issue ... the reputational effects of these scandals can be devastating, so the power of NGOs plus the new set of moral universals is immense. Certainly, this power can be misused. But if you pretend it's going to go away, if you think you can avoid a partnership relationship, you may be well on the way to destroying your reputation or corporation. This is a new frontier where both sides have power and I think corporations have considerable difficulty understanding how power relations have changed. They've got so many assets, they've got 50,000 employees in 26 countries ... they simply don't realize the enormous power that NGOs and this new system of moral universals have in destroying reputations.

You have to have accountability on the NGO side as well as on the company side. Many corporations have good reason to feel burned by their relations with human rights NGOs, environmental NGOs, humanitarian NGOs. They've had to learn to be professional, and it's perfectly possible to have a non-collusive, adversarial relationship that is ongoing, structured by agreements, kept by both sides. Each side keeps the other side honest. That's the key dynamic in the partnership. And if it works, it's the most productive area in human rights, international development and the environment. It's just much more important than state-to-state relations.

A final partnership example: the Chad Pipeline Project. This is a project in which a consortium of banks and oil companies have gotten together to build a $3.7 billion pipeline to carry crude oil 650 miles across neighboring Cameroon to the Atlantic. The oil companies have brought in the World Bank as a moral guarantor. The bank, in turn, has imposed conditions, both on the oil company and on the government of Chad. Together, the partners have begun to write a new charter that requires the Chad government to take some of the revenue stream and develop the country

55

with it instead of buying weapons or palaces. How do you oversee that? There are six or seven major players on one single development issue. But the stakes here are the lives of the Chadian people. If the partners get this right, the Chadian people have better lives; if they get it wrong, the same old nightmare continues.

Thank you.

The conversation was conducted by Susan Stern

Michael Ignatieff

Michael Ignatieff was born in Toronto in 1947. Carr Professor of Human Rights Policy at the Kennedy School of Government, Harvard University and Director of the Carr Center. Recent publications include a biography of Isaiah Berlin; *Human Rights as Politics and Idolatry, Empire Lite: Nation-Building in Bosnia, Kosovo and Afghanistan* and *The Lesser Evil: Political Ethics in an Age of Terror.*

Ernst Ligteringen and Paul Hohnen

A New Issue, a New Partner-ship, a New Tool

Among the various contributions to the advancement of a partnership-based approach to sustainable development made by the 2002 United Nations World Summit on Sustainable Development (WSSD), one in particular invites special attention. This is the reference (in paragraph 17 of the WSSD Plan of Implementation) to the Global Reporting Initiative (GRI) *Sustainability Reporting Guidelines,* the only 'global public policy initiative' to be specifically referenced in the Summit outcomes.

A decade earlier, at the 1992 Rio de Janeiro UN 'Earth Summit', the concept of sustainability reporting did not yet exist. Five years ago, at the 1997 'Rio + 5' Summit, the GRI did not exist. This chapter seeks to explain how the GRI came to be mentioned by leaders of the world's nations at Johannesburg, how it operates, and some of the potential problems and challenges this unique partnership faces over the coming years.

A brief history

The story of the GRI began with the recognition by leading thinkers in the United States that no real or lasting progress would be made towards 'sustainable development' unless (1) all organisations could reach a common understanding of the meaning of the term in relation to their own activities and (2) a framework for measuring and reporting their progress towards this goal could be constructed.

57

At the initiative of the US-based Coalition for Environmentally Responsible Economies (CERES), and in partnership with the UN Environment Programme (UNEP), the GRI began in late 1997 as a project to develop, promote and disseminate a generally accepted framework for sustainability reporting. This was defined as reporting on the economic, social and environmental performance of an organisation, also referred to as 'triple bottom line' reporting. Its mission was to make sustainability reporting as credible, comparable and routine as financial reporting.

Noting the absence of a relevant global institutional framework, and conscious of the potential of partnerships and trust-building experiences in institutional dialogues (e.g. Alternative Conflict Resolution, Participatory Rural Appraisal), the GRI adopted a multi-stakeholder approach as its modus operandi. The motivation was simple: for reporting indicators to be generally accepted as legitimate, both report-makers and report users should be brought together in a process that fostered debate and consensus on which aspects of sustainability performance should be reported, why and how.

From 1998 to late 2001, the GRI worked on a twin-track approach. A multi-stakeholder Steering Committee developed plans for the GRI's governance and organisational structure. In parallel, a number of multi-stakeholder working groups held consultations around the world on the development of the first-ever set of generally applicable sustainability reporting guidelines. The first pilot version of the GRI *Sustainability Reporting Guidelines* was released in March 1999 and revised and reissued in June 2000 following testing and feedback by stakeholders.

In 2002, the GRI was formally established as a new international institution. Highlights of the year included the release of the *Sustainability Reporting Guidelines,* formal recognition by the WSSD, the establishment of a Board of Directors, a permanent secretariat in Amsterdam and the first meeting of the GRI Stakeholder Council. In less than five years, some 150 companies around the world had begun using the GRI's main product, i.e. the *Guidelines*. It was perhaps this rapid progress from an innovative concept to a globally applied framework that led to WSSD endorsement by the world's governments and which prompted UN Secretary-General Kofi Annan to observe that the GRI:

> brings together like-minded actors from all sectors of society in a coalition for change towards greater sustainability, respect for human rights and labour standards. By offering a new framework for corporate reporting, the GRI has a unique contribution to make in fostering transparency and accountability of corporate activities beyond financial matters.

GRI: A process and a product

The GRI is a product-development partnership. It uses a multi-stakeholder process, in which all partners are equal members, to develop generally agreed products that can be used by all stakeholder constituencies. Because it is also a learning forum, discussions on indicators and issues on which agreement is not reached also contribute to learning and the evolution of the product. In short, the GRI's distinguishing characteristics are a *process* and a *product*.

Process

Integral to the GRI multi-stakeholder process from the outset was a commitment to seven core principles:

1. Accountability: the GRI's governance ensures answerability.
2. Adaptability: the GRI is designed for continuous improvement.

3. Balance: the GRI seeks balanced input from the main stakeholder groups.
4. Inclusiveness: the GRI is open to inputs from all interested stakeholders.
5. Independence: the GRI is not beholden to any one stakeholder group.
6. Technical excellence: the GRI leads innovation in sustainability reporting.
7. Transparency: the GRI's activities are open to public scrutiny.

These operating principles are integrated into the fabric of the GRI's governance, structure and procedures at every level. All the GRI institutions comprise representatives from five main constituencies: business, accounting experts, mediating (e.g. academic) institutions, trade unions and non-governmental organisations (NGOs). Participants from all regions of the world, widely recognised as leaders in their respective fields, engage in the GRI in a personal capacity.

Overall direction of the GRI is provided by the GRI Board. The Board is advised on broad policy, and in part, elected by a 60-member Stakeholder Council which in turn is elected by the GRI Organisational Stakeholders, an open-ended body of organisations that choose to sign up in support of the GRI mission. The Board will also receive advice of a more technical nature from a soon-to-be-established Technical Advisory Committee. Finally, ad hoc multi-stakeholder working groups are created to develop specific products.

These different forums all have clear prescribed functions and a limited number of seats at the table to ensure their functional effectiveness. Participants are selected through a broad consultation with the different stakeholder constituencies, aimed at identifying the most knowledgeable parties prepared to engage constructively in a multi-stakeholder dialogue with a predetermined balance between the number of representatives from different stakeholder groups, geographic regions, genders and cultural identities.

Product

At the product level, the GRI is responsible for the strong momentum in the development and adoption of the *Guidelines* which, at the time of writing, are used by well over 350 organisations (mainly corporations) in the preparation of their sustainability reports, a figure that has more than doubled since the launch of the *Guidelines* in 2002.

In addition to the *Guidelines,* the GRI has also developed four additional categories of product: *Sector Supplements* providing additional industry sector specific indicators; *Technical Protocols,* guiding measurement indicators in relation to issues such as water, energy and child labour; *Resource Documents* on specific topics of frequent interest such as HIV/AIDS; and *Complementary Reporting Briefing Documents* on the interface with other global initiatives such as the UN Global Compact and the OECD Guidelines for Multi-national Enterprises.

Any multi-stakeholder partnership faces a diverse range of operational challenges. At the broadest level, such bodies can only be effective if participants take ownership of the process and recognise that the total outcome of their collective efforts will contribute to the furtherance of their individual interests. So why does the GRI continue to attract active engagement from stakeholder constituencies and enjoy increased use of its *Guidelines* and other outputs? What are the main challenges it faces?

Challenges: process

At the process level, the GRI has been largely successful in attracting and maintaining the engagement of a wide spectrum of stakeholders as evidenced by the level of interest expressed in improving the 2002 *Guidelines* and in developing *Sector Supplements*. There is now literally a community of well over a thousand individuals from around the world – from industry, the financial world, academia, professional consultancies, labour unions and NGOs – who have or are taking part in working groups developing one or more of these GRI products.

Choosing the moment

Multi-stakeholder dialogues depend critically on the level of basic trust between the parties at the table: trust that a dialogue can achieve the agreed mission. It is therefore essential that the right moment is chosen for any initiative: too early – e.g. a multi-stakeholder dialogue on a reporting framework for the pharmaceutical industry immediately following bruising global exchanges over pricing of life-saving drugs – and the chances are that the parties will not be ready to trust the potential of a constructive dialogue. On the other hand, choosing a sector which different stakeholder groups would not consider relevant to their current priorities would lead to difficulties in getting relevant players to the table. To be successful, a stakeholder dialogue needs to be relevant to the moment and there needs to be trust in the feasibility of the dialogue.

Staying mission-focused

Stakeholders need to trust that they can work effectively on the agreed mission with the parties at the table. In the GRI's case, stakeholders meet to agree the definition of information that would be relevant for measuring and reporting the impact on sustainability. By definition, the relationships between business, labour unions and social interest groups have a history that pre-dates the GRI and there is always a risk that this might spill over into the GRI dialogue. For example, in a dispute between a company and a labour union, the issue in question may not be directly relevant to the GRI. However, the dispute could still undermine the parties' trust in the feasibility of the GRI dialogue and the future use of the GRI product they are working to develop.

Participants in a multi-stakeholder process need to recognise that a wider set of differences between them will always exist. The challenge is to agree that issues in other arenas can be worked out separately in their own space without inhibiting progress on work in areas of common ground in the multi-stakeholder process.

Who pays for a free 'public good'?

Many of the GRI's 1000+ voluntary collaborators (and their employers who allowed them time off), have a right to feel ownership of the *Guidelines*. The *Guidelines* can be regarded as a 'public good', freely available for use by any organisation that wishes to measure and report its contribution to sustainable development. Consequently, there is a separation between the use of the GRI's products and revenue generation. Beyond its start-up phase, a voluntary partnership such as the GRI needs to develop a sustainable stream of revenue from parties who have a stake in its success. As a result of the lack of an immediately visible return on individual investment and the relative unfamiliarity with the new multi-stakeholder model, the GRI's revenue has not kept pace with the use of its products.

For a voluntary partnership such as the GRI to succeed, stakeholder groups need to be persuaded that there is value in voluntarily using the products, participating in the process and supporting it financially – support at all three levels is vital to the success of the initiative.

Challenges: products

Global or national responses to global problems?

There is a risk that national and regional corporate social responsibility (CSR) policies and measures may undermine existing global initiatives. While there are many international conventions (e.g. ILO, Kyoto) and global initiatives (e.g. Global Compact, OECD MNE Guidelines, GRI, AA-1000) central to sustainable development, these will not be successful if initiatives at the national and regional level are not expressly developed to ensure their full implementation, or are inconsistent with them. Although the WSSD emphasised the importance of adopting a global approach, some national and regional authorities still chose to develop CSR legislation or guidelines that do not optimise the use of existing global tools.

National and regional policymakers have to make a choice when seeking to advance CSR practices in their territories: they can either make their policies subsidiary to global policy initiatives or adopt independent national or regional policies, leaving any harmonisation at a supranational level to a negotiation process between regions and nations. By definition, subsidiary national or regional approaches tend to support and strengthen a consistent and coordinated global approach, while unconnected national or regional initiatives tend to undermine initiatives already agreed or operational at the global level.

The development of disconnected national and regional level policy approaches remains a risk to the GRI and other global CSR initiatives. Fragmentation of the policy framework can confuse users in a globalising world and thereby actually reduce relevance, constrain uptake and increase costs.

Free riders

As mentioned above, the GRI *Guidelines* are a public good, available for use by any organisation free of charge. Among the.many potential 'free rider' problems is the use without acknowledgment of indicators developed by the GRI – judging from reports by some organisations, and guidelines prepared by others, these are being widely used without due recognition. Recognising that sustainability reporting is relatively new, and that some organisations may require time to test and assess the *Guidelines*, the GRI accepts that this practice is in the interests of increased long-term uptake.

Mandatory or voluntary?

The GRI is a voluntary initiative: it is a partnership of the willing who seek to establish best practice and policy in reporting in the global arena. The policy choice between an exclusively voluntary approach and hard or soft regulation or legislation will, in all likelihood, be determined by specific conditions in any specific area. The need for mandatory measures will be felt less where there are high levels of trust, where a strong voluntary ethos exists and where reporting is developing well. In the absence of these conditions, pressures for adoption of a mandatory approach are more likely to develop.

Experience to date seems to indicate that the voluntary adoption of the GRI framework is associated with a strong growth in voluntary reporting. However, should the growth of voluntary reporting stagnate or if the development in the quality of voluntary reporting were to prove inadequate, arguments about the need for a mandatory approach might be expected to gain strength.

Lessons for multi-stakeholder approaches in global policy-making

The potential of the GRI can be assessed at many levels. Like any organisation, the critical element for the long-term success of a multi-stakeholder process is that it should

65

achieve its goals in a cost-effective manner. In this context, the GRI's challenge is to attain its mission of becoming the generally accepted sustainability reporting framework. Early indications suggest that the GRI's model is regarded as successful – whether measured in terms of uptake, use or participation, it is clear that stakeholders are prepared to work together in advancing sustainability reporting. In turn, this reinforces understanding of the potential of transparency and accountability to contribute concretely to sustainable development.

If the GRI continues its record of doubling the number of reporters every year, it will bring closer the time when most, if not all, organisations – corporations as well as governments and other bodies – will use the GRI framework to routinely measure and report their contribution to sustainable development. In this way, the GRI can make a major contribution to raising awareness about the problems of, and solutions to, sustainable development.

Without a means of translating international laws, codes of conduct and standards on sustainable development into everyday language, there is a risk that these will remain unimplemented. The GRI is a powerful tool for helping organisations understand and use these laws, as well as instruments such as the OECD *Guidelines for Multinational Enterprises* and the UN Global Compact.

It is said that an organisation cannot manage what it doesn't measure. The GRI facilitates identification of the risks and opportunities of sustainable development challenges. It is perhaps not surprising, therefore, that feedback from organisations using the GRI for their reporting consistently indicate a high internal benefit felt by both their employees and management. In this sense, the GRI offers a means of unlocking vast organisational potential to acknowledge and respond to sustainable development challenges.

Because the GRI's approach involves learning and adapts to experience, it can encourage a cycle of continuous improvement without which sustainable development is unlikely to be achieved. The synergies of sustainable ecological, economic or social systems cannot be realised unless all social partners are transparent and accountable. Increasingly, sustainability issues are generating complex policy questions which cannot be adequately dealt with in traditional governance institutions. Stakeholder initiatives such as the GRI can play a crucial role in helping to develop, and implement, cost-effective policy responses.

By adopting a partnership approach, the GRI has brought parties together who sometimes find it difficult to relate to each other in existing institutional and political structures. The GRI's multi-stakeholder dialogues have created a space where participants can develop trust and even pride in the utility of their joint effort, and thus improve the overall quality and focus of dialogue about sustainable development.

In doing so, the GRI has demonstrated the potential of mission-focused multi-stakeholder engagement to create new products and innovative partnerships to respond to the policy gaps that have emerged from traditional forms of governance on the issue of sustainable development. At the end of the day, however, the success of multi-stakeholder dialogues will continue to depend on the art of choosing the right issue at the appropriate time, gaining the active participation of a balanced group of key constituencies and achieving government support for their vital contribution.

Paul Hohnen

Paul Hohnen was born in Sydney in 1950. Director of Strategic Development with the Global Reporting Initiative, Amsterdam. A former Australian career diplomat, Director of Greenpeace International's external relations (1993–1999). Since 2000, private consultant to a range of UN, company and NGOs on the advancement of sustainable development.

67

Ernst Ligteringen

Ernst Ligteringen was born in the Netherlands in 1955. Chief Executive of the Global Reporting Initiative (GRI), Amsterdam. Oxfam International's first Executive Director, International Federation of the Red Cross' Director of Program Coordination. Returned to his home country for the GRI assignment after 24 years of work and study in former Zaire, the Dominican Republic, Colombia, the UK and France.

Benjamin R. Barber

Global Governance: Malevolent or Benevolent Interdependence?

Global governance remains the world's most pressing business and its most daunting challenge. Despite almost 60 years of productive common experience, Europe has yet to achieve common democratic governance. The seams in its tacked-together common union are in danger of coming apart – the Swedish 'No' vote on the Euro, the continuing Danish and English skepticism and the complications engendered by the effort to extend the market to Eastern Europe and Turkey. The United Nations, the great hope of the post-Second World War world, remains an unwieldy conglomerate of quarrelling factions and adversarial blocs in which both the First and the Third World feel underrepresented. And the United States, the architect of the new international system that came out of the Second World War, appears to have turned its back on its own creation and in pursuit of security prefers to depend on unilateralism and war rather than on multilateralism and law. In short, as the need for regional and global governance has grown, the likelihood of actually achieving it seems to have diminished.

And yet, and yet! The devastating events of September 11, 2001 that made evident how far the world is from a common peace, also spoke with a vengeance to the reality of a growing global interdependence that makes global governance not only necessary but probably inevitable. For the real lesson of 9/11 points to a common world's ever more common destiny.

Europe learned the lesson of interdependence from the Second World War, if not before, while the Third World, deeply dependent on what happens in the First World, has never harbored any illusions of real independence. But the US, the key to global governance today, has been and remains the world's leading promoter of the idea of independence. After all, 228 years ago, in the belief that liberty and the autonomy of the sovereign nation went hand in hand, America proclaimed its independence. For more than two centuries it has pursued the sovereign ideal as the premise of the rights and social justice in whose name it has striven to become both democratic and free. Speaking not just for itself but for other nations, it has (as President Bush did recently at the UN) insisted that democracy is premised on national liberation and that personal liberty requires national independence.

A little less than 15 years ago, peoples in Budapest, Prague, Warsaw and Moscow reasserted the powerful connection between liberty and independence by declaring their own liberation from the dominion of Soviet communism – reclaiming their liberty by reasserting their right to be self-governing. Yet although today these same nations are pressing to join Europe, in other parts of the world as different as Afghanistan, Liberia, Kosovo and Brazil, nations continue to reassert their sovereign independence from domestic tyranny and foreign imperialism as the condition for the liberty of their people.

With recent history as their tutor, however, nations that have long cherished their independence or recently struggled to achieve it are learning the hard way that freedom, equality, safety from tyranny and security from terror cannot be achieved on the basis of independence alone. That in a world in which ecology, public health, markets, technology and war affect everyone equally, interdependence is a stark reality upon which the survival of the human race depends. That where fears rules and terrorism is met only by 'shock and awe', neither peace nor democracy can ensue. That while we have yet to construct those global institutions that might offer us a benevolent interdependence, we are beset by global entities that impose on us the costs of a malevolent and often anarchic interdependence. That in the absence of a new journey to democratize our interdependence, we may lose the blessings conferred by the old journey to democratic independence.

Where once nations depended on sovereignty alone to secure their destinies, today they depend on one other. In a world in which the poverty of some imperils the wealth of others, where none are safer than the least safe, multilateralism is not a stratagem of idealists but a realist necessity. The lesson of 9/11 was not that rogue states could be unilaterally preempted and vanquished by a sovereign US, but that sovereignty was a chimera – that HIV/AIDS, global warming, international trade, nuclear proliferation, transnational crime and predatory capital had already stolen from America the substance of its cherished sovereignty well before the terrorists displayed their murderous contempt for it on that fateful morning.

The irony is that while sovereignty remains the first principle of international affairs for the US, its reality has already been fatally compromised by the realities of interdependence. So that even as the US refuses to place its troops under foreign commanders and promulgates a preventive war doctrine that gives it the sovereign right to decide when and where and against whom it will wage war, it suffers from an ever weakening sovereignty in other key areas. Despite its global economic hegemony, Washington can no longer prevent a single job or factory or company from leaving the US in the quest for greater profits, cannot stop alien viruses from entering its territory, cannot control financial capital, and cannot prevent intellectual piracy on the Internet. Sovereignty remains a powerful word and the justification for a great deal of what nations do today, but as a reality it has lost much of its potency. Terrorism itself, like all international crime, testifies to the insufficiencies of sovereignty. The US could protect neither the capital of finance   **71** at the World Trade Center nor the headquarters of its vaunted military machine at the Pentagon, despite the fact that the 'invading force' was armed only with box cutters and fanatic zeal. Indeed, the hijackers came from inside the US, not outside, and the 'states that harbored them' prior to the attack were not Afghanistan and Iraq but New Jersey and Florida – so much for sovereignty!

Yet America still seems to prefer to play the Lone Ranger – Gary Cooper in the film *High Noon* in which the sheriff must meet four desperados all by himself on Main Street. Recent events suggest this is a world, however, where only global posses, communities working together, have a chance of succeeding. For interdependence is now our reality and the acknowledgment of interdependence the necessary starting point for prudent foreign policy. After all, terrorists are not nations, and whether or not they are supported by rogue states, they are in effect malevolent NGOs that operate in the interstices of the international system. They use the new transnational networks of finance, telecommunications, transportation and trade to carry out their business across national borders. If the states that confront them cannot use international tools at least as effectively as the terrorists use them, there is little hope that terrorism can be overcome.

Yet while international cooperation is desirable and necessary, it is clear that the obstacles that still confront those who seek new institutions of global governance are as various as they are intractable. The refusal of the US under the Bush administration to negotiate an understanding that might allow it to sign the Landmines Treaty (already ratified by over 140 nations) is an example. The US has good reasons to expect the Treaty signatories to recognize its special responsibilities as a global policeman and the role mines can play in protecting thinly deployed troops. But by the same token, the US has an obligation to work hard to draft a treaty it is able to sign. Some of the same problems face the new International Criminal Tribunal. The US believes with some justification that this new court could end up as a kangaroo court for troops it deploys on behalf of the UN or other peace-keeping missions. But the imperatives of interdependence call for negotiations that will allow the US to join under reasonable conditions rather than obstinate American unilateralism or obstinate international high-mindedness that chooses hypocritically to overlook the special responsibilities shouldered by the US.

In other words, whether it is the Landmines Treaty or the Criminal Court or other obligations such as the Kyoto Treaty on Global Warming or the anti-ballistic missile treaty, the current atmosphere makes the US a stubborn loner and its international interlocutors ineffective suitors for American cooperation. The battle in the UN prior to the war in Iraq was typical of an America too anxious to act without multilateral cooperation and a UN afraid to act at all. This is in part because sovereignty remains the first principle of the UN. It is a congress of nations and, the Secretary-General's Office notwithstanding, represents those nations rather than the people of the world. It is not a 'we the people' but a 'we the nations that represent peoples' organization. The US is quick to play the sovereignty card, but so are the other nations of the UN when their vital interests are at stake or when they believe their interests are better advanced outside rather than inside the General Assembly. Nor is America's recent critic 'old Europe' (in Secretary of Defense Rumsfeld's dismissive phrase) itself free of blame for obstructing international cooperation. Its hypocritical support of agricultural and cultural subsidies for its own afflicted economic sectors, despite its putative adherence to free trade doctrines even as it puts pressure on Third World countries to drop their own trade restrictions, is evidence of this hypocrisy which destroyed the trade talks at Cancun in the autumn of 2003.

Citizens need not await presidents or governments to embrace interdependence and work to construct a civic architecture of global cooperation, however. Indeed, they cannot

73

wait. For the challenge is how to get 'sovereign' political policy to catch up with global realities. The lessons of the above tutorial suggest that global governance must be built bottom up, not top down. That it is more likely to come from transnational civic cooperation and the work of NGOs and economic organizations than from states. This is in any case how democracy is ideally constructed: create a foundation in education, free institutions and citizenship and build a political edifice on top of that foundation once it is settled. In other words, the continuing reluctance of governments to commit in practice to the global governance ideals to which they are committed in theory need not prevent citizens from working towards greater international cooperation.

Global governance will depend in the first instance on global citizenship which in turn will have to rest on the fashioning of a global civil society and civic education. For citizens, whether local or global, are made not born; they are educated and socialized into their roles rather than natural inhabitants of those roles. That was the lesson taught by the American founders when Thomas Jefferson and John Adams both recognized that without educated citizens, the experimental new constitution would never work; that, in James Madison's words, a bill of rights and a constitution were not worth the parchment on which they were written in the absence of educated citizens who could make those documents work in practice.

The challenge today then is to create the foundations for global governance before trying to transform the UN and the Bretton Woods systems into institutional global government. The tools will be technologies such as the Internet – which is already being used by malevolent NGOs (such as al-Qaeda) and international right-wing movements (e.g. the neo-Nazis) – and cooperation among NGOs on the model of the Community of Democracy and Jubilee 2000 (whose aim is to erase Third World debt). Their spirit will be expressed in the new Declaration of Interdependence, promulgated in 2003 and celebrated in a first Interdependence Day festival in Philadelphia and Budapest on September 12, 2003, and to be celebrated again in 2004 in Rome and many other world cities.

The Declaration of Interdependence captures the spirit of civic globalism:

DECLARATION OF INTERDEPENDENCE

We the people of the world do herewith declare our interdependence both as individuals and legal persons and as peoples – members of distinct communities and nations. We do pledge ourselves citizens of one CivWorld, civic, civil and civilized. Without prejudice to the goods and interests of our national and regional identities, we recognize our responsibilities to the common goods and liberties of humankind as a whole.

We do therefore pledge to work both directly and through the nations and communities of which we are also citizens:

- *To establish democratic forms of global civil and legal governance through which our common rights can be secured and our common ends realized;*
- *To guarantee justice and equality for all by establishing on a firm basis the human rights of every person on the planet, ensuring that the least among us may enjoy the same liberties as the prominent and the powerful;*
- *To forge a safe and sustainable global environment for all – which is the condition of human survival – at a cost to peoples based on their current share in the world's wealth;*
- *To offer children, our common human future, special attention and protection in distributing our common goods, above all those upon which health and education depend;*
and

75

- *To foster democratic policies and institutions expressing and protecting our human commonality; and still at the same time,*
- *To nurture free spaces in which our distinctive religious, ethnic and cultural identities may flourish and our equally worthy lives may be lived in dignity, protected from political, economic and cultural hegemony of every kind.*

Interdependence Day and the Declaration of Interdependence (whose promulgation it marks) allow new global citizens to affirm the creative potential of what is for now merely a grim reality. The simple fact is that no American child will ever again sleep safe in her bed if children in Baghdad or Karachi or Nairobi are not secure in theirs. That Europeans will not be permitted to feel proud of liberty if people elsewhere feel humiliated by servitude. This is not because America is responsible for everything that has happened to others or because Europe was once the imperial colonizer of the world, but because in a world of interdependence the consequences of misery and injustice for some will be suffered by all.

Global governance is much more than a utopian dream: it is a necessity of interdependence to which there is no realistic alternative. But for it to emerge, there must first be global civil society and a global citizenry. To create them, bottom up, is the challenge.

Benjamin R. Barber
Benjamin R. Barber is Gershon and Carrol Kekst Professor of Civil Society at the University of Maryland and a director of the Democracy Collaborative. DaimlerChrysler Fellow at the American Academy, Berlin (spring 2002). Publications include *Strong Democracy: Participatory Politics for a New Age, Jihad vs. McWorld* and *Fear's Empire*.

Betty Sue Flowers

The Primacy of People in a World of Nations

'Imagine'

At the end of the First World War, the League of Nations was created – and even though it failed to prevent the Second World War, it formed the basis for a more robust institution to take its place. At the end of the First World War, the United Nations was created – and while it may have had some influence in preventing a Third World War, it seems powerless to resolve the most pressing global problems we face today. Now that the Cold War has ended, we need a new form of global governance, one that recognizes that the nations of the world cannot, *as nations,* solve global problems.

This chapter is a beginning exploration of what it might mean to create the next system of global governance. It is an act of practical imagination, limited by what can be done as a next step, but with a radically different assumption as its starting point: that the structures of global governance for the 21st century must be based on *the primacy of people rather than on the power of nations.*

Thinking about global governance

Thinking about 'global governance' is both daunting and frightening – daunting because a political project that requires nation-states with varying degrees of power to reach agreement about a shared architecture of power seems impossible, and frightening because *ideas* of good governance often have a way of becoming tyrannies in practice. When it comes to consciously sitting down to design 'global governance', the first response of many people around the world is a strong resistance – 'Leave us alone.'

And yet it is almost impossible to be 'left alone' – we are so bound together through trade, mass media, and the ecological health of the planet that the geographical and cultural boundaries that in the past gave nations a basis of sovereignty are crumbling. Nation-states can no longer control violence, their own currency, the genetic make-up of their crops, the information that reaches their citizens, and many other basic areas over which they once had authority.[1] And the body comprised of nation-states – the United Nations – is hampered by a structure that reflects the self-interests of individual nations, not the interests of the whole. The new problems emerging from globalization and interdependence are not solvable at the nation-state level or by a collection of nation-states.

People around the world experience this seismic shift not just as a challenge to national sovereignty, but also as a direct threat to their personal lives. Jobs are outsourced where labor unions can't protect them; children are influenced by the morals of pop culture imported from alien value systems; the very air they breathe is polluted by sources from countries in which they have no influence on policy. Thoughtful observers see that since nation-states are powerless to solve these problems within their own boundaries, something must be done at a global level – so much in fact that global 'governance' as distinguished from global 'government' seems to be a necessity.

Whenever the need for better governance arises, the temptation is to dream up a system – Plato's republic is not the only utopia to emerge fully formed from the mind of a thinker – but if we truly intend to make headway on the daunting task of global governance, we must resist the temptation to systematize by focusing instead on *principles* and *processes.* We must pay less attention to the architecture of global governance and more to the principles and processes by which we can encourage forms of community and partnership with each other.

First principles and supportive processes

The technology that helped to create this crisis of power also has the potential to help resolve it. For the first time in human history, a significant fraction of people can interact with each other directly – actively through the Internet and passively through the mass media – rather than through the mediated power structures of their national governments. At this point, the technology outstrips our imaginations: we can use the Internet and mobile phones to organize resistance to global organizations and to make certain national abuses of power better known. But we're only just beginning to imagine how this ad hoc power can be used to help with the challenge of governance. Even so, inherent in this technology is a revolutionary possibility: the organization of global complexity that reaches down to the level of the individual.

Complex human social systems are most powerful when organized around values, which later become embedded in laws and customs. Values are important to the beginning of any governance enterprise because, unlike laws and policies, they exist at a level of generality that allows people to communicate with each other and reach a 'fuzzy' common ground. As laws and rules based on these values begin to be articulated, those involved in dialogue become aware that there are more areas of disagreement than they might at first have supposed. But the common ground already established acts as a powerful magnet, drawing people together in dialogue even as they explore their differences.

These dialogues around shared values must work towards explicit processes of governance with attendant penalties for

79

ignoring these processes. One reason for the UN's powerlessness is that while nations can agree upon sanctions, for example, they seem unable to agree on the appropriate action required if sanctions or mandates (such as arms inspections) are ignored. In part, this inability to enforce its 'laws' is caused by a lack of consensus about what values these 'laws' support. A 'disarmed' Iraq was still able to purchase arms (or the capacity to make them) from nations that had supported the sanctions. 'Disarming' a dictator is not a strong enough positive value to unite around, either rhetorically or practically.

Around what value might this worldwide dialogue towards consensus begin and how could it be nourished to allow a global consensus that will lead to action? What hope exists that such an enterprise could produce practical results?

The central value for global governance

The single most important principle of global governance is its basis in the human being: not the king, not the priests or ayatollahs, not nation-states – and not even the United Nation-states – but the individual human being. It may take years for consensus to be reached as to what universal rights each human being can claim, but one right has already emerged: the dignity of the individual human life. More specifically, governments cannot be allowed to systematically kill particular portions of their populations.

In the late 1990s, when the society of Western nations under NATO chose to intervene against Serbia, it did so against it own rules – after all, the intervention was in response to the internal affairs of a sovereign nation. In this case (and notably not in the case of non-European nations), human rights took priority over national sovereignty, setting a precedent for putting a principle above the power of a sovereign state. The leader of that state, Slobodan Milosevic, was then taken to an *international* court of justice.

This is a hopeful beginning for a system of global governance based on people rather than nations. But its popular legitimacy is flawed in three significant ways. First, many people feel that choosing the principle of human rights over the principle of sovereignty only succeeded in this case because Serbia was a relatively powerless nation. Had Serbia been more powerful, i.e. had it possessed weapons of mass destruction, such a breach of sovereignty might never have happened. This 'double standard' points to the necessity of solving the problems inherent in the power differential between those nations possessing WMDs and those who have not yet developed or bought them. The process of articulating human rights must go hand-in-hand with another, nation-based process of controlling WMDs.

The second flaw in this application of an overriding principle of human rights lies in the narrowness of its application to a European context. The society of nations was seen to ignore the same, or worse, violations of this principle when they occurred in Africa. If the principle of human rights is to have any power, it must be applied in all cases, even where no national self-interest appears to be involved.

The third flaw lies in the perception of many that the self-interest of the United States was the deciding factor in the outcome. Key to all thinking about global governance for the 21st century must be an international consensus about the role of the US. When the League of Nations and the UN were founded, a number of nations could be said to be roughly equal in power. But now, the US is so much more powerful than any other nation that a special role, with particular rights as well as obligations, must be spelled out for it. Practically speaking, this cannot simply entail a scaling back of US power or the naive expectation that the US will ignore its own self-interests before risking its treasure and the lives of its citizens. More effective would be an exploration of how the long-term self-interests of the US can coincide with those of people worldwide.

81

Institutions and long-term self-interests

Just as the UN grew out of the League of Nations, so the most promising process for establishing the new institutions of global governance is to explore what is possible based on our existing institutions. Rather than one source, the UN, there are four likely sources for emerging institutions, problematic though their interactions with each other might be:

1. UN agencies such as the World Health Organization, which can be strengthened through tighter oversight and greater transparency.
2. International NGOs, which can assume more legitimacy with greater transparency and public oversight.
3. Membership organizations, such as the WTO and the European Union, in which the common interest and long-term self-interest are already seen to coincide in those who apply to join.
4. The emerging citizenship culture of multinational corporations. This last group may seem an unlikely candidate at first sight, but as the CEO of Canon, R. Kaku, asserted many years ago, multinationals, when operating globally, are the only entities whose long-term self-interests coincide with the interests of the world as a whole.

The processes of self-determination

What all four sources for global partnerships have in common is that they operate as voluntary associations, not through coerced allegiance. In the case of multinationals, for example, partnerships with NGOs and greater transparency have led to pressure to make improvements in social responsibility. Eventually, best practice can become standard operating procedure, making an enormous difference to individual lives and to the environment, especially in those parts of the world where corporations have significant power in relation to governments.

The evolution of these structures into a kind of virtual global community architecture is accompanied by the growing capacity of people to discover the sources of power and coordinate individual action to push for change. At the same time that many people feel a loss in power to influence politics or the economy as a whole, they can experience an increase in power enabling them to transform their personal lives.

Building hope

Media and information technology are so ubiquitous that even people in very remote parts of the globe often have knowledge of particular movies, TV shows, and sports celebrities. In addition, we are living under the first truly global 'myth' or story of reality – the economic myth – where a kind of global consensus about the desirability of increasing material prosperity has already been achieved. The notable exceptions to this, the 'resistance to modernity' sometimes seen in fanatical religious groups, highlight both how far consensus in relation to this myth has come and how much is omitted that former myths, such as religious myths, gave to the cultures operating within them.

Any group of diverse global citizens meeting together is likely to come to agreement about very fundamental desires such as safety, health, prosperity for their children and the freedom that gives dignity to human lives. Where we differ is in the choice of forms of persuasion or coercion to be applied to *nations* when they thwart these desires for their own citizens.

As a small next step, a series of multi-stakeholder dialogues around the world, organized in scenario form (multiple possible paths forward), and disseminated using global marketing techniques would allow people of different ages and educational backgrounds to explore options *in principle* before technocrats begin to tinker. The aim would not be to choose a path into the future but to create a conversation that could build to a consensus about practical ways to move forward. In scenario form, even new structures of governance can be explored in a general way. For example, the idea that the power to propose global rules should be given to a body of citizen representatives while the decision to accept or deny such proposals should be the responsibility of individual nations.

In the last 30 years, such a global conversation has led to an emerging consensus and the *will to do something* about the problems of the global environment. So successful has been the grass-roots or people component of this movement that one could imagine a scenario in which institutions that already help to manage our interconnectedness – the WTO and the various environmental agreements, for example – become the platforms for developing global governance for the 21st century.

In working to set up the League of Nations, US President Woodrow Wilson said, 'What we seek is the reign of law, based upon the consent of the governed, and sustained by the organized opinion of mankind.' While the eventual reign of law will be the foundation for the effective application of principles, the next step for achieving effective global governance may be reliant on the last of these aims: organizing the opinion of mankind.

Note

1 For a fuller discussion, see Philip Bobbitt, *The Shield of Achilles*, 2003.

Betty Sue Flowers
Betty Sue Flowers is the Director of the LBJ Library at the University of Texas at Austin, where she is also Professor of

English. Poet, editor, and business consultant. Hosted 'Conversations with Betty Sue Flowers', moderator for executive seminars at the Aspen Institute for Humanistic Studies. Publications range from poetry therapy to the economic myth, including four television tie-in books in collaboration with Bill Moyers, among them, *Joseph Campbell and the Power of Myth*.

Amr Hamzawy

Good Governance in the Arab World

Crisis or conspiracy?

Whenever the Arab world is the subject of discussion in the West, there is a sense of impending crisis. In the 1970s and 1980s, concern focused on the slow pace of modernisation and the threat of an Islamist takeover based on the Iranian model. Since the 1990s it has shifted to the faltering progress of democratisation and liberalisation as well as the spread of radical terrorist networks. This bleak picture of a region perpetually embroiled in conflict is darkened even further by new waves of violence emanating from the Arab-Israeli conflict, unresolved since 1948. The events of the past three years, in particular the attacks of September 11th and the collapse of Saddam Hussein's dictatorship, have highlighted this reality and brought the Arab world back onto centre stage after a decade of relative marginalisation.

Viewed from this perspective, the lack of free elections, the failure of state institutions to exercise political responsibility towards their citizens, human rights violations and the lack of transparency or any fight against corruption are merely the most prominent items on an apparently endless list of deficits. Despite their different 'takes' on the region's problems, North American and European researchers appear to have run out of ideas for effective ways of tackling them. Nothing seems to work – development aid, the offer of economic partnership, dialogue between cultures and religions, programmes of democratisation, political pressure on the ruling elites and even military intervention; their impacts appear minimal in societies characterised by endless social injustice and brutal repression.

Meanwhile, the Arab world suffers from the fact that politicians and intellectuals persist in blaming the West for its ongoing plight by advancing various conspiracy theories and painting quasi-prophetic 'we are the victims' scenarios. While it is certainly important to discuss the role of external actors and their interests in the Middle East, it is still shocking to see how short-lived and marginal the moments of self-criticism are in Arab public discourse. Even after the overthrow of Saddam and the numerous revelations about his regime of terror, internal Arab opinion has only been concerned with either criticising derailed American policy in the region or warning of the dangers of renewed military intervention.

Despite the serious situation, public interest is not focused on seeking potential answers to the problems. No doubt some Western governments will face a range of accusations – from covert support for Arab dictators through to pursuing a brutal politics of self-interest – but public criticism of the West merely serves to absolve Arabs collectively from taking responsibility for the failure to implement democracy and development. Local debates give the impression of a region that is devoid of acting subjects and is merely awaiting the next onslaught by hostile foreign forces.

Both patterns of perception – crisis on the one hand and conspiracy on the other – are based on monolithic interpretive paradigms, which either structurally marginalise gradual processes of change and partial efforts at reform in the Arab world, especially by non-state actors, or remain completely silent. The fact that occasionally Western political discourse speaks of the region in terms of *best practice* while Arab public discourse is constantly heralding 'transformation' alters nothing about this one-sided approach. Such terms refer almost exclusively to large-scale modernisation projects decreed by nation-states, whose fate over the last three decades can be summed up in just one word: failure. **87**

However, a shift in perspective to take systematic account both of the achievements brought about by non-state actors and the gradual changes that have taken place in Arab societies enables us to draw a differentiated picture of the region, particularly with regard to democracy and good governance.

Arab forms of rule and non-state partnerships based on shared responsibility

One way of doing this analytically is first to subdivide the forms of rule in the Arab world into three categories: those in the process of becoming democratised; semi-authoritarian; and authoritarian. Over the past few years, functioning civil societies have become established in Morocco, Bahrain and Qatar, and their sphere of activities is constantly being extended, despite certain state-initiated setbacks. Religious and secular – traditional and modern – NGOs carry out important tasks in the areas of education, health, financial support of poorer families, monitoring of state authorities, fighting corruption and legal aid for political prisoners; through these activities they stimulate the emergence of a pluralistic, consensus-oriented public sphere. The ruling elites now see their role less as one that is normatively superior to that of other social actors; a number of developments suggest that they perceive themselves as a shaping force in the democratic sense, seeking consensus with other actors. Vivid examples include the participation of opposition parties in governing coalitions in Morocco, the last free elections in Bahrain and the current debate on the constitution in Qatar. In these countries the concepts of political responsibility and good governance are topics that structure public discourse and provide a point of reference for articulation of the democratic social contract.

We are seeing ongoing processes of democratisation, which, in the case of Morocco since the 1980s and Bahrain and Qatar since the 1990s, have been completed successfully and – unlike, say, in Eastern Europe – have involved the participation of formerly authoritarian ruling elites. True, there are still certain negativities associated with the development of the three 'paragons' of the Arab world – the place of women in society, individual rights and religious freedom – nonetheless, the gradual, process-like character of their attempts at reform should not be ignored.

By contrast, the current political situation in Algeria, Tunisia, Egypt, Jordan, the Lebanon and Yemen points to a number of serious obstacles to the emergence of a democratic relationship between the state and society. Processes of economic liberalisation were introduced in these countries up to and including the late 1980s. The expectation in political and intellectual circles that this would bring about a gradual process of democratisation was based on the popular assumption, prevalent in political science research on transformation, that economic liberalisation brought with it political pluralism in the medium term and democratic conditions in the long term. The fact that civil society activities were permitted and that a flourishing media landscape developed reinforced this attitude of expectation both within and outside the region. However, these hopes were dashed. Even today, the form of rule that exists in these countries can be characterised as semi-authoritarian for many reasons.

First, the ruling elites have managed time and again to nip all signs of social pressure towards democratisation in the bud, deploying a variety of different strategies. Whereas in Algeria the military had to intervene at the start of the 1990s in order to prevent the winners of the parliamentary elections, the Islamists, from forming a government, Tunisian President Bin Ali prohibited all oppositional movements by decree at the end of the 1980s. In Egypt, Jordan, the Lebanon and Yemen, on the other hand, two methods have traditionally proved successful: restrictive legislation and co-optation. Emergency laws, state committees for authorising political

89

parties, bureaucratic authorities charged with monitoring the financing of NGOs and the manipulation of electoral districts are vivid examples of the first method. Additionally, by co-opting actors in civil society, such as trade unions and human rights organisations, state apparatuses succeed in destroying any remaining potential for liberation – leaving the all-powerful state apparatuses and a politically ineffective opposition.

Another issue is the show of democratisation put on principally to avoid antagonising the donors among the Western governments. The political domain in every semi-authoritarian country displays a pluralistic façade that gives the appearance of a multi-party system and a modern separation of powers. The official discourse juggles with politically correct terms such as civil rights, transparency, protection of minorities and de-militarisation of the public sphere. In parallel, the political and intellectual representatives of the regimes concerned think up convoluted ways of explaining to their 'rank and file' that these are all long-term processes of transformation, whose success depends on their patience and obedience. In this context, the meaning of good governance is reduced to efficient modernisation of state structures and the creation of highly efficient technical-bureaucratic procedures within the state power apparatuses. Normative elements such as legitimacy and representation, both substantial elements of good governance, are swept under the carpet.

Despite this, functioning democratic partnerships are emerging in the sphere of civil society within these semi-authoritarian forms of rule and are struggling against the autocratic regimes in power. An increasing number of organisations are operating in the sphere of human rights and the struggle against corruption. The number of cases of state violence and disregard of legal regulations revealed to the public by these actors has gradually been on the increase. Even if these partial approaches have not been sufficient to force the ruling elites into serious democratisation at the present time, they still have the unmistakeable effect of sensitising large segments of the population and convincing them of the necessity of comprehensive reform. Added to this is the fact that the regimes in the countries mentioned above have failed to deliver in the vital areas of poverty reduction and equality of opportunity. In spite of massive public demonstrations of power, their credibility is fading inexorably. It won't take much more for the mask of democracy to fall away altogether from the ugly countenance of those who now rule in splendid isolation. They and their power apparatuses are incapable of following the path of democratisation. This second category can be summed up by the phrase 'blocked reforms'.

Finally, countries such as Saudi Arabia and Syria are typical examples of the third category of Arab forms of rule. They display all the characteristics of authoritarian regimes. Governance is the domain of traditional and/or military elites, who have complete control over the society's resources and their distribution, thereby cementing their power over other social actors. Freedom of information, civil rights, political freedoms and separation of powers: none register on the scale. And yet since September 11th – not least due to pressure from the Americans – a debate about reform has begun to emerge whose rhetoric revolves around the concepts of democracy and good governance. The ruling elites in both countries now organise regular debating forums and conferences aimed at devising future strategies for 'gradual transformation'. They seek to give the impression of liberalism and generosity by inviting intellectual and political representatives from different groups and political persuasions to these events and encouraging them to give their ideas free rein. The documents that have emerged from these meetings are no doubt very interesting, but their function is merely consultative, and prospects for democracy degenerate in this context to rulers making decisions based solely on expediency. Social forces are present only in isolation, democratic partnerships hardly at all.

Agents of democratic change

Having established a typology of Arab forms of rule, we can now inquire about the social agents of democratic change. Since reforms have either been blocked or are non-existent in those countries that make up the second and third categories, this question takes on an enormous significance there in particular. What do democratic partnerships consist of in Egyptian or Jordanian civil society? Which actors, say, in Saudi Arabia or Syria, could transform the current mood for reform into genuine pressure for reform? The answer is ideological dynamite: moderate Islamists.

It is absolutely crucial to differentiate between moderate and radical groupings among the Islamists. In response to a recent question as to whether the Egyptian Muslim Brotherhood (the oldest Islamist movement in the region) would be included in the 'democratic national dialogue', the Egyptian information minister Safawat al-Schirif replied: 'Is there a movement in Egypt called the Muslim Brotherhood?' He went on to state clearly that in Egypt religious parties were prohibited and that religious groups were not allowed to participate in the dialogue between the government and the opposition. Religion, according to al-Schirif, had no place in politics. These kinds of statements are typical of many Arab governments and their relationship to religious groups: they deny the political relevance of Islamism as a mass phenomenon, even though they know the opposite is true, or they simply describe it in terms of a security problem. Algeria, Tunisia, Egypt and Saudi Arabia take this approach. By contrast, Morocco and, to some extent Jordan have succeeded in dealing politically with Islamist movements: for some years they have been attempting to integrate the Islamists into the political process.

It began with the Iranian revolution in 1979 and the murder of Egyptian President Anwar as-Sadat by radical Islamists. Both events sparked fears worldwide about the political future of the Arab-Islamic world. 'Islam is both religion and state' became the maxim of religious movements throughout many countries and posed an increasing challenge to secular political systems. In order to fight against Westernisation and the decline in values, both socially and politically, many Islamists demanded that the legal order based on Islamic principles, the *Sharia,* be introduced. The origins of this worrying trend could initially be sought in the domestic political context and in the region's politics. The Egyptian government under as-Sadat, for example, was committed to a strongly pro-Western course. While economic development advanced overall, a majority of the Arab-Islamic population felt excluded from the new prosperity.

As religious groups searched for their own alternatives – a search which increasingly took place outside state structures – they developed the general battle cry 'Islam is the solution!' The lines of conflict became increasingly hardened during the 1980s and 1990s. The activities of Islamist groupings that were prepared to use violence provoked strong reactions on the part of governments. Islamists operating underground or within the covert opposition were jailed in their thousands; many were condemned to death or to long jail sentences. As the scope of their activities consistently narrowed as a result, there was criticism from the population, particularly of their visible brutality. The terrorist attacks in Egypt, for example, led to tourists staying away in droves, thereby depriving many ordinary people of the livelihood on which they depended.

From the mid-1990s onwards a series of new trends emerged. The experience of dealing with authoritarian state power led some Islamist groups to take up the issues of 'parliamentary democracy' and 'human rights' as important objectives. These groups were able to get involved in the existing contexts of civil society. With most points of access to the political sphere barred to religious groups, their moderate representatives became active in other ways – as the founders of Islamic banks and modern welfare institutions. A few radical movements, such as the Egyptian Jihad group and some Saudi Arabian underground cells, renounced violence. The willingness of moderate Islamists to engage in reform, along with their activities in the sphere of social welfare, has won them a great deal of social recognition.

Moderate Islamist movements are hugely important for democracy and good governance in the Arab world. They frequently represent the only effective, socially embedded opposition to semi-authoritarian and authoritarian Arab regimes. Unlike these movements, secular actors from civil society, such as professional organisations, human rights organisations and women's associations, often operate in isolation and limit themselves to a specialised expert discourse. This is not to say that the existence and activities of such actors is not indispensable for the emergence of a pluralist public sphere; it is simply that they are unable to exert any serious pressure for reform on the ruling elites. Only moderate Islamist groups, both traditional and modern, are anchored in society and are in a position politically to mobilise large sections of Arab societies. When they are not excluded and when their moderate tendencies are encouraged, they are the true agents of democratic transformation. The ever-recurring contrasts drawn between Islam and democracy, between religious movements and the norms of an open society, are merely based on outmoded enemy images, which fail to recognise the diverse nuances of reality.

The West must engage in a serious dialogue with moderate Islamist groupings. Most Arab governments will criticise such a re-orientation, while secular moralists and hard-nosed politicians in the West will also sound their note of warning. They will dismiss such approaches as irrational or create destabilisation in the region by emphasising the difficulties involved. Nonetheless, dialogue with moderate Islamists is the only way of developing momentum for democracy in the region.

Amr Hamzawy

Amr Hamzawy was born in Cairo in 1967. Currently Assistant Professor in the Department of Political Science at Cairo University. Studied political science in Cairo, Amsterdam and Berlin. Has written and edited a number of publications addressing contemporary Arab debates on democracy, civil society, Islamism, globalisation and relations with the West.

Charles Handy

Partnership and Trust

The 21st century opened with a series of catastrophic events, most notably the attack on the twin towers of the World Trade Center, the bankruptcy of Enron and the resulting disintegration of its auditors, Arthur Andersen, and then, more recently, the invasion of Iraq. Traumatic for all those affected, these dramas also carried symbolic messages for our modern times.

On that bright sunny morning on the 11th September in 2001, America was shocked to discover that the might of her armed forces, the sophistication of her information systems and the financial muscle of the corporations inhabiting those twin towers counted for nothing when set against a partnership of 19 determined and passionate individuals, part of a globally scattered network with no known centre. What happened then could, metaphorically, happen to any corporation or organisation. Size and sophistication is in itself no protection against invasion by unforeseen enemies nor is it any guarantee of safety. Bigness can even be a disadvantage, as the twin towers proved, if the bigness is gathered together, because, once penetrated, its own weight conspires to collapse the whole. Maybe we have to learn from our enemies and create more loosely jointed partnership organisations so that damage to one part does not bring down all the others.

To some extent that has already been happening with the spread of quasi-federal corporations that combine small strategic centres with autonomous operating parts, linked together by technology so that they can boast of being simultaneously both global and local. But unbundled organisations cannot be managed by information systems alone – there must also be a cause or mission that unites the partners.

Without that sense of a compelling cause, few will be willing to give their trust or loyalty to such insubstantial virtual organisations, often known only by their initials. Trust in our new world is increasingly given to individuals not institutions – the latter have too often proved unworthy of that trust and their mission too self-seeking to merit our commitment.

Enron and the aftermath of its collapse provided a powerful lesson of the consequences of that erosion of trust. It was not only Enron's employees who were left to rue their faith in what had been lauded as one of America's most admired businesses; the once mighty partnership of Arthur Andersen literally evaporated when it became apparent that no clients or government would ever trust it again. Evidence of malpractice at other corporations forced the United States government into urgent action to bolster trust in the whole capitalist system. That trust is still fragile. The tradition that capitalism is a partnership between society and businesses to work for the benefit of both no longer seems so secure when some businesses so clearly put their own interests before those of the surrounding society.

Two years later, still trusting in its own might, the American government felt impelled to invade Iraq in order to remove a widely feared dictator, against the instincts and protests of much of the world. Mighty armies can trample opposition and often work best on their own, but managing a peace requires partnership and trust, as conquering armies have discovered to their cost down the centuries. As businesses as well as governments have begun to realise, to be successful globally you have to be trusted locally, with local partners. Building those partnerships and the foundations of that trust is the urgent challenge for every business and every government both within their own countries and internationally.

At the start of the 21st century it is becoming clear that the balance of power has changed fundamentally. The traditional sources of power in institutions – information and formal authority – have lost their potency. When information is hard to corral because of the remorseless growth in the power of technology, especially the Internet, every operation becomes more transparent. When subordinates know as much as their superiors, those superiors need the acquiescence of those beneath them in order to exercise their authority. When both sides know as much as the other, then decisions cannot be imposed so easily. No longer are people so ready to assume that elders and seniors know best or can be trusted to act in everyone's interests. Nor, to be fair, are those seniors so confident in their ability to manage complex situations in a more interlinked world without the help of others involved. Totalitarian regimes have been crumbling, in business as much as in politics, because of this lack of trust in the ruling authority.

Elsewhere, too, there has been a noticeable decline in deference as people assert their rights as individuals and demand a respect for their views and their personal dignity. No longer, for instance, does ownership provide unilateral control over property or individuals. Shareholders and their agents, the managers, are required to take other interests into account. Hierarchy, generally, is losing its legitimacy while partnership is in the ascendant as different interest groups flex their muscles and individuals start to take back control of their lives from organisations and governments. In the business world, employees are now increasingly described as members, clients and customers are constituents, contractors are partners and associated companies or organisations are alliances – and they are all stakeholders. Language is the herald of social change. When the words change we need to take heed and change our ways.

Effective partnership depends on transparency and trust. It was nicely symbolised once by the old partners' rooms that were to be found in the offices of lawyers, bankers and stockbrokers in Britain. All the partners sat in one room within earshot of each other. Their desks were wide enough to accommodate one partner on each side, facing each other. Each partner's decisions were binding on all the rest, so it was important that all knew what was going on and could both see and hear it, for trust depends on good information, received through all the senses, and on shared and tested experience. No longer can partners expect to share a room, a desk and their daily working experience. Technology of all sorts has to be called in to aid instead, but the requirements remain the same – a shared vision, transparency and trust.

A different sort of trust is at work when we drive our car along a country road. Approaching a blind corner we do not slow down but hug the left-hand side of the road, trusting that anyone coming the other way will do the same. We do not need to know the name of person approaching or anything about them, only the rules of the road (bearing in mind that in many countries the rule requires us to keep to the right not the left) and to feel confident that the system is widely respected and enforced. This is systemic trust, the willingness to rely on the rules of an institution or system. Much of our daily life depends on systemic trust. When this breaks down, because people lose confidence in the governing authority, life in a country or an organisation becomes unpredictable, even dangerous.

Rules are needed in every relationship, whether it is with a state, an institution or a person. Without mutually understood rules, every event has to be treated as a unique situation, something that consumes unnecessary time and energy. The rules may be codified, written or implicit, but without rules there is often too much unpredictability which itself breeds distrust. The rules may include codes of behaviour, values and standards, critical areas for professional bodies where the public are asked to take expertise and competence on trust. Partnership only works if there is at least an implicit agreement on what is right and what is wrong in the way the work is done.

99

The paradox is that rules can suggest distrust rather than trust, implying that the persons instituting the rule do not trust others to act properly and sensibly on their own initiative. The best rules, therefore, are self-enforcing, because all involved see the reason for them and the sense in keeping to them as a way of making life more manageable. Bad laws, laws which do not carry the consent of the people, seldom work because it becomes too costly to enforce them. Good rules, therefore, are usually the result of a partnership process in which all interested parties have their say. In the same way, democracies, for all their faults, produce better laws than dictatorships because the people, or their representatives, have had their chance to express their views.

The First Principle of trust, therefore, is that trust and partnership, in some form, go together. One without the other will not work. When partnership breaks down, trust evaporates and vice versa. Workers disillusioned by their employing organisation will feel free to cheat it in some way or other, forcing the employer to create more and more control devices, which themselves suggest a lack of trust. This in its turn feeds the disillusion. The spiral of distrust that results is hard to reverse. Because trust cannot be assumed or demanded, every relationship – whether with an institution, a professional body or a person – has to incorporate some sense of partnership. Trust has to be earned and deserved and it is only the other party who can validate it, which is why it is hard to trust those whom one never meets, businesses which take no account of one's needs, institutions whose mechanisms or procedures seem obtuse and excluding, or governments who have lost credibility.

The Second Principle reinforces the first: trust, as well as partnership, thrives on transparency. The more everyone knows, the less reason there is for suspicion or worry. One organisation once asked a cross-section of its staff to estimate the salaries of their colleagues. Almost invariably, individuals thought the salaries of their colleagues to be far higher than they actually were. The levels of dissatisfaction plunged when the organisation decided to publish all salaries and to make clear the rules for fixing them. The new transparency that is being forced on organisations by technology not only reinforces the idea of partnership in place of hierarchy, it removes more of the suspicion which fuels distrust.

The Third Principle recognises that trust needs bonding. Devolved responsibilities can generate strong relationships of trust within the autonomous group or unit but may result in a loosening of their connections to the bigger body. Federalism, the newly fashionable form for large organisations, requires that there be a sense of twin citizenship in the organisation. This is the idea that it is possible to belong to more than one overlapping body – that one can be a citizen of Texas and of the United States of America, owing loyalty to both. This is necessary if, on occasion, the needs of the larger organisation have to override the needs of the local unit. Too often the need to reinforce the commitment to the bigger body is overlooked. But without a shared sense of mission throughout the organisation or the partnership, the centre may start to distrust the parts and seek to impose controls or pull in the boundaries, fuelling distrust. Bonding can't be done remotely. The annual congresses that institutions and businesses arrange for their members pose as learning opportunities but in reality are bonding rituals, reminders of the bigger loyalty. Newsletters and email circulars are no substitute for people in the flesh and en masse.

The Fourth Principle recognises that trust needs boundaries. Few people are prepared to give anyone complete freedom. Organisations lay down the limits of authority for groups and roles. Governments may advocate individual freedom but restrain it with laws and regulations. Even the closest of marriages will have areas that are the especial responsibility of one of the partners, areas in which the other does not have complete licence. The new devolved businesses maintain control by results rather than by close monitoring of the processes, with the devolved units allowed to get on with the delivery of their agreed goals. Those in control can rest more comfortably and trust more readily if the limits of discretion are known and respected, if the boundaries are established.

The Fifth Principle is that trust needs to be tough. The harsh reality is that not everyone lives up to the trust that has been invested in them. When rules are repeatedly broken, boundaries exceeded or goals missed, trust in that person or group will gradually be withdrawn, inhibiting the progress of the organisation. If there is no sign of learning and improvement, the culprit has to be sacrificed for the good of the whole. One weak link damages the chain. It is better, however, to trust more freely and amputate if necessary than to ration trust to the few of whom one can be sure. That can too easily result in an inner core of cronies or trusties, alienating the rest and spreading resentment and distrust.

The Sixth Principle, therefore, is that trust and partnership both depend on an ability to learn and develop. If partners are going to continue to be able to rely upon each other as the world advances and changes around them, then everyone will have to keep up or be discarded. A lasting partnership depends upon a learning culture, one in which new approaches are encouraged, where people are trusted to develop new ideas and to learn from those that don't work. A key feature of such a learning culture is a willingness to share knowledge and information. As in the old-fashioned partners' rooms, there should be no walls or barriers.

The Seventh Principle, and the last, is that trust and partnerships need leadership. But in a partnership it will not be hierarchical leadership. A typical example comes from sport, in particular from rowing, where a crew of eight oarsmen, plus one cox is required to go backwards as hard as they can without speaking to each other, steered by the one person who is too small to row but the only one who can see where they are going. It is, it has to be, the perfect partnership, each doing their own thing but in concert with all others, trusting that each person is doing their job as best they can. 'Who, in this case,' I once asked an Olympic oarsman, 'is the leader, since all groups have leaders?' 'We don't use that word,' he replied, 'but there are various candidates. There is, to begin with, the official captain. He selects the crew and is responsible for keeping discipline and morale, but in the boat he is just one of us, an oarsman. Then there is the cox, the one who steers the boat, he has definitely got a leadership role. But so has the stroke, the lead oarsman who sets the pace which we all follow. And don't forget a person who isn't in the boat at all, the coach on the bank, whose role as teacher and mentor can make all the difference.' 'Take your pick,' he said, 'they all have a leadership task at different times.'

So it is in effective partnerships. The leadership role changes with the situation. There may be a senior member who represents the partnership, the equivalent of the captain of the boat, but the task leadership rotates so that the right person for the job is always in charge. For this sort of leadership to work, mutual trust is essential. Partnerships of all types need a measure of continuity in order to create the shared experiences that alone can nurture real two-way trust.

The implications

The redistribution of power in society has significant implications for every institution and for every relationship. Increasingly things won't work unless the key players embrace a partnership model. In an interlocked world each player has enough negative power to halt everything, be it a commercial deal or a personal relationship. No one will commit to an enterprise unless they can see the benefit to themselves and in very few instances will it make sense to use physical or economic power to compel them. Partnership implies an agreement on goals and purposes as well as on who

103

does what and on the distribution of outcomes. This makes for lengthy negotiations at the start but the bonus is the foundation for mutual trust that can result and the smoother operations that will follow.

Trust, however, is fragile. Like a pane of glass, once broken it will never be the same again. The seven principles of trust are an essential guide. They are not easy to follow in a rapidly changing world: one in which we are encouraged to be wary, to question before we decide; one where commitment to anything or anyone is seen by many as equivalent to mortgaging one's future, where trust can seem foolhardy and partnership risky. There is, however, no alternative if the world is not to succumb to totalitarianism with all the enforced controls that inevitably accompany it.

Charles Handy
Charles Handy is an author and broadcaster living in London. Has written many books on the changing shape of work, organisations and personal life; his latest is *The Elephant and the Flea*.

The Business Contribution

Jürgen E. Schrempp

A Corporate Contribution to the Fight against HIV/AIDS

As a company expands its network across the world, its unavoidable social responsibility obligations grow apace. Economic success and commercial size demand socially responsible actions in all those global markets in which we operate. DaimlerChrysler has imposed this duty upon itself, and I personally endorse unreservedly and wholeheartedly our acknowledgement of our social responsibility commitment.

We are firmly convinced of the benefits of globalisation: open markets, free trade, and transfer of knowledge across borders. Globalisation leads to enormous progress in technology and science, higher standards of medical care and more efficient use of resources. Last but not least, international dialogue also heightens one's awareness of the need for observance of human rights. Contrary to what many critics would have us believe, globalisation does not therefore lead to a decline in social standards. It leads instead to an increase in global prosperity.

There are many arguments supporting this theory, but the strong opposition wind of the large anti-globalisation lobby shows that we have not yet managed to communicate convincingly the benefits of globalisation. The open, constructive – if at times controversial – dialogue between the very diverse

105

interest groups is exactly the kind of discourse that is needed. It ensures that no one is excluded from globalisation. We are sure that transparency is the one quality that will enable us to dispel fear and prejudice while building trust.

Ultimately, we need this trust in order to form a greater number of new partnerships around the world. Globalisation requires partnership between politics and business; it requires partnership between corporate management and employees; and it requires partnership between companies and society at large.

As a global company that operates in some 200 countries around the world, we can – at the start of this 21st century – demonstrate many examples of our dynamic commitment to the principles of social responsibility. We base this commitment on clear recognition of the principles of the Global Compact, which we were among the first to embrace. Our *Principles for Social Responsibility,* agreed in concert with our global employee representatives, are based upon the provisions of this United Nations initiative. These principles are practised worldwide and applied where there are varying cultures and diverse values. Thus, they provide a proper foundation for optimisation of the human aspect of irreversible globalisation.

I am convinced that social responsibility is a vital factor in the long-term success of any company. Only in this way can we contribute to lasting global peace and prosperity. However, fulfilling this responsibility presupposes that we are and will remain permanently competitive. In this respect, the economic self-interest of the company and 'social responsibility' are by no means mutually exclusive, but are rather like two sides of the same coin.

There is no clearer evidence of this than the horrific threat posed by the global spread of the HIV/AIDS pandemic and industry's approach to it. According to UNAIDS, at the end of 2003, 40 million people worldwide were infected with HIV. Last year, around three million people – more than the population of Berlin or Washington and their outlying districts – died from this fatal immune deficiency disease. The experts agree unanimously that this pernicious trend is one of the greatest threats to mankind.

Aside from the personal tragedy of each individual case of infection, HIV/AIDS also destroys established structures and societies in many countries. It impedes economic development in the very countries where an increase in prosperity and social security is so desperately required. As a consequence, and an important one at that, HIV/AIDS has become an additional major risk to international security. Among the millions of people dying from AIDS are teachers who can no longer impart their knowledge, doctors who can no longer cure their patients, skilled workers who can no longer produce goods and, finally, customers who can no longer consume goods.

One of the worst hotspots of the epidemic is southern Africa, which is home to approximately 30 percent of the people infected with HIV worldwide, even though the region comprises less than 2 percent of the world's population. In the Republic of South Africa alone, around 35 percent of 25–34 year-olds are now infected with HIV. Over the last few years, average life expectancy has fallen. By 2008 it is expected to decrease further, from 65 to 45. That is what it was in 1950.

DaimlerChrysler has a long corporate history in South Africa. In our plants there, with a total workforce of some 4,500 people, we manufacture around 55,000 vehicles a year. These are exported all over the world. We recognised early on that HIV/AIDS was also going to affect our company. Absence due to illness, the stigmatisation of sufferers, the loss of highly trained skilled workers and the need to appoint replacements with all the recurrent training costs involved such as growing health care costs – all these are factors that require action by the company. After issuing strict guidelines on non-discrimination towards infected employees as early as

1991, and being the first major company in South Africa to begin offering free medical care to employees suffering from AIDS in 1996, we developed and introduced a comprehensive strategy to fight HIV/AIDS in our workplaces between 2000 and 2003.

We were able to implement the programme in a close and extremely successful public–private partnership with Deutsche Gesellschaft für Technische Zusammenarbeit (GTZ). This secured the key skills crucial in the development and start-up phase of the project. Cooperation with the South African government, the national automotive trade union, NUMSA, and international organisations such as UNAIDS and the International Labour Organization (ILO) proved to be equally important.

Our workplace programme in South Africa offers all employees, and their families, extensive support in the fight against HIV/AIDS. The main objectives of the 'Workplace Initiative on HIV/AIDS' are: to avoid infection through education and prevention; to break down stigmatisation; to alleviate the consequences of the disease through health care subsidies and a comprehensive health care concept; to ensure that we have appropriate staff and corporate development programmes; to plan and manage social welfare benefits; and to strive towards the practicable sensitisation and active involvement of the people outside the plants.

The implementation of the programme relies heavily on 'peer education' involving specially trained members of staff. They contribute significantly to acceptance of the programme and play a major role in eliminating taboos and stigmatisation of sufferers. However, these employees are not only active within the company but, more importantly, also act as an interface between the workforce and the company. A broad-based community outreach is achieved through the deployment of 'peer educators' who work at the grass-roots level of the company – in other words, within the families of company employees and their communities. In addition, we have begun to extend the workplace project to suppliers, contractors and dealer networks, and also support other HIV initiatives within the country. Educational campaigns in schools and child care centres, as well as support of national aid programmes through provision of in-house expertise and close cooperation with regional non-governmental organisations (NGOs) are examples of how industry and commerce can reach beyond the workplace programmes to society at large.

Of course, we have only just reached the end of our three-year start-up phase – since January 2004, DaimlerChrysler South Africa has now been running the workplace programme under its own auspices – and it is still too early for a comprehensive quantitative analysis. However, on the plus side, the programme has been widely accepted among the workforce, and absenteeism due to HIV/AIDS has already been cut in half. Initial estimates also show that the prevention of one case of HIV infection will save the company around three to four annual salaries. In this respect, humanitarian progress and economic benefit are irrefutably and inextricably linked.

The positive results and considerable awareness generated by our activities confirm my strong conviction in calling for even greater commitment on the part of industry and commerce. Within our company, we plan to apply the measures developed in South Africa to companies in other countries, adapting them to the individual needs and special regional features. However, we also recognise that in the so-called developed countries, the threat posed by HIV/AIDS is so large that we need to take greater precautions. We are therefore refocusing on this issue in our vocational training in Germany.

If entrepreneurs around the world took up the fight against HIV/AIDS on behalf of, and with the help of their employees with sufficient energy, they would create enormous synergies with which industry could support very effectively the all-too-often hesitant efforts of international politicians. The Global Business Coalition on HIV/AIDS (GBC), of

109

which I became chairman in the summer of 2002, has set itself the objective of calling for precisely this type of commitment. With more than 130 major international member companies, the fast-growing GBC has not only become an excellent source for spreading 'best practices', but is above all a vital partner to politicians and society. If industry passionately and wholeheartedly devotes its innovative power and flexibility to society in its fight against HIV/AIDS, we are not only fulfilling our self-imposed duties as 'good corporate citizens', but are also acting in our own economic interest.

The recently concluded co-investment agreement between the GBC and the Global Fund to Fight AIDS, Tuberculosis and Malaria, under which companies use their own health care facilities in joint projects with public institutions, is another major step in a new era of partnership. The hugely positive response to the work of the GBC from representatives from the political arena, and the acclaim from experts and media interests, are both an encouragement and vindication. All serious parties involved recognise that large donations from industry and commerce represent a mere drop in the ocean, and industry and commerce cannot take on the role of governments. The efficient and practicable role of industry is to accept its global social responsibility – in partnership, and with long-term perspective.

Jürgen E. Schrempp
Professor Jürgen E. Schrempp is Chairman of the Board of Management of DaimlerChrysler AG and Chairman of the Global Business Coalition on HIV/AIDS.

Henning Kagermann

A Fair Share of Responsibility

Companies, and particularly the executives that run them, are today faced with enormous pressures to succeed, streamline costs, grow shareholder value and innovate, while at the same time be flexible and agile, and be good corporate citizens, harnessing their influence and strength to better not only their company but also the society in which they live. This begins with effective governance within each corporation. Beyond company borders and outside a vacuum, corporate governance also requires strong partnerships and dedication between companies, government and society. So what do these partnerships mean? And how does a management team balance all of this in a reasonable way that does not require enormous amounts of money and resources?

Role of corporate governance

This balance begins with effective corporate governance, which provides a framework for responsible, value-oriented management and control of a company. Good and effective corporate governance starts with will and management attitude (this is all-important). There must be a long-standing commitment by the management team that is augmented by compliance with legal regulations. The commitment cannot simply be a directive set in stone never to change, nor can it happen overnight. The company, its management team and all employees must pledge to support clear communication and transparency over the long term.

In many countries, laws and regulations have been enacted to stem the tide of scandal and restore confidence

111

in both investors and the public, and provide guidelines to corporations on how to be transparent and true to their stakeholders. It is unfortunate that companies have not been more proactive on this front and that it has taken a continuing wave of the legislative hand to bring about positive change.

The most prominent among these acts is without a doubt the Sarbanes-Oxley or Public Company Accounting Reform and Investor Protection Act of 2002 in the United States. Sarbanes-Oxley is designed to increase disclosure requirements to ensure integrity of corporate management and transparency of business processes, and improve the quality of financial information provided to authorities. It actually goes far beyond just financial information and includes risk management, controlling, internal auditing, investor relations, advisory boards and IT. Another national example is the German Corporate Governance Code, which provides recommendations for the governance of German companies. The Code's aim is to support the transparency and clarity of German corporate governance. It also clarifies the rights of shareholders and describes the dual board system (Executive Board and Supervisory Board) required under German law. Further regulations are in the pipeline, both on the European and German levels and in several countries worldwide.

Of course, we must ask whether any act can permanently prevent inappropriate actions on the part of a corporation. Corporations, governments and other stakeholders must work together to find a balanced answer to this to drive stakeholder value and sustain a viable company.

Corporate governance at SAP:
our role, insight and use of software

I view corporate governance from three angles: as CEO of a global corporation; as a software vendor with responsibility for helping our customers and partners use our product most effectively to support compliance; and from the unique perspective of a German-based company listed on the United States stock exchange whose major competitors have their headquarters in the US.

From my perspective as a CEO, the questions I ask myself are:

- Are we doing everything we can to create true transparency?
- Do we have a clear governance structure?
- Are we creating an atmosphere of all-round trust: internal, customer, investor, supervisory and public?

These questions must be answered and dealt with in a way that meets all the needs of business, government and society, but at a cost that is fair and reasonable. For any CEO, this means working closely with all the members of his ecosystem to illustrate what his company stands for and what it is doing to demonstrate good corporate governance. In addition, company resources must not be wasted or tied up to an extended degree, but rather, should allow maximum flexibility. The entire process must be relatively simple, easy to implement and clear to all.

For me and for SAP, regulations such as Sarbanes-Oxley and the German Corporate Governance Code can help drive this, but there is a thin line between effective regulation and overregulation. We must ensure that there is a balance between regulations and economic flexibility. We are fully behind and applaud legislative actions to create effective corporate governance, and we are ready to go the extra mile

113

to comply. In fact, in the fourth quarter of 2002, we started an extensive project to ensure compliance with Sarbanes-Oxley.

The biggest barrier to making this process simple is the fact that there are differing national standards around the world. In today's global economy, where some of the biggest companies in the world have locations in numerous countries, we need to start working with our partners toward mutual recognition in the medium term and international standards in the long term. We are cautious of uncoordinated national efforts across the globe. We do recognise that both the US and the European Union have the same goal, i.e. ensuring good corporate governance. And the US Securities and Exchange Commission (SEC) has focused on creating the best balance of Sarbanes-Oxley rules for foreign companies that conduct business in the US. But these multiple national efforts create an undue burden on companies.

The process towards reducing the burden begins with recognition by a number of companies and governments that this is what we need to drive business and economic growth. Currently, meeting national regulations can be costly. This is money that could be spent far more wisely, increasing both our innovative capability and stakeholder value. We must also be very careful about creating an undue burden on companies and tying up their resources with highly complicated regulations. By 'we' I mean businesses and governments, valuable partners in creating leading-edge business and economies. Once we recognise the need for international standards, we can move towards that goal. The road will not be easy and we will need to take small steps along the way. Until international standards are in place, we should begin by at least mutually recognising audits. This is the short-term goal. Mutual recognition would reduce this burden for everyone – for business and for government.

In the short term, companies also need to look at how they themselves can reduce their resources in driving compliance and effective corporate governance. An often overlooked area is software. In fact, most companies have actually had systems in place for years that can ensure good accounting practices and provide management with a clear, transparent overview of the company. But many systems have been underused, as has been shown by recent surveys of CIOs. While I realise that not all companies can easily integrate all their data into one system, it is a goal to work towards since it reduces complexity and increases visibility of operations and transparency of data.

While compliance ultimately lies in the hands of each company, proper IT support can help companies comply more effectively and efficiently with the regulations. An integrated system across the company can help to achieve the clarity and transparency a company needs to ensure it has effective corporate governance. One overview of the company, easily accessed by management, is the answer. Within SAP, our entire company is contained within one system, which greatly simplifies the management of our company. IT is a powerful tool for meeting today's business requirements and preparing a company for tomorrow's challenges. The talk of IT being a commodity is exaggerated – IT does matter and will continue to do so.

Growing and sustaining partnerships

Software, however, cannot create ethical behaviour. This must be inherent in the company which is why a corporate ethics policy is so important. I am a strong believer in a high level of transparency and good corporate governance; I also believe an ethics code should cover more than just executive management, which Sarbanes-Oxley limits the requirement to – it should be adopted by the entire company. This is what we have done at SAP with our 'Code of Business Conduct', adopted by the SAP Executive Board in January

2003 and by the entire company in a global rollout, completed in 2003.

Another important challenge within effective corporate governance is risk management. This is something we recognised would be critical in today's economy and that is why we have extended our risk management programme to include a corporate risk management function to harmonise the numerous, but as yet mainly stand-alone risk management efforts we have made at SAP.

Beyond effective corporate governance, a partnership with society to demonstrate leadership in governance is essential. The United Nations Global Compact is an opportunity for companies to begin a dialogue with society. Through this interdisciplinary collaboration, all sides can benefit. Companies can learn from the experiences of the UN and the participating non-governmental organisations (NGOs) and in their turn can support these organisations with their extensive business expertise. The Global Compact Portal, which SAP helped to build, is the central management and communication platform for this initiative. The Portal consolidates information from numerous sources such as applications, databases and the Internet. This supports and promotes a worldwide network and the exchange of best practices.

Another hindrance for good governance practices is corruption, which can cause the economy of an entire nation to suffer, as in Nigeria. In many countries, corruption is obstructing economic growth and the development of society. For example, it may not be possible to build or extend educational institutions because the resources allocated to such projects have disappeared into illegal channels. Through corruption, many lose for the benefit of a few. Our products can help to promote transparency in companies as business processes can be closely followed and monitored. In addition, SAP partners with organisations such as Transparency International to discuss fair business practices with other companies. INTEGRITY, one of the first sponsored projects was initiated by an SAP employee, Soji Apampa, Managing Director of SAP Nigeria. The goal of this project is to grow a network of companies, government agencies and private individuals who voluntarily agree to commit to fighting corruption. This demonstrates how the attitude of one individual can make a difference.

The future of governance

Our vision of the future sees globally recognised standards and regulations that apply to all companies. In addition, we see a new corporate vision begin to take hold, one that reflects more closely the virtualisation of our world. Looking at today's companies and the increasing use of outsourcing, new fiscal, accounting and business models will have to be developed to answer the question of how to report finances in companies that may be moving towards more of a fiscal fiction. Where does the company begin and where does it end? Twenty years from now, we should also have moved closer to global tax standards. Government regulations must match the reality of economic globalisation.

Beyond just accounting and internal governance practices, companies must continue to renew themselves with partnerships with all their stakeholders. A company is only as strong as its ecosystem and an organisation must be proactive in all areas.

All these factors come into play to create a leading-edge company, one that is integrated into the surrounding society, one that has created trusted relationships and one that recognises the importance of strong corporate governance. For me, this is doubly important, as an employee of a software company and as its CEO.

Henning Kagermann

Henning Kagermann was born in Braunschweig, Germany, in 1947. Chairman of the Executive Board of SAP AG and CEO. Taught physics and computer science at the Technical University of Braunschweig and the University of Mannheim in Germany from 1982 to 1992 while at SAP.

Paolo Scaroni

Plugged into Society

Enel is Italy's major power company, providing electricity since 1962. While no longer a state-owned monopoly, the company continues to occupy a central place in Italy's economy, producing up to 50 percent of the electricity generated in the country for about 30 million customers. Over time, our responsibilities have extended beyond those of a simple industrial operator and evolved into a close relationship with our customers.

With the advancing liberalisation of the energy industry, Enel must increasingly judge itself against an ever more competitive marketplace – a substantial change for a company that has operated as a monopoly for 40 years. But our mission is straightforward: to remain the leader in the production, distribution and sale of electricity and gas in Italy. This implies not only economic success, but transparency and openness towards all stakeholders, with an emphasis on ethics and respect for the environment. We are convinced that this will enhance both our competitiveness and the strength of our brand.

Maintaining that relationship of trust with our customers implies action in several key fields:

- corporate ethics,
- environmental friendliness,
- social responsibility and
- sustainability.

Corporate ethics

Enel operations are governed by a company-wide Code of Ethics and Organisational Model; all company managers are required to sign the Code and all 67,000 employees receive a copy. Employees are also asked to attend an online course that explains the Code and presents specific cases, with questions and answers, against which they can measure their own standards. Our commitment to correct and ethical procedures also extends to our suppliers and commercial partners, all of whom receive copies of the Code and are expected to abide by its rules. In fact, our supply contracts contain resolution clauses to ensure that the rules of the Code are followed. This is how we operate in Italy.

For the last two years we have also been active outside of Italy: in Spain through the Viesgo group; producing energy from renewable sources in Central and North America; and in Bulgaria, where we control a large thermoelectric plant which we are restructuring to increase both its efficiency and environmental friendliness. We are also participating in the privatisation process – for both generation and distribution of electricity – in a number of Central and Eastern European countries, where we can utilise the knowledge and experience gained by our own transition from a state monopoly to a publicly quoted company with 2.5 million shareholders.

The most effective international expansion is one that brings with it principles of social responsibility. We apply the same standards to our overseas companies as we do to our operations in Italy. We expect the same level of sustainable ethical behaviour from all employees and all stakeholders, regardless of the countries in which they operate. For its companies operating in the so-called 'countries at risk', Enel has prepared several specific clauses on ethics that will be progressively inserted in supply contracts. The clauses will oblige suppliers not to employ, either directly or indirectly, any person below the minimum age established by law in the country in which they will operate. Regardless of this minimum age, any work entrusted to minors (i.e. under 18 years of age) must not impair their health, safety or morality. Furthermore, suppliers will be obliged to allow Enel access to registers and/or documents containing the personal data of all employees less than 18 years of age. The ethical clauses will also cover the treatment of personnel in general, dealing with issues such as safeguarding union rights, discrimination, abuse, harassment and forced labour, as well as health and safety issues.

We have already seen a positive response from investors. Ethical funds now hold 8.4 percent of Enel capital, with the number of shares held by such funds climbing from 76 million to 93 million in the last six months (at the time of writing). Our inclusion in a number of ethical indices is a determining factor for the many funds that guarantee their clients investment in companies with the highest ethical standards. Ethical funds raise tens of billions of euros each year and interest in them continues to grow. This is because corporate social responsibility (CSR), in addition to guaranteeing the respect of ethical norms, implies a series of internal checks and procedures, as well as managers' personal involvement, to reduce to a minimum the risk of inappropriate or reckless behaviour that can be highly detrimental to a company's credibility and the value of its shares.

To strengthen the company's corporate governance and as evidence of its commitment to ethical behaviour, Enel was the first Italian company to adopt the Management and Organization Model, a legal requirement making companies liable for crimes against the civil service (e.g. bribery, extortion etc.) and for corporate crimes (false accounting etc.) committed by directors or employees for the benefit of their company. Enel's model (approved by the Board of Directors in July 2002) is comparable to those that exist in the United States and represents a further step towards compliance, transparency and a sense of responsibility in both internal and external relations. At the same time, it provides shareholders with the best guarantee of efficient and fair management.

Environmental friendliness

Enel has reported on environmental issues since 1996 and has embarked on a substantial investment programme aimed at increasing the environmental friendliness of its plants and reducing greenhouse gas emissions following Italy's ratification of the Kyoto protocol. In power production, business sustainability and environmental sustainability are inseparable.

Our environmental report is a detailed document that lists, plant by plant, the effects of our activities on the environment and the improvements made to reduce any harmful impact. This transparent approach has resulted in a close relationship with many of Italy's environmental organisations, some of which have become principal stakeholders. Together we have done much to protect and improve the areas surrounding our power plants, such as developing hiking trails, investing in the local flora and fauna, and opening power plants of all types to the public.

Environmental certification will be extended to all power plants through environmental governance instruments, alongside efforts to reduce both emissions and the consumption of natural resources. We believe that the relationship between enterprise and the environment must result in a strategy that is compatible with the economic aspects of the group and the need to protect the environment. Involving all stakeholders in our environmental policy is another fundamental step in this direction. We have also reinforced safety precautions in the workplace and protection of the workplace itself, outperforming the standard requirements.

Social responsibility

Enel has adopted the London Benchmarking Group's model. This identifies the main categories of social contributions to communities: from the activities least connected with characteristic corporate management and more intrinsically bound to the company's sense of social responsibility to the activities typical of the company's core business. Following this model, projects are divided into charity programmes, investment in communities, commercial initiatives with social impact and socially sustainable business initiatives.

In close accordance with the principles of the Code of Ethics and Organisational Model, Enel has set up (together with several of its units) a non-profit association, Enel Cuore. The association – whose activities focus on fostering social solidarity and community wellbeing – provides charitable help, promotes amateur sports for disabled people and defends the civil rights of disadvantaged persons, particularly those who are ill, children and the elderly.

Sustainability

Enel's first sustainability report was published in 2003. The report aims to guarantee greater transparency and strengthen relations with local communities. As well as providing economic and financial data, the sustainability report measures the company's progress in developing customer relations, its quality of service, workplace safety, and the professional growth and organisational efficiency of its employees. It also lists all initiatives taken to improve corporate governance and managerial transparency.

Social responsibility, concern for the environment and financial performance are interconnected – in this respect the sustainability report can be regarded as a triple bottom line document. This interconnection is evident in Enel's power generation strategy, which aims for a significant conversion of production capacity, a better fuel mix for our thermal power plants and a total rationalisation of the primary materials' supply chain. To implement these important changes, Enel has engaged a wide range of stakeholders: shareholders, investors, suppliers and employees. We have also modified our organisation and systems of corporate reporting by establishing a CSR office and nominating a sustainability controller.

To develop the sustainability report, which is verified by the Board's Audit Committee, over 700 key performance indicators (KPI) for the measurement of an organisation's sustainability were analysed; of these, 180 were selected as being the most suited to Enel. We have identified over 50 data owners within divisions, business units and directorates and transformed them into supporters, reporters and editors of the sustainability report. Via a dedicated server, they access their individual work areas and enter the KPI data they control onto spreadsheets together with an initial comment (the data are ideally updated on a monthly basis, otherwise quarterly or half yearly). The CSR manager and the controller verify the numbers and content in order to ensure a reliable quarterly sustainable operations report – a full sustainability report is published every six months. These data also allow the company's performance to be carefully monitored.

We have selected 76 strategic indicators from the KPI to act as sustainability targets. These targets are part of the CSR plan, which has been integrated into the company's five-year industrial plan. CSR goals are also factored into the remuneration packages of senior managers. With respect to economic, environmental and social responsibilities, each of our divisions and business units have specific and stated actions to pursue within the company's wider industrial plan.

Our efforts have not gone without recognition – Enel won the 2003 'Oscar' for the best sustainability report, an award with a long and prestigious history in Italy. On the international stage, the company gained a Global Energy Award in 2002 for its commitment to and leadership in renewable energy, one of the most important international plaudits in the energy sector. The company was also recently included in the FTSE4Good GLOBAL 100, the index that ranks the top 100 companies in terms of environmental and social sustainability.

The digital meter

Perhaps Enel's ultimate customer–company interaction tool is the new digital meter. Since its introduction in 2001, almost 13 million have been installed to date. The meter allows remote contract management and will provide customers with the opportunity to buy power at different rates according to the time of day. The savings on individual electricity bills are obvious, but what may be less apparent is the potential benefit for the country's electricity system as a whole.

During the summer of 2003 at peak consumption times, Italy's electricity grid frequently came close to overloading. By encouraging people to move some of their electricity consumption to off-peak periods using the digital meter, the threat to the system will be significantly diminished. To further promote the intelligent use of electricity, Enel has entered into agreements with a number of large retailers for the sale of high-efficiency electrical appliances; customers are offered discounts on low energy consumption light bulbs.

Enel sees no contradiction between corporate social responsibility and good economic performance. This is why we are fully committed to the path we have chosen and believe it provides a critical edge in an ever more competitive, global and open world.

Paolo Scaroni

Paolo Scaroni was born in Vicenza, Italy, in 1946. CEO of ENEL SpA since 2002. Graduate of Bocconi University and Columbia University Business School; board member of BAE Systems, Alliance UniChem, and Columbia Business School. Member of the supervisory board of ABN Amro Bank and the executive committee of the Confederation of Italian Industry – Confindustria. Among his publications: *Profession – Manager*.

J.T. Battenberg III

Global Partnership from a Business Perspective

We are what we repeatedly do.
Excellence then, is not an act, but a habit.
Aristotle

Delphi Corporation, a $28 billion leading global manufacturer of automotive and technology systems, was founded in 1999 following its spin-off from General Motors. Its culture is based on principles of excellence, along the lines of Aristotle's thought. To assume that Delphi's commitment to excellence is a banner unfolded only at corporate gatherings and media events would be incorrect. Excellence is the commitment we make to ourselves, our colleagues, our customers, our shareholders and the communities in which we work – Delphi is making excellence its global habit.

There are many examples of excellence I could mention that have direct bearing on how Delphi achieves the fundamentals of its business strategy. Executing that strategy is after all a lead driver in the creation of shareholder value, the ultimate benchmark in the success of a public company. But the real question is how do we maximize our resources globally? How do we translate the concepts we use in our everyday business – 'lean', 'technology-leading', 'ISO Certified' or 'corporate governance' – into achieving greater success with all of our 4,000 supplier companies, foreign governments and 186,000 global employees? We do it through global partnerships.

Let's start with corporate governance. In preparation for Delphi's spin-off from General Motors in 1999, the late Tom

Wyman, our inaugural lead director, and I set specific guidelines for experience and skill for potential board members. We wanted people who could partner with us by providing insight into running a global company operating in 41 countries. We wanted specific experience in finance, banking, marketing, manufacturing, electronics, computer technology and organized labor.

Today, the make-up of Delphi's 13-member Board of Directors (10 outside; 3 inside) is consistent with our business strategy of growth and future success. We have representation from Europe, Asia and South America; we secured leaders from the manufacturing, consumer products and automotive sales arenas as well as executives from marketing and labor relations. Delphi's Board is active in its commitment to open, honest and leadership-oriented corporate governance that helps drive value to shareholders. Its hands-on relationship with management takes a measured commitment in the extra time the Board spends on issues but in the end, it is this sense of partnership with Delphi management that provides the catalyst for the organization to help meet its business objectives.

This partnership is the reason why Delphi's excellence in corporate governance has been recognized by others. Jay Lorsch, Professor of Human Relations at Harvard said, 'One reason we use the formation of Delphi and its Board of Directors as a case study at Harvard is because the corporation broke new ground when it formed its board. It focused on the best fundamentals of corporate governance – what company managers now refer to as Delphi DNA.' For Delphi, it is excellence in the formation of partnerships that will ensure success.

Maximizing resources globally is the top priority of Delphi's purchasing initiatives, and forming partnerships to achieve that goal is essential. Annually, Delphi spends nearly $15 billion with its suppliers to meet customer demands globally. We can't achieve excellence in supply chain management in a vacuum, nor can we assume that our suppliers understand everything we ask of them given the extreme complexity of the automotive and technology businesses Delphi pursues. In that context, Delphi took the opportunity in 1999 to reach out and partner with its global supply community in establishing understandable common processes which have led to better communication and improved products for our customers.

For example, supplier continuous improvement seminars are now held on a regular basis while in the past these were conducted only as and when problems arose. By leveraging Delphi's expertise in lean manufacturing, process control and materials management across a wide range of suppliers, we have been able to improve on the price, delivery and quality of nearly all parts we use.

A good example of this occurred recently when we worked with one of our suppliers to avoid a $3 million potential price increase. The supplier informed us that it was losing money on manufacturing two parts and indicated that a major price increase would be necessary. Delphi's cross-functional team, made up of engineering, materials management, finance and logistics personnel, established a series of workshops with the supplier to help determine its true costs. We helped the supplier's engineers to improve the manufacturing process, reduce waste and create a lean delivery process including a reduction in labor cost. The result: a 96 percent reduction in the proposed price increase, better quality and an improved relationship with a valued partner.

We have initiated this process with nearly 100 of our major suppliers in North America, Europe and Asia/Pacific and we're seeing cost improvements across the board. Going forward, establishing and managing existing supplier partnerships with proven cost savings and cost avoidance techniques will be key to meeting profitability targets and for maximizing future growth.

Another area in which Delphi strives for excellence is safety. In fact, this area is a terrific example of how partnerships with employees, unions and suppliers, together with open and constant communication, can move the needle forward to become world class. It would be easy to give examples of how Delphi has moved to near the top in manufacturing safety in the past five years, noting the reductions in lost working days, and the incremental savings resulting from these improvements. However, the real message here is that we at Delphi made a commitment to change the way we viewed our operations. We changed the way we interacted with our employees and unions and backed up that change with increased training and timely implementation of process improvements.

It's not magic … it's living a partnership. We asked our employees globally – together with the unions who represent them – to be a part of this process at all times and to hold us accountable for any improvements they might suggest. Many would say that we should have been doing that all along, and they are quite right. Although Delphi conducted safety process training in the past, progress remained slow until the organization assigned it a visible priority, monitored and measured it and held accountable those implementing the changes.

Delphi continues to make safety a top priority in its business, not only for the benefits mentioned but also from the employee viewpoint as it instills pride in the workplace, efficiencies in processes and most of all, a sense of ownership among employees to maintain high standards. For example, over the past 10 years, improved safety procedures and employee awareness at all global locations have helped us to achieve a reduction in lost working days per employee by a factor of 20. That's a recapture of over 5,000 lost working days annually, translating into millions of dollars of cost avoidance and resulting in measurable productivity improvements. At the end of the day, a company cannot force its employees to read from the same book on any given subject; everyone supporting improved safety through a workable and trusting partnership is simply excellence in the workplace.

Manufacturing in the global workplace also requires Delphi to partner with a wide range of social and government entities on programs that affect its employees where they work and live. This can be called community involvement, good business or good government relations but we tend to think it's all of the above. It is also part of Delphi's DNA to be a good citizen in the countries in which it does business. Going forward and partnering with the responsible organizations in those countries where we operate can only result in benefits to all parties from an investment, employment and profitability viewpoint.

For example, of Delphi's 186,000 employees, 70,000 work in Mexico. We have been a corporate citizen there since 1978 (when part of General Motors), and currently have 57 plants and engineering facilities and 14 joint venture plants. In total, Delphi represents a $1.6 billion direct infusion into Mexico's annual economy. During the past 10 years, Delphi has partnered with a government agency in Mexico along with a private US/Mexican joint venture builder to promote and create special housing programs for employees in seven cities. This effort created simple, decent housing for about 6,000 employees with an additional positive economic impact of creating nearly 40,000 jobs to support the construction and material acquisition activities. The added effect of this effort also resulted in investment by local government in new schools and recreation areas, and by private investors in shopping centers to improve the quality of life for everyone.

The results of this partnership have been quite measurable and beneficial to both the company and its employees. Statistics show that turnover at our plants in Mexico among employees participating in this program was about one-tenth of one percent a month – dramatically lower than the historical Delphi average for Mexico of 10 percent monthly. This

131

program, along with initiatives in continuing education, environmentally friendly plants, benchmark-level safe working conditions and being designated by employees as 'The best place to work in Mexico', validate our philosophy of being a partner with all the various parties in countries and communities where we operate.

Being a successful partner also requires that management should adapt to local cultural and business operating practices. Specifically, in 1997, Delphi took unilateral steps to improve women's rights and opportunities in Mexico. Under Mexican law, employers had the right to defer employment if a woman tested positive for pregnancy, regardless of her qualifications for the job. In addition to legal precedence, this was also a cultural practice in the country. Employers also had to assume certain expenses associated with medical coverage for the woman in lieu of governmental health care.

Following consultation with various stakeholders, Delphi decided that pregnancy should not be a reason to defer or deny employment to a qualified woman and implemented a new policy of: 'Hire the best candidate! Period.' In addition, a new pregnant employee is provided with in-plant medical services and counseling. In another unprecedented move, Delphi operations in selected cities with higher proportions of female employees offered a *Sala de Lactancia* – nursing rooms for breastfeeding – enabling new mothers to feed their infants brought to the plant, or to express breast milk in a hygienic atmosphere for safe storage and subsequent transport home. Results of this initiative have proven extremely positive – as well as being much appreciated by female employees, it has gained significant media coverage.

It is ironic that early coverage of this issue by media outlets in Mexico looked at the development in a critical light, claiming a possible affront to traditional cultural mores. Despite this early criticism, Mexican President Vicente Fox recently chose a Delphi plant as the model for women's opportunities and employer care for women.

Since 1999, seven Delphi operations in Mexico have earned the prestigious Shingo Prize for manufacturing excellence, an award often called, 'the Nobel Prize for manufacturing'. Nearly all Delphi-Mexico operations have repeatedly achieved federal recognition – *Industria Limpia* – for environmental excellence. Delphi-Mexico has built its own wastewater treatment systems in locations where municipal systems are lacking and Delphi continues to interact with all levels of government in Mexico concerning competitive issues in an open dialogue and in an environment of mutual respect.

In China, one of Delphi's fastest growing markets, partnerships with government and local manufacturers are essential. Identifying capable, strategic partners locally that can work with us to meet expanding customer needs helps to build an infrastructure that not only benefits the automotive industry but also the country as a whole. While business management challenges exist in any location, we have found strong manufacturing partners in China to help us not only to meet customer expectations but also to allow these ventures to grow sequentially with new investment opportunities as our customers expand their sales.

To support that growth, Delphi also established relationships with several universities in China to provide the training needed for its growing employee base. This relationship has also proven beneficial in the recruitment of graduates to fill the various engineering, finance, sales and manufacturing positions in China, a win-win situation for both the company and the country. Additionally, Delphi has assisted the local communities in which it operates. In Guang' an, Sichuan Province, the company helped the local government (in 1999) to build a new health clinic. Delphi's donation also enabled the clinic to buy new medical equipment such as X-ray machines that serve thousands of residents in the local area.

Delphi has a vision that is constant and unwavering: to be its customers' best supplier. The tools we use to achieve that

133

vision are no different than those used by other companies: leadership, responsibility, innovation, technology and strategy. However, the common link between these tools is excellence – it reinforces who we are and how we operate. Sharing responsibilities as a principle of partnership in business has been and will continue to be a key for future business success. But within that success, it will be the company that demands excellence in the application of the tools used that will be of the most benefit. And the company that draws on the skills of its workers to facilitate the attributes of excellence will find that success not only rewards employees but is also quantifiable to business growth.

Delphi is a hands-on company. Our leadership is challenged daily in the quest to teach employees how to use excellence to make a difference in their job. We operate in a culture of openness and clear ethics. We are a technology and knowledge-rich company with a value-centered leadership that has a track record of consistency and continuity, important to both customers and employees. Our vision, values, long-term financial goals and core business strategies are unchanged. Combine all of these Team Delphi traits and you have our corporate DNA. We have a shared philosophy at Delphi – 'It's not just what we do, it's how we do it.'

In summary, governance in the 21st century – particularly what makes Delphi different – is the full realization and utilization of partnerships to achieve business success. To us, this means simply putting sound business practices into place from the very beginning, seizing the opportunity to form partnerships with key parties and then executing strategies that benefit the enterprise. At Delphi, we work daily to achieve measurable results and to bring success to everyone involved, keeping in mind Aristotle's maxim: 'We are what we repeatedly do. Excellence then, is not an act, but a habit.'

J. T. Battenberg III

J. T. Battenberg III was born in Springfield, Missouri, in 1943. Chairman, Chief Executive Officer and President of Delphi Corporation. Serves on several corporate and academic boards, including the Sara Lee Corporation, Columbia University Business School, and the National Advisory Board for J. P. Morgan Chase. Named Statesman of the Year by the Harvard Business Club of Detroit in 2002. Chairs the Fiscal Policy Task Force of the US Business Roundtable.

The Civil Society Contribution

Claus Leggewie

Flight or Fight? NGOs, Business and the State in an Interconnected World

The 1990s are widely held to be the decade of the non-governmental organisation (NGO). Behind the abbreviation hides a broad and varied spectrum of private organisations with public goals. NGOs have forged a path between the state and the market; that is, they have established themselves alongside those actors that up until now have dominated the international system. NGOs can be defined provisionally according to what they *don't* do: they don't exercise governmental power and they don't pursue profit. However, if we look more closely, we can establish roughly what they are and what they do: they work to achieve all manner of collective goods, from clean drinking water for all, through safeguarding the rights of persecuted cultural minorities, to ensuring that citizens are able freely to exercise their rights. As local as these goods may appear, and as limited as the scope of some NGOs is, these are nonetheless global collective goods. During the last decade, NGOs were the fastest-growing phenomena in our interconnected world. This enabled them to achieve something that until then had seemed barely conceivable: to organise collective interests which are either ignored in the short-term thinking of most business actors or are passed over by overstretched welfare states. What is even more astonishing is that they have been able to do this beyond the borders of national economies and nation-states, thereby helping to renew the old dream of the global citizen.

Many thousands of NGOs have now been accredited by the United Nations and granted an official status that makes it appropriate, in some cases, to speak of 'co-governmental organisations'. Other NGOs have preferred not to take this semi-official route into the conference room and the parliamentary lobby, preferring instead to continue relying on self-help or to mobilise social protest and political opposition. However, many are represented both on the street and at the negotiating table. Recent studies, such as that done by the British consultancy firm SustainAbility, have accorded them the elevated status of 'most influential organisations' of the 21st century.

What is relatively new is that NGOs now negotiate not only with state apparatuses but also with global companies. They are the second actor to have moved powerfully into the limelight over the last few decades, following a period of company mergers and acquisitions of unprecedented proportions which has resulted in the formation of global corporations or transnational corporations (TNCs) whose turnover even exceeds the gross domestic product of most newly industrialised countries. After many years during which the NGOs and TNCs held each other in mutual suspicion, there are now several instances of working contacts and information exchange taking place. The basic idea common to both is that the improvements being sought cannot be achieved by government action alone – on the contrary, bitter disappointment has set in with regard to both nation-states and international organisations. Instead, there is recognition that transnational companies not only share the responsibility, but can be expected to come up with more flexible solutions.

Employers and managers have found that it is often easier to get along and make progress with groups that are firmly rooted in society, rather than with administrations and over-

137

inflated bureaucracies. They make use of their contacts with local NGOs, not least in order to explore how best to undertake investments in difficult territory. What started out as a form of bi-lateral antagonistic cooperation – the conflict-laden coexistence of governments and NGOs – has become a triangle, with the much heralded figure of civil society as a third pillar, alongside the state and the market. For global companies, this is merely a logical expression of the retreat of the state: in this case, the privatisation of global politics.

Of course, this doesn't mean that all is sweetness and light between the NGOs and transnational companies. Many ordinary members of NGOs remain deeply suspicious; anti-capitalist in their thinking, they expect nothing much other than environmental misdemeanours, child labour and political corruption from the 'invisible hand of the market'. In addition, the grass roots of NGOs are worlds apart from the management milieu. On the other hand, employers and managers still have vivid images in their minds of violence in Seattle, Genoa and Gothenburg, where masked militants engaged in skirmishes with their enemy, state power, and in the process wrecked the premises of banks and companies.

Caution should be exercised with regard to these sorts of suggestive images. They cannot conceal the fact that many thousands of peaceful demonstrators want to see a different world brought into being. However one might judge the transnational protest movement against the World Trade Organization (WTO), G8 and EU economic summits, these are the issues that command the much sought-after involvement and participation of ordinary citizens – people whose horizons extend well beyond their own backyard. Most of the protesters are young and it is certainly worth listening to them. There is also a great opportunity here for young people, whose political participation is often sorely missed, to play a role, taking their cue not so much from parties and elections as from the broad swathe of NGOs and their often unconventional, but non-violent, forms of action. Only a fraction of the protesters are prepared to commit violence – the majority take a pacific approach.

In view of all this, is it possible for big business and 'good' people to come together, beyond occasional acts of charity? The answer must be yes, but this will not be without elements of conflict and compromise. The spectacular clashes over Shell's Brent Spar drilling platform, for example, or Nike's use of child labour in its South East Asian supplier companies set the ball rolling. Although these sorts of conflicts are still taking place, compromises are now being reached much more frequently. Global companies have become more cautious now that most NGOs have professional campaign management and resourceful legal departments. Appeals for boycotts are fast turned into action in many locations, causing companies to fear not so much loss of income as loss of image – for a global brand, a poor reputation is fatal. Negotiations nowadays between corporations and representatives from NGOs are less like the heated arguments of yesteryear and more akin to ceasefire negotiations held under the auspices of cool and calculating lawyers.

However, the situation is far from ideal. Some company boards feel thoroughly duped by the NGOs: no sooner have they grudgingly agreed to impose stricter measures in respect of the environment or worker safety than the other side demands yet more – from the very companies that have moved the furthest! Another disruptive factor is the sometimes lax way in which data on toxic emissions have been brought into the public domain, as well as the one-sidedness with which many representatives of NGOs appear to allow corrupt state elites in Africa to get away with anything while coming down hard on any improprieties committed by Western corporations. Still, the other side has no less to complain about – broken promises, manipulated data and, frequently, duplicity as well. How often have NGOs been used, only then to be dropped from a considerable height? **139**

Does the ambition to save the world rule out profit maximisation in principle? Certainly in the short term it does, and probably in the longer term too. This will continue to offer plenty of material for conflict between corporations and NGOs. In the medium term, though, both sides can obviously benefit from greater cooperation. In the past, companies often found themselves up against impassive authoritarian systems which guaranteed them (apparent!) security for their investments, all too often ignoring the consequences of their investments for the ecological balance of the country concerned and ultimately also for the situation of their employees. Nowadays, the objectives pursued by NGOs, such as ecological sustainability, democracy and minimum social standards, also feed into investment decisions. The disaster of the African continent clearly illustrates the kind of situation companies and free trade can find themselves in when non-economic aspects are neglected to such a great extent. One of the basic lessons of history is that political democratisation and economic liberalisation usually go hand in hand – free markets don't work well without democracy and democracy doesn't work well without social safety nets and ecological sustainability.

This political axiom of democracy is combined today with the gentle persuasion of global networks. Integrated thinking disciplines the business operatives of globalisation just as much as it does their critics. Their cooperation is made easier by the fact that those who are all too hastily labelled 'opponents of globalisation' by the media are basically after an 'alternative globalisation' – they are not against the removal of boundaries in the world per se. This is the premise according to which, for example, the NGO working for fair trade, Global Exchange, entered into a contract with the Starbucks chain; the latter now offer 'fair trade' coffee on its menu, which gives the producers in the Third World a better margin than products sourced from conventional suppliers.

Starbucks partnering NGOs that are struggling for fair

trade and against free trade ideology and brand mania? No wonder the NGOs were accused of having sold out, of having betrayed their principles to a brand despised by many critics of globalisation. Historically speaking, social movements have repeatedly been faced with a similar dilemma: should they stick to their maximum demands as fundamentalists (and thereby fail) or should they make concessions according to the demands of realpolitik and thereby achieve a proportion of their objectives – albeit at the cost of their 'squeaky clean' identity? Concerns are increasingly being voiced, even among the political realists, that such tactics could turn NGOs, once self-declared watchdogs, into harmless lapdogs.

Apart from such strategic considerations, people in business-affiliated think tanks have begun to wonder what future shape NGOs could take, including how they might act as market-friendly networks that operate in the markets themselves. SustainAbility predicts the following trends in the 21st century: first, NGOs will change from being outsiders to being insiders, no longer simply uncovering problems but also endeavouring to find solutions to them. They will acquire money and other resources less via moral appeals and more by encouraging donors to invest in a positive future. Finally, NGOs will no longer be single-issue campaigns but will start pursuing multidimensional strategies. They will remain non-profit organisations, but will apply best practice in terms of transparency, accountability and management.

If NGOs follow this route, then they will clearly be taking on an element of the identity and practice of companies, which will make them more attractive to economic actors per se. This was one of the provocative theories with which SustainAbility entered the 'lion's den': the World Social Forum in Porto Alegre (Brazil) in 2003. The organisers of the annual World Economic Forum in Davos are pursuing very similar ideas, and the representatives of the NGOs are now quite at home there. **141**

NGOs as part of the Davos culture? To most of their representatives and spokespeople this is not an attractive prospect, but they have undoubtedly grown in self-confidence in relation to TNCs, just as those who can now envisage entering into a purposeful alliance with specific corporations and enlightened representatives of the World Bank and the International Monetary Fund (IMF) – and perhaps even with the WTO and the G8 bureaucracy – have also grown in number. They are encouraged in this by the exceptionally company-friendly programme of UN Secretary-General Kofi Annan, who in 1999 established the Global Compact, a platform of values shared by the UN and various companies and to which over 1200 members now belong. He did this, first, because he wanted to remind leading economic figures of their obligations in terms of respect for human rights, the environment and workers' rights; in addition, however, the UN does not want to have to rely on the resources and consent of its member states alone – especially the United States – which regularly exercise political pressure and withhold the payments they are obliged to make.

This progress has chiefly met with scepticism on the part of the NGOs. They demand the implementation of clear rules and sanctions for companies that misbehave, instead of non-binding declarations of intent and voluntary contributions that can be revoked at any time. Critics conjecture that the Global Compact is more of a PR stunt on the part of politicians to boost their image and to enable them to pass on their responsibilities to business. They are in effect issuing a reminder that the differences between the market and the state need to remain. In their opinion, there is no way the rapprochement between NGOs and business should be allowed to undermine the already weakened capacity of politics. Indeed, it is true that neither commercial activity nor sustainability and human rights can be advanced without a 'commonwealth of democracies', that is, democratically governed nations. A global civil society that depends on the invisible hand of the market and the moral capital of NGOs lacks political backbone.

Finally, it is worth highlighting the one characteristic that most NGOs and companies have in common of which they are either unaware or do not consider a problem: a striking lack of accountability. Companies are principally concerned with pursuing the profit-related interests of their owners and shareholders, but in reality large corporations frequently take on public tasks alongside and in competition with nation-states, whose political elites they are able to place under enormous pressure. By virtue of this they have acquired a form of political power that has thus far eluded any kind of monitoring or counterweight. The neo-conservative American Enterprise Institute, of all organisations, recently posted a web page accusing the NGOs of lacking legitimacy and accountability – without showing any willingness whatsoever to put its own house in order first.

Fundamentally, however, the accusation aimed at the NGOs is an apt one, even if they rightly insist that they are playing a democratic role by bringing issues into the public sphere which governments, political parties and parliaments have either ignored or played down. Nonetheless, they too are faced with a problem of legitimatisation as soon as they are no longer merely informing and mobilising the global public but are contributing in either actual or formal terms towards political decision-making. One might say that the NGOs are faced with a paradox of democratisation. Who has given them a mandate? Who monitors their activities? Democratic governments and international organisations have been given a mandate, either directly or indirectly, from the people who elected them, while NGOs, like large companies, have nothing of the kind, even though both are increasingly involved in political activity in today's global society.

Transparency and social responsibility in the sense of *corporate citizenship* are appropriate ways of eliminating this deficit, at least in part. But it shows once again that political

143

actors with a democratic mandate have by no means become superfluous. In an interconnected world it is more and more important that entrepreneurial activity, political frameworks and citizens' initiatives are fine-tuned. It is impossible to imagine this network without the NGOs.

The consequences of this for statehood and diplomacy at the start of the 21st century are plain. In future, more state and interstate functions will be carried out by *private–public partnerships*, and foreign policy will often mean foreign economic policy, i.e. requiring close communication with global corporations as well as those at home. Certainly, diplomats will seek to make better contacts with representatives of NGOs and will have to cultivate *public diplomacy* – greater transparency and openness. But the political character of diplomacy must remain intact and not become overly detached from the state. Ultimately it is in the interests not only of businesses but also of the 'third sector', for civil society's economic and citizen-based projects to remain within a political context under democratic control. Not every political task can be privatised or outsourced. What is needed instead at the start of the 21st century is a political renaissance, meaning not merely or even principally statehood in a national guise. It is by this route, using trial and error, that *global governance*, i.e. governance beyond the nation-state, will take shape.

Claus Leggewie
Claus Leggewie was born in 1950. Professor of Political Science at the University of Giessen, Germany, since 1989. Guest professor at a number of universities including the University of Paris at Nanterre and New York University. Author of numerous publications.

Patricia Wolf

Partnership for Change: Shareholder Advocacy and the Faith Community

Introduction

In 1971, several clergy from Protestant denominations, concerned that they were profiting from the system of racial apartheid in South Africa and the Vietnam War, founded the Interfaith Center for Corporate Responsibility (ICCR). Although they didn't know it then, they also founded a movement. The group's first social policy shareholder resolution was filed the same year, calling upon General Motors to withdraw from South Africa.

By 1975, ICCR membership embraced 12 national Protestant Church agencies and 28 Roman Catholic organizations. The increasing involvement of the Catholic community coincided with a deepened consciousness of the integration of faith and action and the internalization of the 1971 World Synod of Catholic Bishops' document *Justice in the World,* which states:

> Action on behalf of justice and participation in the transformation of the world fully appear to us as a constitutive dimension of the preaching of the Gospel, or, in other words, of the Church's mission for the redemption of the human race and its liberation from every oppressive situation.

Today, ICCR's membership numbers 275 Protestant, Catholic, and Jewish institutional investors, including denominations, religious orders, pension funds, foundations, health systems, and dioceses. Its members connect their mission to their investment strategies and decisions. Commonly adopted principles for investment activity include upholding human dignity, environmental responsibility, and the achievement of world peace.

In 1995, a growing connectedness and networking among faith-based organizations led to the collaboration between three religious shareholder groups – ICCR, the Ecumenical Council for Corporate Responsibility (ECCR) based in the United Kingdom, and the Taskforce on the Churches and Corporate Responsibility (now called KAIROS) with its headquarters in Canada – to develop *Principles for Global Corporate Responsibility.*

The concerns to which this project gave voice were then on the margins of public debate. Now, those same concerns, such as global labor standards and access to life-saving drugs, have moved to center stage. Faith-based and socially responsible investors have played a major role in building this recognition and momentum.

In 2002, the third edition of the *Principles for Global Corporate Responsibility* was published, heralding a new era of partnership among the faith community and non-governmental groups in both 'developing' and 'developed' countries. A unique product of collaboration among groups from north and south, east and west, in addition to the initial architects of the first edition, members include the Christian Centre for Socially Responsible Investment (based in Australia), the Hong Kong Christian Industrial Committee (based in Hong Kong), the Bench Marks Foundation of Southern Africa for Corporate Responsibility (based in South Africa), and Censat Aqua Viva, Friends of the Earth (based in Columbia, South America).

The Principles for Global Corporate Responsibility: Bench Marks for Measuring Business Performance

The long-range goal of the *Bench Marks* document is to transform the way corporations relate to people, communities, and the environment. It is designed to promote positive corporate responsibility. It is *not* a set of reporting standards such as the Global Reporting Initiative (GRI). It is *not* a set of principles to be endorsed by corporations in an effort to gain public credibility and legitimacy. Rather, the document states expectations of corporate behavior based on internationally recognized standards and norms, and the experience of individuals and organizations in many parts of the world. Written in the context of faith, it calls for new relationships between corporations, communities, and ecosystems built upon equitable relationships that include those most affected by the activities of corporations. From the perspective of faith, the context for all human activity is the totality of creation. Therefore, we need to use our power to live in harmony with creation, affirm the interdependence of everything on earth, and the dignity of all living creatures.

The *Bench Marks* document is divided into three categories: Principles, Criteria, and Bench Marks.

1. By *Principles* we mean a statement of business philosophy fundamental to a responsible company's actions.
2. By *Criteria* we mean particular company policies and practices that can be compared for consistency with the *Principles.*
3. By *Bench Marks* we mean suggested specific reference points of measurement to be used in assessing a company's performance in relation to the *Criteria.*

For example, in the section addressing the contract supplier system, that structural dimension of globalization that drives **147** corporations to move from country to country in the quest for low-cost labor, we state:

1. *Principle:* The company accepts responsibility for all those whom it employs either directly or indirectly through contract suppliers, sub-contractors, vendors, or suppliers.
2. *Criteria:* The company has a strong code of conduct for vendors and suppliers which includes, but is not limited to, child labor, forced labor, harassment, non-discrimination, healthy and safe workplace, freedom of association and the right to bargain collectively, sustainable living wages and benefits, hours of work, the environment, supportive social and physical community infrastructure and monitoring mechanisms for compliance.
3. *Bench Marks:* The company clearly communicates to its suppliers, vendors and licensees the company's code of vendor/supplier conduct and its process of enforcement. Violations of the code are effectively addressed. Cancellation of a contract is used only as a last resort.

The balance between yield and impact

Before discussing the application of the *Bench Marks* document through shareholder advocacy, it is important to acknowledge the wide range of attitudes toward corporate responsibility and whether a social investment approach is consistent with fiduciary responsibility. Often it is assumed that yield is sacrificed through the implementation of socially responsible investment (SRI) strategies. We do not believe this is the case. The ICCR is not a social investment firm, but its members are all long-term investors who expect a competitive rate of return on their investments to support retirement funds, endowments, and other needs. Our philosophy of investment is evident in the *Bench Marks* document. We believe that social and environmental factors do have an impact on risk and long-term financial performance.

Increasingly the research supports this position. A joint study by Morgan Stanley Dean Witter Bank and the independent rating agency, Oekom Research, tested the idea that sustainable investments lag behind the market in terms of financial performance and found that sustainability leaders in the MSCI World Index financially outperformed sustainability laggards over the past four years (31 December 1999–27 October 2003). The study analyzed the share price movements of 602 companies which together make up approximately 80 percent of the market capitalization value of the MSCI World Index; of these 186 were judged to be sustainability leaders in their respective sectors. On a year-to-year basis, the best-in-class portfolio outperformed the MCSI World Index by 3.76 percent.

Innovest Strategic Value Advisors, an investment research and advisory firm specializing in finance and the environment, reported on research conducted on behalf of a major US public pension fund that wanted to investigate whether or not environmental and social (SRI) analysis could be used as part of decision-making in its investment process without having an adverse impact on the risk adjusted returns of its portfolios. The results generally indicate that using the firms' proprietary environmental values rating in the investment process had a positive effect on five of six investment portfolios.

However, Innovest goes further in its conclusions, positing that there is every reason for fiduciaries and their money managers to believe that SRI considerations will become a greater factor in the future. Global 'mega-trends' which can be expected to increase the *financial* importance of SRI factors include: the globalization and intensification of industrial competition, particularly into emerging markets, exponentially increasing the level of environmental and social risk for major corporations and investors; growing pressure from the international non-governmental organizations (NGOs), armed with unprecedented resources, credibility, and global communications platforms; and changing demographics for both consumers and investors, substantially increasing the saliency and financial stakes of companies' environmental and social performance.

ICCR shareholder advocacy approach

This vision of civil society leads us forward to the mission of ICCR: to hold corporations accountable and to advance the cause of justice with a particular emphasis on the oppressed, impoverished, and exploited. We implement and advance the mission by using our leverage as shareowners to open up direct dialogue with corporate leaders, file shareholder resolutions, and collaborate with other NGOs. With the *Bench Marks* document as a guide, these strategies represent our approach to effective corporate change and a response to systemic issues raised by the globalized economy.

One such issue is the contract supplier system. We believe companies are accountable for the labor, social, and environmental conditions under which their products and services are produced. The challenge is to persuade companies to ensure that their suppliers, vendors and factory management respect the dignity of the workers by creating a safe and healthy workplace where the rights of workers are enforced. Companies need to understand that this type of corporate behavior actually is good business practice. ICCR's goal is for companies to adopt a strong code of conduct to include a full range of worker rights, to issue transparent, comprehensive public reports, and to collaborate with NGOs in training and monitoring. Three companies addressed by ICCR are Gap, Disney, and the Coca-Cola Company, all strategic leaders in their industry sector.

ICCR members have engaged Gap in shareholder dialogue and action since 1995. The *Bench Marks* document has informed that dialogue, leading to some significant breakthroughs in the implementation and monitoring of codes of conduct in clothing supplier factories in Central America. Following six months of letter-writing by religious and community groups and face-to-face discussions with the company, Gap agreed, in 1995, to explore independent monitoring at Mandarin International, a factory making Gap products in San Salvador where labor violations had been uncovered. The Independent Monitoring Working Group (IMWG) was established with representatives from ICCR, Gap, and Business for Social Responsibility. The IMWG assisted Gap to define independent monitoring and identify key religious, human rights and labor rights groups in San Salvador in order to monitor the Mandarin factory and oversee the re-hiring of workers previously dismissed for attempting to form a union. Four local non-governmental groups formed the Independent Monitoring Group of El Salvador (GMIES). GMIES began monitoring Mandarin in 1996 and now monitors a number of Gap-sourced factories in El Salvador. In addition GMIES has monitored labor conditions for other companies and issued public reports on its findings.

This development is historic. Gap is the first company to agree to develop an independent monitoring mechanism for its contract suppliers. Other companies have hired auditing firms to monitor codes of conduct, but GMIES was the first independent monitoring group working in the clothing sector made up of local NGOs who know the local culture, language, factory context and who also have the trust of workers.

This major advance in supplier monitoring and corporate accountability came about because ICCR brought Gap into the process; the company used its influence to help improve the working conditions of employees. Following pressure from shareholders for accountability, local groups with the necessary skill, dedication and expertise to identify problems that needed to be addressed were engaged. Today in Central America there are independent monitoring groups in Guatemala, Honduras and Nicaragua.

In 1996, a group of ICCR members and associates began

discussions with the Walt Disney Company on codes of conduct, implementation and monitoring. For three years, shareholders filed resolutions calling on the company to adopt the International Labour Organization core labor standards. We urged it to utilize independent monitors as a part of its compliance program and issue public reports on its progress. There were infrequent meetings with Disney top management and little progress was made. However, since the year 2000, due to a change in social compliance leadership, considerable progress has been made and the ICCR shareholder group has developed a constructive relationship with the company. This has resulted in improvements in Disney's code of conduct: workers now have the right to organize a union and bargain collectively; ICCR is allowed to observe and comment on Disney's monitoring process in a supplier plant in the Dominican Republic; and Disney has made a commitment to work with local NGOs to enhance the company's monitoring and training efforts. The company has also been encouraged to be more transparent by issuing public reports on its labor compliance efforts.

There is continued in-depth shareholder involvement, addressing issues such as sustainable compliance with labor codes of conduct, what systems need to be put in place at the factory level to ensure compliance over time, and the role of education and training of workers and managers in order to improve the working conditions in supplier factories.

ICCR shareholders are also currently engaged in discussions with the Coca-Cola Company on two issues: contract suppliers and, as a large employer in sub-Saharan Africa, the impact of HIV/AIDS on its operations and the company's response to this health pandemic. Central to the discussion is Coca-Cola's relationship with its bottling suppliers. ICCR believes enforcement of the company codes of conduct should extend to the bottlers, but the company maintains that its abilities to impose enforcement are limited as it has no direct control over the bottling businesses.

The *Bench Marks* document calls upon companies, operating in those countries lacking in government provision of universal health coverage, to provide adequate health facilities for employees and dependents. This includes supplying necessary essential medicines such as antiretrovirals for HIV/AIDS sufferers.

HIV is a core business problem for Coca-Cola in Africa. In the early stages of dialogue with ICCR, the company agreed to provide treatment for their direct employees immediately. Although there is a limited accountability structure between Coca-Cola and its bottlers, the company has come under increasing pressure from ICCR and other NGOs for failing to meet its responsibilities to bottler employees. Nonetheless, Coca-Cola's transparency has been laudable. The Coca-Cola Africa Foundation estimates (at the time of writing) that 5,000 of their 60,000 bottler employees are HIV positive, 909 have tested positive, and 25 are receiving antiretroviral treatment.

A Coca-Cola bottler has been accused of human rights abuses in a plant in Columbia and a lawsuit based on the Alien Tort Claims Act is currently in the US District Court for the Southern District of Florida. In addition, there are moves toward an international boycott of Coca-Cola. Loss of reputation is a key financial risk factor and it is becoming increasingly difficult for Coca-Cola to distance itself from the behavior of its brand bottlers. With ICCR's assistance, the company is currently trying to re-establish an accountability structure but its history and culture make this a difficult goal to achieve.

Conclusion

More than 30 years ago ICCR was considered naive and frivolous when its members used their shareholder power to address the role of corporations in maintaining the apartheid structure in South Africa. Today no institution is more closely associated with social policy shareholder resolutions than ICCR, and no one individual is more closely associated with influencing corporate social policy than the members of the faith community. We have tackled major social problems and urged corporate leaders to understand and look at their responsibilities and obligations in new ways. The message has been heard in civil society. The socially responsible investment movement is now global and the faith community is a critical partner within it.

Patricia Wolf

Patricia Wolf was born in New York City in 1944. Member of the Sisters of Mercy of the Americas since 1963. Began shareholder advocacy work in 1975. Executive Director of the Interfaith Center on Corporate Responsibility (since 2001). Holds an MA degree from Manhattan College and an Honorary Doctorate from Mercy College, Dobbs Ferry, New York.

Peter Eigen

Coalition Building –
The Secret of Success

Civil society can register its disagreement with the course of globalisation in myriad forms, but the goal must be to effect change – change that improves the lives of the most vulnerable, change that creates a more level playing field for national and international actors who demonstrate integrity in their endeavours. Just as laws to clamp down on bribery require teeth – namely, prosecutors with the resources to enforce the law – so the angry crowds require a sound grasp of the process of effecting change if they want to do more than shout or throw stones from the sidelines.

The actions of the anti-globalisation protesters in Seattle, Prague, Gothenburg and – with tragic consequences – Genoa, were targeted at global financial and intergovernmental institutions. These protests may grab the headlines, but civil society organisations need to engage with each other, and also with governments and the private sector, so that their voice is heard and taken seriously by policymakers at all levels. That is the key to our approach at Transparency International (TI), the international non-governmental organisation (NGO) devoted exclusively to fighting corruption.

As Pascal Lamy, the European Commissioner for Trade, expressed it recently, 'TI, contrary to many of its sister NGOs, is far more than just an agenda-setter: by joining forces with governments and business, Peter and his troops have managed to shape a range of international instruments to curb corruption, ranging from the OECD to the Council of Europe and the UN.'[1]

Over the past two years, TI has been working to pressure governments to agree on the UN Convention against Corruption. The Convention, signed by 95 countries in Mexico on 9–11 December 2003, marks an important development in strengthening international cooperation on preventing and criminalising corruption, in particular, the breakthroughs made on mutual legal assistance in the return of assets stolen by corrupt leaders.

The Convention is not perfect, and there are regrettable omissions – there is no mandatory criminalisation of corruption in party political funding for instance, and the outlawing of private sector bribery is also only optional. Nevertheless, it is a watershed, a powerful signal that there is now a global consensus that corruption must be stopped. In addition, the UN General Assembly has agreed to declare 9 December, the day the Convention was signed by heads of government, as an annual International Anti-Corruption Day. This should be a potent opportunity for heightening public awareness of the problems of corruption on a sustained basis, year-in, year-out, and for calling governments and businesses to account; to live up to the high standards laid out in the Convention.

Corruption can be defined in a general way as the abuse of entrusted power for private benefit, and it is the poor and the sick who suffer most from its consequences. For this reason, civil society organisations owe it to ordinary people to achieve results that can improve their livelihoods. The average urban Kenyan pays 16 bribes a month, according to the Kenya Urban Bribery Index, a survey carried out in 2002 by Transparency International Kenya. This amounts to a burden of bribes of KSh 8,185 (US$104) per month – compared with an average monthly income among the survey respondents of only KSh 26,000 (US$331). Public servants receive the most bribes – 99 percent of the total value. The worst offenders were found to be the police: six out of 10 urban residents reported paying bribes to the police.

TI is now working with a new government in Kenya to turn this desperate situation around. John Githongo, former Executive Director of TI-Kenya, is now Permanent Secretary for Governance and Ethics in the Office of President Mwai Kibaki. TI-Kenya will continue to be vigilant in monitoring the work of the new administration, but – equally importantly – TI has joined forces with the World Bank to ensure that its new interest in Kenya promotes good governance and does not tolerate bribery; that the financial support it provides serves the people, not corrupt politicians and public officials.

TI will work to effect change and also to push forward the thinking of key players. For instance, in March 2003, I led a TI delegation, including representatives of national chapters, in a full day of talks with the World Bank. The Bank's president, James Wolfensohn, discussed our concerns for the whole day, and progress is already emerging: the World Bank has dropped its provisions circumscribing adoption of TI's Integrity Pact.

Under an Integrity Pact, bidders competing for the supply of goods and services provide a binding assurance that they have not paid any bribes in order to obtain the contract, and an undertaking that they will not do so in future. Pre-agreed sanctions come into force if this undertaking is breached, including blacklisting. TI now has to ensure that the World Bank endorses the Integrity Pact and actively encourages its implementation in its country offices.

This combination of engagement and persuasion has marked TI's approach in its interactions with governments and international institutions. As Pascal Lamy puts it, the relationship between TI and the European Commission has been 'constructive, although not always comfortable'.

Private sector, government and civil society need each other

A clear example of the new frontiers brought about via globalisation are conflict zones where the trade in arms, diamonds and oil has exacerbated the ferocity of the fighting and the rampant abuse of human rights. The conflicts in Angola, Sierra Leone and the Democratic Republic of Congo (DRC), for instance, which embroiled surrounding states, were fuelled and protracted by a scramble for natural resources by politicians, generals, and international companies alike.

Corruption not only impinges on macroeconomic aspects of economic management, but also on the development of the private sector, especially small businesses. If a licence to start a business can be obtained only by bribing a public official, and continuing subsequent payoffs to a multitude of corrupt inspectors and law enforcement officials, the whole country's economic development is effectively stunted. With the abject failure of government-led development efforts in most parts of the world, the private sector is seen as the key to future economic development. As long as corruption reigns so supremely, however, such economic prospects simply remain an impossible dream.

We can now see, for the first time, the start of a serious dialogue between major NGOs and key players in the private sector. The latter's newfound respect for civil society is largely due to the recognition that consumers, especially when galvanised by NGOs, have the power to influence corporate behaviour through their consumption preferences. The private sector can no longer conduct all its business with governments; it has become too exposed and governments have become too weak. The willingness of the private sector to engage civil society is evidenced by the rapid growth of the social accountability movement and the adoption of social reporting. This will be costly and painful, but it is as necessary as it is unavoidable.

TI works with other NGOs in coalitions such as the Publish What You Pay (PWYP) coalition with Global Witness, Oxfam and many others, pushing for international companies to disclose what they pay to host governments and state oil companies, and for financial regulators in London, New York and elsewhere to make such disclosure a mandatory requirement of stock exchange listing. In November 2003, TI brought together Nigerian President Olusegun Obasanjo and executives from oil companies, successfully eliciting a commitment from Obasanjo to publish what his country earns, as well as requiring foreign oil companies in Nigeria to publish what they pay.

In the United Kingdom, the national chapter of TI is actively partnering the British government on the Extractive Industries Transparency Initiative (EITI) to work towards the day when oil, gas and mining companies publish taxes, fees, royalties and other payments made to each host government as a condition for being listed on international stock exchanges and financial markets.

While mandatory disclosure is the objective of the PWYP campaign, voluntary corporate disclosure is being explored under the EITI initiative. With the involvement of governments, the EITI complements the PWYP campaign, strengthening the pressure on – and incentive to – the industry leaders to take this seriously. If they do not, companies will continue to face and fear discrimination by host countries if they breach confidentiality clauses. For instance, BP's ambitions to 'publish what you pay' in Angola drew threats of concession termination from the Angolan state oil company, Sonangol.

Making the OECD Convention work

The OECD Convention on Combating Bribery of Foreign Public Officials in International Business Transactions (known as the OECD Anti-Bribery Convention), aimed at

159

curtailing the bribing by OECD exporters of foreign public officials in order to win or retain business, is a striking example of the importance of the coalition-building approach. The 35 signatories to the Convention account for more than 90 percent of foreign direct investment worldwide. The key to securing support for the OECD Convention, which came into effect in February 1999, was the backing of large companies. TI secured the support of the International Chamber of Commerce, and 20 European companies signed a letter we drafted to their ministers encouraging them to sign the OECD Convention.

We managed to get business on side by offering an escape route from the prisoner's dilemma in which they found themselves (as we are doing with the Integrity Pact). Businesspeople are not naturally inclined to bribe (it costs money), but in the past they had no choice – they found themselves at a competitive disadvantage, with contracts in China and Indonesia, for instance, worth billions of dollars, at risk. Under the OECD Convention, all major competitors in the world market are legally bound to cease the practice of bribery simultaneously. For example, French or German companies can now be charged under their home countries' laws for bribing African, Asian or Latin American officials.

It is this cooperative approach that is essential to success in tackling an issue as complex as corruption in a global marketplace where it had become almost the norm. The coalition-building approach enables the three parties – government, the private sector and civil society organisations – to find areas of common interest where no single government or company would otherwise be willing to unilaterally apply more responsible standards of behaviour.

It is all the more important, therefore, that each country feels confident that the other signatories will not only introduce the appropriate legislation to implement the Convention, but also that they will effectively enforce that legislation. A follow-up process is underway at the OECD to translate this into law and practice, and civil society organisations, led by TI, are providing input and monitoring the follow-up. In November 2002, TI national chapters campaigned to ensure that their governments made up the shortfall in the budget for monitoring the enforcement of the Convention in signatory countries via a peer review process. That met with initial success, but TI still has to continue to apply pressure to ensure that the monitoring process is adequately resourced.

In the Bribe Payers Survey – a TI poll of 835 senior managers in 15 emerging market economies, conducted by Gallup International between December 2001 and March 2002 – only one in five respondents knew anything about the Convention. These are the managers at the frontline where bribery takes place, and the results are damning evidence that OECD governments have failed to make businesses understand the new legislation.

The message is gradually getting through – too slowly, but getting through nevertheless – that bribery will continue unless companies operate on a level playing field. The practice will be stopped only when companies know that bribe-payers will incur fines and blacklisting, and that executives will be put behind bars.

It used to be an uphill battle to persuade businesses, particularly small and medium-sized companies, that the benefits of operating on the basis of honesty outweighed the costs of losing business while competitors bribed their way into winning contracts. Economists were inclined to agree that in a bribe-demanding environment, the pursuit of profit would induce all competitors to behave equally.

But the mood has changed dramatically. At the March 2002 UN Conference on Financing for Development in Monterrey, a succession of ministers from donor countries joined World Bank and International Monetary Fund (IMF) officials in a common judgement: that wherever corruption reigns, development aspirations will remain an unattainable dream. **161**

Bribery hampers competition

The Enron, Global Crossing, WorldCom and now Parmalaat scandals have jolted shareholders and pension fund managers into reality: the public no longer has any confidence that a given corporation's books show a true and fair statement of its finances. The implications for the efficient operation of capital markets are far-reaching.

Companies must establish codes of conduct, including detailed rules designed to combat bribery at home or by their subsidiaries abroad. To this end, together with companies including BP, Shell, Tata and General Electric, TI has developed a set of business principles for countering bribery. The proposals include training programmes with guidance for all employees to ensure that bribery – direct or indirect – is eliminated. Under the guidelines of another NGO project, the Global Reporting Initiative (GRI), participating companies are asked to describe their policies and procedures for addressing corruption, including how the organisation meets the requirements of the OECD Anti-Bribery Convention.

The International Federation of Consulting Engineers (FIDIC) has produced its own guidelines for 'business integrity management' based on the premise that companies must continually document the information underlying their claims of integrity. The Mining, Minerals and Sustainable Development project, launched in April 2000, has been working with TI to encourage companies to publish basic information about revenue generated from particular projects and monies paid to governments.

The economic case is overwhelming for governments and business to join with civil society organisations in tackling corruption. The OECD estimates that annual budgets for government purchases worldwide run to $5 trillion. The scope for large sums diverted in bribes is frightening, as are the lost opportunities when public expenditure is diverted away from basic needs such as education, health care and housing.

Civil society is taking the lead

In Uganda, civil society organisations were at the forefront of attempts to pressure the government into making its methods of awarding tenders more transparent. During 2001, they petitioned the World Bank to send a panel of investigators to establish, among other things, whether there were any elements of corruption in the Power Purchase Agreement (PPA) between the government and the US multinational AES to construct the US $550 million Bujagali dam. The World Bank did subsequently send an inspection panel; its report criticised numerous aspects of the project, including the World Bank's decision to keep the PPA secret. In June 2002, the World Bank announced it was suspending its loan for the dam because of corruption allegations.

TI has succeeded in putting transparency, good governance and the fight against corruption at the centre of the agenda of the world community. Everybody – from James Wolfensohn to Kofi Annan, who is close to making anti-corruption measures a 10th principle of the UN Global Compact – is now talking about the devastating impact of corruption on development and the need to tackle the problem. We have to ensure that this level of awareness to the devastating effects of corruption does not fade from public conscience in the midst of the many pressing issues facing humanity today. Tackling corruption is indispensable if sustainable solutions are to be found to global issues such as poverty, inadequate health care provision, and decent housing and education for all.

But the solution requires partnership. It is not always comfortable; but the results can be highly constructive.

Note

1 Pascal Lamy, European Commissioner for Trade, 'Curbing corruption in a globalised world: a tribute to Peter Eigen and Transparency International', *Reader's Digest* European of the Year Award 2004, Berlin, 8 January 2004. **163**

Peter Eigen

Peter Eigen was born in Augsburg, Germany, in 1938. Chairman of Transparency International (which he founded in 1993). Honorary Professor of Political Science at the Free University in Berlin. Declared European of the Year 2004 (*Reader's Digest* magazine).

Manfred Güllner

Politics and the People – Case Study Germany

Disenchantment with politics – or plain dissatisfaction?

For over a decade, cultural critics and cultural pessimists in Germany have been using the phrase 'disenchantment with politics' to describe the relationship between ordinary people and politics. Even former President Richard von Weizsäcker made himself a mouthpiece for the sceptics at the start of the 1990s – with the result that the proportion of respondents who declared themselves indifferent or undecided when asked about their voting habits rose to record levels not repeated since, in spite of all the political crises that have taken place.

'Disenchantment with politics' suggests that people are turning away from politics, that they are tired of it and are therefore no longer interested in what goes on politically. But this generalised assessment does not actually match the reality. Germans are still as interested in politics as they ever were. The viewing figures for news and information programmes on television have not fallen over the past few years – if anything, they have gone up. Newspapers have not lost readers because people are no longer as interested in politics, but because the competition with other media, in particular the Internet, has become very keen, especially among younger people.

Two examples may serve to illustrate how avidly Germans follow political events. Interest in the party funding scandal which rocked the Christian Democratic Union (one of

Germany's two largest political parties) at the start of 2000 remained high over a period of several weeks: more than two-thirds of all German citizens – regardless of age, professional status, level of school education etc. – thought that this affair was the most important issue in the country, even after several weeks of detailed media coverage. And more than 80 percent of Germans were eager for more information about the scandal at the time despite the intense coverage.

Further proof that people in Germany follow events in politics attentively is also demonstrated by the fact that in answer to a question posed by *forsa* every day for more than 10 years – openly and with no closed answer options – about the most important issues reported by the media, nearly all the respondents have been able to give a detailed response. This high level of interest in political events may well be due to the (at times) arduous process of transformation from subjects to state citizens that Germans have gone through since the end of the Second World War. Today they see no alternative to the democratic system. Even at the height of the CDU funding scandal, with all the indignation it triggered, 71 percent of German citizens (74 percent in the West and 54 percent in the East) said that they were happy with the political system in Germany. And in January 2000, 70 percent (72 percent in the West and 67 percent in the East) of the population said that parties were necessary for the political system in Germany to work.

For the first time ever in their history, Germans have become committed democrats. They identify with the political system and also accept the political parties – contrary to what cultural critics would suggest. People in Germany are not at all tired of politics; rather, they have politically come of age.

Part of becoming a politically mature citizen involves continually making judgements about current affairs rather than maintaining a neutral stance with regard to political events. And this is where there is obvious unease – overall satisfaction with the political system notwithstanding – about the way in which some political figures perform their duties. Former Chancellor Helmut Kohl (CDU), for example, attracted people's indignation by his defiant withholding of information (he refused to divulge names of major donors) during the funding scandal. Kohl, it will be remembered, had been voted out of office in 1998 because people no longer trusted him to break the reform logjam in Germany; nonetheless after 16 years as Chancellor, he enjoyed much personal support as the 'father of reunification'. In the year 2000, however, around three-quarters of all German citizens were either disappointed with Kohl or felt angry about his behaviour. Only a few people (16 percent) displayed any understanding or sympathy towards him. And 71 percent of the population reject the notion that a person's word of honour is more important than the law as Kohl continues to insist to this day – 62 percent even called for him to be taken into coercive custody to force him to name his donors.

It should be noted, however, that Kohl's behaviour was judged less as an exceptional case than as a symptom of the behaviour people expected from political actors and parties: 72 percent of all Germans think that irregularities in party financing are common practice; 85 percent believe that politicians are open to corruption and 89 percent say that other parties are also afflicted by problems with financing similar to those affecting the CDU. These are all clear indicators of a process of alienation between citizens and politics. It stands to reason, then, that a mere 15 percent of Germans believe that the parties care about what 'ordinary' people think.

But it is not only politicians and political parties that have lost the people's trust; so too have other large organisations. Institutions such as the courts and the police do continue to enjoy high levels of confidence, both among the population as well as among journalists. The various media, with the exception of the Internet, also enjoy relatively high levels of trust – the most highly regarded being daily newspapers and the radio.

167

Alongside political parties, though, it is the churches, trade unions, management, PR and advertising that are accorded the least trust. With the exception of the churches, journalists' trust in these other institutions is even lower than among the population as a whole. Dissatisfaction about the way the political system operates and about the themes and personalities presented at the different levels of politics is also manifested very clearly by the numbers staying away from the polls. The mature German voter clearly expresses his or her dissatisfaction about political figures and political parties by withdrawing from the electoral process. But how can institutions that have forfeited their prestige, such as political parties, regain the trust that has been lost?

Ways out of the confidence crisis

Two options that seem to offer a way of attenuating the processes of alienation between citizens and politicians are frequently mentioned in political debate: greater privatisation of tasks so far fulfilled by the public sector, and an increase in opportunities for citizens to cast a direct vote on specific issues.

However, there is some doubt about whether these options are really capable of bringing about the desired goal. First, the privatisation so far of services previously provided by the public sector has by no means given people greater confidence in politics and its institutions or in other large organisations. The only positive impacts made by privatisation have been with regard to the availability of cheaper products and services, for example telecommunications. But privatisation – or rather, liberalisation – has not led in every instance to price reductions, and only to a limited extent has it engendered a better quality of service or a greater understanding of people's needs. On the contrary – some privatisations, such as in the waste industry, have led to poorer service at local levels and thus to a further loss of confidence in the ability of politicians to deliver.

Rather than relentlessly pursuing the sale of further public bodies for purely fiscal reasons, be it in the area of transport or housing provision, hospitals or other similar institutions, the state should examine carefully which tasks it must continue to fulfil itself and which ones it could privatise without incurring any negative consequences – and preferably even to positive effect – for its citizens.

One goal that goes far beyond mere privatisation should definitely be pursued, namely a significant slimming down of bureaucracy and, with it, a reorientation of the objectives of public administration. This would be one way of reducing the sense of being oppressed and 'ripped off' by state bureaucracy. If the state were oriented more towards the needs of its people rather than towards the criteria of 'state liability', this might help it to regain the confidence of its citizens.

It is likewise questionable whether the second proposal that is frequently aired – namely, more referenda on specific issues – could increase public confidence in politics. Greater citizen participation is certainly useful – both for the state and for the people – but any opportunities to participate via referenda must be genuine, not just a token attempt to give the appearance of participation. For example, hearings conducted in the context of development schemes have little to do with actual participation. Rather, they provide interest groups and fringe groups with an opportunity to articulate their particular ideas – frequently against the wishes of the majority of those affected by the construction plans.

The other point is that citizens themselves may say superficially that they are in favour of holding referenda, such as for the direct election of mayors, Lord Mayors and the President of the Republic; but in reality, they believe that decision-making processes in a complex society ought to be based on a division of labour, i.e. politicians elected by parliament should be responsible in the first instance for grappling with difficult problems and decisions. And they understand that solutions to multi-layered problems, such as in the area of transport, cannot simply be found by using yes/no questions in the context of a referendum.

What is remarkable in this connection is that voter participation in local government elections in the state of Hesse was extraordinarily high when city councillors were elected in a straightforward system of proportional representation. However, once personalised electoral procedures were introduced, voter participation in Hesse fell significantly.

The only way in which politics can overcome the current crisis of confidence is by taking greater account of the needs of the people on the one hand and by showing firm leadership on the other. This does not mean using short-term tactics to score points against one's political opponents in the media. Leadership means preparing and implementing projects over a whole parliamentary term, regardless of the media response at any given time. The media thrive on reporting specific current events. But politics should not see itself as a short-term reaction to media coverage or media attacks. Politicians certainly have to take note of the media – just as they also need to judge the mood of the electorate via opinion polls. But just as they should not base their actions on the ebbs and flows of political tides or majority opinions, neither should they take media coverage too seriously – their first duty is to the needs of the people. Only by being fully recommitted to the task in hand, and seeking proximity to the people rather than to the media, will the political elite be able to regain lost confidence.

Manfred Güllner

Manfred Güllner was born in Remscheid, Germany, in 1941. Studied sociology, social psychology and business management in Cologne. Member of the management of the Institute for Applied Social Sciences (Infas) (1970–78); Director of the

Office of Statistics in Cologne (1978–83). In 1984 founded the *forsa* Society for Social Research and Statistical Analysis. Awarded an honorary doctorate by the Free University in Berlin in 2004. Author of numerous publications.

The Art of Tackling Issues: Pooling Know-how

If partnerships between the state, the business community and civil society are indeed our best hope for effective global governance, how can they tackle the daunting challenges we are facing? They need to rebuild war-torn societies; alleviate poverty; address global pandemics such as HIV/AIDS; protect human rights, combat corruption; enhance the stability of global financial markets; promote sustainable development – the list is long. The key to the success of these strange-bedfellow partnerships lies in the innovative approaches their combined know-how and experience can invent and implement to solve age-old problems in new guises.

Sustainability

Stephan Schmidheiny

Partners, Governance and Governments

The most revolutionary new partnerships I know of are those between not-for-profit organisations and companies trying to conduct business with the poor in ways that benefit all concerned. Some big companies are getting involved in this kind of business – termed *pro-poor, base-of-the-pyramid* or *sustainable livelihoods* – for a variety of reasons. Many executives feel that business can and should play a role in reducing global poverty; many have been affected by demonstrations at World Trade Organization meetings that seem to be as much anti-business as anti-globalisation; many who regard the markets in Europe and North America as stagnant perceive a new market of billions of potential new customers in the developing world; and many are reacting to all of the above.

A recent World Bank report divided the world population into three groups, with 11 percent in the richest bracket, 11 percent in the middle income group and 78 percent categorised as poor. Companies that disregard the latter group are ignoring roughly 4.8 billion people – a serious business oversight.

The framework conditions in developing countries – for example, legal systems, infrastructure, government transparency and political honesty – seem to be improving, albeit slowly. Political Risk Services, a group that specialises in risk analysis, reported that during the period from 1993 to 2003, their average risk score in low and middle income countries improved from 59 to 64; and almost three times as many countries showed an improving risk climate as did a deteriorating one. As a result, the sphere in which multinational corporations can profitably operate is expanding.

My viewpoint on pro-poor business is influenced mainly by my experience of the World Business Council for Sustainable Development (WBCSD), the business group I founded in 1991 to report to the Earth Summit in Rio de Janeiro in 1992. The WBCSD now includes over 170 of the world's more important companies and runs a Sustainable Livelihoods Working Group to promote business with the poor. This latter type of business rarely distracts a company from its core business, nor does it impinge on the quality of the product or service offered. What it does do, however, is change the nature of the transaction so that those less well off can afford or have access to those goods or services. Let me offer some examples.

Eskom, the South African utility, wants (and is mandated by the government) to provide electricity to remote neighbourhoods, but as the people in these areas tend not to have bank accounts or even addresses, they cannot be billed. By selling them the equivalent of tokens to use in their home electricity meters, the company lowers its transaction costs, customers can purchase power in affordable chunks, and local jobs (such as selling tokens, installing meters) are created.

DuPont wants to sell agricultural inputs to corn farmers in Colombia, but by planting time, the money earned from harvests has often been spent and the farmers cannot afford good seeds, pesticide or fertilisers. So the company went into partnership with the Ministry of Agriculture, Finagro (the agrarian bank), the National Agriculture and Livestock Board, and the State Bank of Compensation and Security, among others, to develop a scheme that creates contracts between farmers and agro-industry companies to buy the future harvests at a fixed price. The farmers are not obliged to buy DuPont products, but by providing training programmes and advice systems, the company gains a head start in the market. DuPont became so excited about this business that it recently generated 75 pro-poor business ideas in Mexico and following a selection process, is pursuing seven of these.

In another approach to the 'affordability problem', Pioneer Hybrid changed the way it sold seeds, fertiliser and pesticides in Kenya. These were traditionally sold in bags weighing 50 kilos or more. This represented an investment of several weeks' income for most farmers, and the bags were impossible to carry home without transport. A local NGO worked with Pioneer and farmers in the Siaya district to repackage the goods in affordable mini-packs. Farmers can now buy a chewing-gum sized sachet of 250 seeds of a local vegetable for five shillings (6 cents), and for another 10 shillings (12 cents) they can purchase a pack of fertiliser for 150 planting holes. A good farmer can earn between 2,000 and 4,000 shillings ($25–50) by using these packs, and Pioneer's sales have increased as a result of this new selling technique.

GrupoNueva (a Latin American holding company I used to own) recently held a contest among its 15,000 employees that generated over 200 pro-poor business ideas, nine of which are being converted into business plans. The company became interested in such efforts after an Argentinian subsidiary almost went bankrupt in the economic crash a few years ago. It loaded products – plumbing materials – onto trucks and set off into the poor neighbourhoods of Buenos Aires to sell to tiny, storefront outlets. The project generated sufficient revenue to keep the company afloat. Now that the crisis is waning, mobile sales have increased and the practice has spread to other cities. In these examples, the companies remained true to their core businesses; the same products were sold to both the poor and the better off.

Another aspect that many pro-poor business projects share is the need for partnerships such as those formed by DuPont

177

in Colombia and Pioneer Hybrid in Kenya. Partnerships are becoming more common now partly because there are far more civil society organisations (CSOs) made up of people willing and able to work with businesses to achieve their own non-business goals, such as improving the underprivileged's access to water, food, credit, housing, transport, communications, and general economic security. With the help of CSOs in all areas of the business spectrum – from product development to sales and distribution – companies are finding it easier to operate in low-income countries/areas. Moreover, the CSOs help companies to achieve their stated goal of benefiting the poor while conducting business transactions. There are many successful partnerships I could mention – the following are but a few.

Procter and Gamble (P&G) worked with the UN Children's Fund (UNICEF), the Micronutrient Initiative and Cornell University to develop a flavourful children's drink that contains essential micronutrients such as iodine and iron, the lack of which can stunt physical and intellectual growth. It was intended that the drink should be sold in poor neighbourhoods where children's diets are likely to be deficient.

When in 2000, Aguas do Amazonas (AdA), the Brazilian subsidiary of the international water company, Suez, won a 30-year concession to provide water and sanitation services in Manaus, it immediately joined forces with the CSO, ESSOR, to enable it to reach the poor areas inhabited by 60 percent of the population. Together, AdA and ESSOR conducted a joint survey targeting four poor communities to help the company identify their needs and adapt its business model to meet them. ESSOR acted as a 'broker' between the company and the communities by working with local leaders and volunteers to raise awareness of the need for clean water, to assess the people's ability and willingness to pay for the service and to mobilise the community to help maintain and manage the water connections. ESSOR was instrumental in convincing people of the advantages of becoming AdA's formal customers.

Some of the companies most interested in working with the poor are the big oil and mining enterprises. They often drill and dig in remote areas among the world's poorest people and feel a responsibility for their livelihoods. Although it is difficult for them to 'do business', many have programmes to hire and train as many local people as possible, and to help small local businesses become effective suppliers.

One obvious non-business partner for such companies is the state. In the Philippines, BP Solar engaged in the vast Municipal Solar Infrastructure Project (MSIP), undertaken with the Philippine and Australian governments. The project, completed in May 2001, has helped to provide health, education and governance benefits to more than 721,140 poor Filipinos in 11 provinces. In total 1,145 packaged solar systems were installed in 435 villages, powering health centres, water systems, schools and municipal halls. The project cost US$27 million and funding was provided by the Australian government – a grant of 33 percent plus a soft loan for the remaining 67 percent. According to BP, it undertakes such projects because they are good business, both in terms of profitability and in terms of environmental and social responsibility. Rural infrastructure projects now form the core of BP Solar's business strategy, and it intends to 'clone MSIP' in other regions.

As the subject of this book is governance, it is worth asking if these partnerships need any sort of special outside 'governance' or regulation. I do not think so – it would be very difficult for major multinationals to try to disguise exploitation as 'pro-poor', and one of the roles of the non-business partners is to ensure that the business partners remain focused on the *pro* in 'pro-poor'. Conducting commerce with low-income communities is still in its infancy and at the experimental stage. As it is not yet profitable – more an act of faith – there is no real scope for corporate greed. DuPont

CEO Chad Holliday put it into perspective when he said of pro-poor business: 'This is an investment in the future. And although I think we can have some theory and some very good demonstration projects in the next two or three years, I believe it will take five to ten years before it starts making a difference to my bottom line.'

Even in its early stages, such business can be controversial. There will always be arguments about boundaries, and how much good or harm is being done. For example, in South Africa, Coca-Cola has an entrepreneur development scheme which trains thousands of young people each year in basic business skills such as book-keeping, marketing and sales. The programme exists so that the young people can sell Coke in remote areas not well served by stores. It could be argued that the poor certainly do not need more dark, sweet fizzy water; but it could also be argued that for societies to flourish, young people need such business skills which, once acquired, they will have for life.

What these new business/CSO partnerships need rather than outside governance is good governments. I am constantly amazed at how hard most governments work to make it difficult or impossible for their poorer citizens to start and build up legal businesses, and to make effective use of the resources they possess.

Two excellent books on these issues were written by Hernando De Soto of Peru. In *The Other Path: The Economic Answer to Terrorism,* he documents the months of dealing with government bureaucracy it takes to set up a simple business in Peru. Thus most enterprises remain 'informal', a euphemism for being not so much illegal as 'unlegal', i.e. outside the law. While such enterprises may not pay taxes, they pay as much or more in bribes. By operating outside the law, they have no access to bank credit or to any government development schemes. De Soto argues that changing laws to encourage such businesses to operate within the formal economy and thus become partners of the government would rob terrorist movements of their appeal. Although he writes about Peru, his arguments are applicable to almost any developing country.

In his more recent and even more profound *The Mystery of Capitalism: Why Capitalism Succeeds in the West and Fails Everywhere Else,* he documents the surprisingly large number of resources the poor possess de facto but cannot use because they lack legal title to houses, lands, workshops, etc. He explains the complex infrastructure, the paper trails, the laws, the systems of plats and maps and credit ratings that capitalism needs to thrive – an infrastructure taken for granted in the West.

The lack of this infrastructure is also taken for granted in the developing world. Yet sustainable economic development requires democracy and the accepted rule of law; effective intellectual and physical property rights; reliability of contracts; absence of corruption; equitable trade terms and respect for comparative advantage; ordered competition among businesses; fair and transparent accounting standards; accountability and predictability of government interventions; investment in education and enabling technologies; and reform of taxation so that it funds collective investments rather than penalises income.

No country is perfect, perhaps not even satisfactory, in all of these areas, but without such a set of framework conditions, business cannot be an effective part of development. I make this fairly obvious argument for two reasons. First, 'governance' is a very fashionable term and much clever work is being carried out on new forms of governance. But let us first help countries achieve old-fashioned 'good government' that creates and maintains a common wealth with equal opportunity for all. Secondly, without good government and sound framework conditions, it is not only business that suffers – the sort of partnerships I have described cannot function.

P&G developed its drink to combat micro-malnutrition and launched it in the Philippines. There were a number of

181

problems of affordability and distribution, but one serious problem that contributed to the failure of the product was the fact that local manufacturers started selling nutritionally worthless products while claiming that they possessed more nutritional benefits than P&G's product (enforced truth-in-advertising laws did not exist). P&G later relaunched the drink in Venezuela under a different name, and it is developing other similar pro-poor products.

In 1950, the US multinational SC Johnson launched Raid, the first commercial aerosol insecticide using as a basic active ingredient pyrethrum from the pyrethrum flower grown in the highlands of Kenya. This became very important to the highland farming community and its economy, providing livelihoods for over 400,000 Kenyan farmers and their families. The company worked with CSOs to improve both its relationships with the farmers and farmers' skills. Despite the introduction of lower cost synthetic alternatives, the company decided to maintain its ties with the community and it has worked for 30 years with the Pyrethrum Board of Kenya (PBK), a parastatal agency, to maintain a high quality, consistent supply of pyrethrum from Kenya. When the Kenyan government changed recently, it unilaterally altered its relationship with the company, interrupting the supply of pyrethrum and forcing the company to consider looking outside Kenya for its pyrethrum supplies.

It is not only the framework conditions in the developing world that are of concern. Wealthy countries have conspired to keep Third World agricultural countries poor by giving huge subsidies to their own farmers, allowing them to better compete against some of the world's poorest farmers. It is hardly fair to ask business to be a force for economic development when many of the policies of the developed countries hinder such development.

We should all encourage governments to adopt basic framework conditions to provide an environment in which these fascinating new partnerships can work. It has become almost a slogan these days for the WBCSD that 'business cannot succeed in societies that fail'. A global society of over four billion poor is beginning to look suspiciously like failure.

Stephan Schmidheiny

Stephan Schmidheiny was born in Switzerland in 1947. Founder of the AVINA Foundation; Honorary Chairman of the World Business Council for Sustainable Development (which he founded in 1991). Publications include: *Changing Course: A Global Business Perspective on Development and the Environment* and *Walking the Talk: The Business Case for Sustainable Development*.

Kader Asmal

Environment and Sustainability: Looking to the Future

> *Sustainable Development is a flag of convenience under which diverse ships sail without an agreed theoretical core.*[1]

At the beginning of the 21st century, we can look back at the previous century as an era of development failure – failed theory, failed policy and failed projects – but we can also draw encouragement, perhaps even hope, from recent signs that a new 'partnership principle' is emerging in our understanding of the necessary link between environmental responsibility and sustainable development. With due regard for the theoretical complexity of the subject, in the following chapter I propose to outline what I see as the practical steps we need to take if we are to make meaningful progress in sustainable development. After briefly considering some basic assumptions (and frustrations) about sustainable development, I will reflect on the importance of the 'partnership principle' within two areas – environmental rights and multilateral cooperation – in which I have been involved.

I shall then reflect on a remarkable example of multilateral collaboration, the World Commission on Dams (WCD), which I was honoured to chair for its duration from 1998 to 2000. Drawing upon the active participation of both proponents and opponents of building large dams, the Commission was a model for what can be accomplished in making environmental rights a reality.

Although we certainly need to keep working on clarifying our conceptual frameworks and refining our situational analysis, I shall argue that sustainable development can be advanced by involving ordinary people in the critical process of moving back and forth between the principles of environmental rights and the practices of multilateral cooperation.

Sustainable development

The United Nations World Commission on Environment and Development, chaired by Gro Harlem Brundtland, Prime Minister of Norway, in 1987 produced the benchmark definition of sustainable development as 'development that meets the needs of the present without compromising the ability of future generations to meet their own needs'. Since then there have been many operational definitions of sustainable development but most are variations on the Brundtland Commission's work.

Although the Brundtland principles have been widely repeated, we do not really have an inviolable, universal or timeless definition upon which to base our understanding of sustainable development. Detractors of the Brundtland Commission definition have accused it of being a formula designed to promote consensus rather than clarity. Other detractors, viewing the Brundtland report as representative of 'mainstream' sustainable development thinking, accuse it of suggesting that growth and over-consumption are the root causes of the current problem, but calling nevertheless for continued economic growth of up to 5 to 10 times the output existing at the time the report was published in 1987. Thus the powerful myth that growth equals development remains firmly entrenched even in certain sustainable development circles.

As we know, since the publication of the Brundtland Commission report, global economic output has certainly increased, but poor countries, in terms of relative wealth, have become poorer. Depending upon the method of calculation, we find that the relative gap between rich and poor countries has widened by as much as 60 percent. Moreover, **185** the percentage of the world population living in poor countries with per capita GNPs of less than $500 (in 1987 US dollars) has remained at about 60 percent.

The solution to this growing inequality and persistent poverty cannot lie in the ruling classes trying to convince the world that the best way out of our current problems is for the rich to continue to increase consumption in order to prime the growth engine of the international economy. It is estimated currently that the rich countries use 75 percent of the world's resources and produce 75 percent of the world's waste.

We have consumed more of the world's natural wealth in the brief period since 1950 than in the entire history of humankind. This natural wealth is non-renewable and should be regarded as 'natural capital'. It is a well-known economic truth that to treat capital as current income is a recipe for disaster. As William E. Rees has expressed it, 'total consumption by the human economy already exceeds natural income; humankind is both liquidating natural capital and destroying our real wealth-creating potential. In this light, efforts to expand our way to sustainability through deregulation and trade can only accelerate global decline.'

Many critics have argued that environmental responsibility and sustainable development have been frustrated because governments are more accountable to international capital (through transnational corporations, the World Bank, the International Monetary Fund and other such bodies) than to their own citizens, while, as Vanadana Shiva observed, a 'global monoculture is being propagated based on the conception that a child thirsty for clean water really needs Coca-Cola and a young girl dreaming of going to school really wants a pair of Nikes'.

Factories throughout the developing world churn out an unending stream of those Nike running shoes and bottles of Coca-Cola using non-unionised workers, often women, working 50-hour weeks for a few dollars a day. Globally the combined wealth of the world's 350 richest individuals exceeds that of the world's poorest 2.5 billion people.

On the environmental front, we continue to treat the varied and complex natural ecosystems, on which all life depends and on which the human economy is based, as both limitless and, for the most part, free. Yet we have not even achieved sensible methods for the treatment and disposal of waste products, including toxic chemicals and, of course, nuclear waste. We continue to undermine the principles of sustainable development by utilising non-renewable resources at an increasing rate and failing to develop renewable resources effectively. Sustainable development requires that non-renewable resources should be depleted only at the rate of creation of renewable substitutes.

These concerns, as we know, have given rise to prophecies of doom and promises of utopia, which were both strangely fixated on the millennial year 2000. In its 1972 report, *Limits to Growth,* the Club of Rome predicted environmental catastrophe by 2000. The Brundtland Commission, as mandated by the UN, set out to make recommendations that would achieve sustainable development by the year 2000. Clearly, neither the prophecy of doom nor the prophecy of sustainable development was fulfilled. Yet we still live with the same challenges that gave rise to those concerns. What can we do about it? What are our practical options, available in the present, for protecting the integrity of our environment and the sustainability of development for future generations? Viable options, I propose, are available in our ongoing work to extend the scope of human rights to the protection of basic environmental rights.

Environmental rights

The United Nations Conference on Environment and Development held in Rio de Janeiro during June 1992 produced the

Rio Declaration on Environment and Development. The same conference produced *Agenda 21,* a 40-chapter blueprint for action on specific issues relating to sustainable development. *Agenda 21* set out what needs to be done to reduce wasteful and inefficient consumption patterns in some parts of the world while encouraging increased but sustained development in others. It offers policies and programmes to achieve a sustainable balance between consumption, population and the Earth's life-supporting capacity. A major theme in *Agenda 21* is the need to eradicate poverty by giving poor people more access to the resources they need in order to live sustainably. Since Rio there have been a variety of other UN initiatives to promote *Agenda 21*. Although progress has generally been frustrating, these initiatives continue to place environmental responsibility and sustainable development at the forefront of the international struggle to realise basic human rights.

At the time of the Rio Earth Summit in 1992, I was privileged to play a significant role in the drafting of the new constitution for South Africa. It is not often that one is presented with such a unique opportunity to design the essence around which a country decides to build its political, social and economic future.

The South African Constitution is probably one of the few in the world that constitutionalises the concept of sustainable development. Section 24(a)(iii) of our Constitution reads:

> Everyone has the right to have the environment protected, for the benefit of present and future generations, through reasonable legislative and other measures that secure ecologically sustainable development and use of natural resources while promoting justifiable economic and social development.

In the Bill of Rights section, rights to adequate housing, to health care services, sufficient food and water and social security are also entrenched (obviously within the limits of the resources available).

Of course the challenge for South Africa and our government is to ensure that these clauses are acted upon efficiently and effectively rather than allowing them to be merely dictums for good governance which are dusted off on ceremonial occasions and then forgotten.

As an example of our efforts to link human rights and human development, South Africa's Ministry of Water Affairs and Forestry is the lead ministry for the 'Working for Water' programme which, to the consternation of many North Americans and Europeans, specialises in cutting down trees! More than 40,000 previously unemployed people are working in South Africa to eradicate alien vegetation in water catchment areas as part of a long-term demand management process to conserve water, a precious and scarce resource in South Africa. Besides providing a valuable service in the pursuit of sustainable development and the creation of employment, the programme is used to promote public health and welfare campaigns.

Demand management, we have found, is crucial to the sustainable use of our water resources and our Department of Water Affairs and Forestry already has a policy to ensure that no new plans to construct dams are approved before a proper demand management study has been undertaken. For example, the City of Cape Town has been waiting for some years for approval to build a new dam while demand management studies are undertaken.

At an international level there is progress as well. Building on the Declaration of the Right to Development of 1986 and the Rio Earth Summit of 1992, in May 1994 an international group of experts on international human rights and environmental law convened at the UN in Geneva and drafted the first ever declaration of principles on human rights and the environment. Clause 1 of the draft principles of the declaration states: 'Human rights, an ecologically sound environ-

189

ment, sustainable development and peace are interdependent and indivisible.' Like other basic human rights, these rights are indivisible, but in their interdependence they assume the character of a collective right. This collective 'ecology' of environmental rights calls for collective, multilateral efforts in their promotion and protection. A good illustration of such a collective effort was the work carried out by the WCD.

Multilateral cooperation

As Cabinet Minister of Water Affairs and Forestry in the first democratic government of South Africa, I agreed to serve as Chair of the WCD because I believed that it would provide an unusual and unique opportunity to address one of the most intensely debated issues in sustainable development. The construction of large dams has become the subject of intense scrutiny and I believe the WCD has contributed by clarifying many issues and assisting with decisions and planning about water resource utilisation in the future. In our deliberations, the Commission was guided by the principles and values of sustainable development. As a result, it produced properly reasoned criteria and guidelines that are broadly acceptable to all the role players who have an interest in the building of large dams and the utilisation of water.

The fact that both dam proponents and critics reached consensus on creating the Commission and continued to work together signalled a significant step forward. In this respect, I believe that this Commission was unique among international commissions and it provided considerable promise for the future. Without the open and honest approach adopted by all the Commissioners, we would not have been able to reach consensus in carrying out the Commission's mandate.

Nevertheless, as a commission we faced a number of critical challenges, particularly in the areas of the relocation of affected peoples and the questions of compensation, viable alternatives to large dams, alternative sources of energy, and the need to balance environmental and ecological concerns against increasing development demands. There was considerable debate about the extent to which hydropower can really be considered a 'clean' form of energy. The issue of carbon dioxide reduction targets is important as part of the concerns about global climate change and much of this is dependent on choices of power generation.

While serving as a remarkable example of international cooperation, the WCD was also a model for what I would like to call 'globalisation from below', since it relied for its success upon the active participation of ordinary people from all over the world who were most immediately affected by the impact of dam-building and other development projects.

In drawing up a set of guidelines for good practices in building dams, the final report of the WCD found that advancing sustainable development, which also meant enhancing human development, depended on putting a strategy in place that we called 'Rights, Risks and Negotiated Outcomes'. Having recently participated in the successful outcome of a 'negotiated revolution' in my own country, I found this emphasis on negotiation essential. As a strategy for decision-making in large-scale development projects, the model for negotiated outcomes proposed by the WCD was truly revolutionary. The Commission envisioned a 'negotiated revolution' in the decision-making process. Instead of proceeding only in terms of conventional economic calculations of costs and benefits, decisions have to be driven by an inclusive, consultative process that moves back and forth between basic human rights and anticipated human risks, particularly those posed to the most vulnerable people affected by any development project.

This necessary connection between risks and rights, I believe, marks an important advance in both the theory and practice of sustainable development. While recognising that public and private developers of large dam projects, the **191** 'voluntary risk takers', manage a complex range of technical, financial and even political risks, we also have to acknowledge that many people become 'involuntary risk bearers' in the process. They have rights that must be protected, but they also have voices that must be heard by being included in the negotiating process. People who are affected by the building of a dam are not objects but agents in the negotiation of outcomes for sustainable development. By creating a framework for an inclusive decision-making process based on affirming rights and analysing risks, the WCD advanced a new 'partnership principle' for sustaining both human rights and human development in building dams.

In principle, this framework of rights, risks and negotiated outcomes could be extended to other arenas of conflict involving environmental protection and sustainable development. As independent analysis of the WCD concluded, the Commission stood as a model for multilateral cooperation and negotiation in arriving at sustainable solutions. With all of our international, multilateral institutions and initiatives currently at risk in a unipolar world, we need models such as the WCD to remind us of what is possible.

Critics of global capitalism, especially anti-globalisation purists, may have felt that by placing the financial risks of developers on the same negotiating table with the involuntary risks faced by the poor in developing countries – especially given the devastating and disproportional risks borne by women and children, the unemployed and homeless, and the indigenous communities so often displaced or deprived by development projects – we had 'sold out'. Aware of this criticism, the WCD included in its final report a brief statement by one of our commissioners, Medha Patkar, who categorically rejected the 'unjust and destructive dominant development model' prevailing under global capitalism. Opposition, rather than negotiation, can only follow.

Based on my long experience of oppositional politics, serving an anti-apartheid struggle that refused to negotiate away our human freedom, rights and dignity, I understand this position. But the negotiated revolution in South Africa, while not changing everything, certainly taught us that genuine gains could be achieved in the pursuit of justice through negotiation. As an inclusive model for negotiating outcomes, the guidelines worked out by the WCD establish basic terms and conditions for advancing sustainable development that are real because they can actually be achieved.

Conclusion

Against the background of this brief review of environmental rights and multilateral cooperation, what is our theory of sustainable development? Although our efforts might not have a single, 'agreed theoretical core', they can still be informed by a theoretical framework, like the guidelines proposed by the WCD that seek to make theory practical. Integrated into our practice, our theoretical reflections must be directly engaged with the conditions of possibility for affirming rights and assessing risks in ways that are most inclusive because they will also be most faithful to our reality. If development is to be sustainable, it must proceed alongside sustainable processes of negotiation in which people participate freely in social, political and economic decision-making.

Sustainable development must be premised on the concept of equity, on the concept that all people, now and in the future, are entitled to a life of dignity, a life in which their basic human needs are met and they are free to develop their human potential. These commitments to human dignity, freedom and equity, of course, require putting people before profits, but these basic rights can also be protected and promoted through responsible development projects that take us forward (not backward) within the natural order of our environment. A sustainable future depends upon merging human rights and environmental rights; it depends upon situ-

193

ating human development within the context of environmental protection; it depends upon opening options in the present for all people without foreclosing the possible options for future generations.

Note

1 Bill Adams (1993), 'Sustainable development and the greening of development theory', in Frans Schuurman (ed.), *Beyond the Impasse: New Directions in Development Theory* (London, Zed Books), p. 218.

Kader Asmal

Kader Asmal was born in Stanger, Natal, South Africa, in 1934. Minister of Education of South Africa since June 1999; member of the National Executive Committee of the African National Congress (ANC) since 1991. Founder member of both the British and Irish Anti-Apartheid Movements. Member of the Constitutional Commission of the ANC; Minister of Water Affairs and Forestry (1994–1999). First Chairman of The World Commission on Dams.

Daniel Yergin

The Rules of the Game

An Interview

How do you foresee partnerships working in the 21st century in terms of supplying the energy needs of the world so that is not divisive, so that countries do not suffer from having oil, or now, liquid gas?

We are living in the second age of globalization. The first age was the period at the end of the 19th century and early 20th century that was so optimistic and ended so disastrously. It took more than seven decades to rebuild a global economy. A whole host of obvious things happened at the end of the 1980s and the beginning of the 1990s, such as the fall of the Berlin Wall and the Gulf War. Some of the events that took place were less obvious, such as the crisis in India, the introduction of reforms there and the integration of the country into the global economy. At the same time, Chinese reform really gathered speed, and the growth of global capital markets took off. Technological change, especially in communications and information, but also in transportation, underpins the entire development.

The pressing question now concerns the new rules of the game for this new age of globalization. How do governments work together? What are the roles of the private sector, civil society and non-governmental organizations (NGOs)? This is not self-evident. It is clear that any system needs rules – explicit or implicit – whether on capital flows, on the environment, on privacy or on the operation of the Internet. What we have to tackle is how these rules get made and by whom. The important question of sovereignty often gets brushed aside. But civil society is also a self-defining concept. NGOs are becoming much more active and influential – they are also proliferating across the spectrum. This raises important questions. Who do they represent? What is their role? This is often a very sensitive issue in the developing world. In developing countries I hear government officials say, 'We're the ones who've been elected to represent the interest of our people and improve their standard of living. Who says we can't have trade and investment?' I remember South Africa's finance minister saying just that. At the same time that we have witnessed the growth of the global company and a rapid increase in the number of NGOs, we have also seen an explosion of democracy. Yet NGOs are not elected. We have to give some thought to this question.

NGOs may lack legitimacy, but they do raise important issues such as corruption, for example.

The issue of corruption has really moved to the fore, both on moral grounds and because of the conviction that large-scale and widespread corruption is a real drawback to achieving economic growth and development. It deters people and distorts the process. Hernando De Soto, who is carrying out important work on obstacles to growth, has come to the conclusion that a major obstacle is the absence of property rights. As a result, poor people are unable to turn what they quasi-own into capital they can do something with and build upon. I believe the nexus of property rights, corruption, flows of funds and distribution is clearly an important part of this discussion. Corruption is encouraged by systems that have weak property rights accompanied by widespread controls and permission/approval requirements.

Where does business come into this?

I'll answer the question by talking about oil. What is the international oil business? It's a commercial business that ties together resources, technology, economics and politics. It provides what consumers want and need in an industrial society. As we have seen, especially in the 1970s, it acquired very confrontational characteristics as in the 'North–South divide'. However, in recent times, I think we have witnessed a decrease in the level of confrontation. There's far more dialogue and interaction between consumers and producers than existed in the past. In general, relationships are more cooperative but that doesn't mean that there aren't and won't be disruptions. There were three major disruptions in 2003: one in Venezuela, related to a quasi-civil war within country; one in Nigeria involving regional conflict; and of course, the interruption to Iraqi production because of the war. The system is vulnerable to disruptions of various kinds. It creates great interdependency. We can see similar questions emerging with the liquefied natural gas (LNG) industry, which is moving from being a rigid regional business into a flexible, global market in order to meet the world's rapidly growing demand for natural gas as a fuel. There are clearly certain fundamental common interests – consumers need supplies and producers need markets – and these help to create the foundation.

The energy industry has come under heavy fire. Oil companies are often accused of exploiting various parts of the Third World. Company misconduct is part of public perception.

Much of this language, while deeply ingrained, is also many decades out of date. What are the companies being blamed for – providing revenues for nation-states? Something like 80 to 85 percent of the oil revenues from any given field go into the coffers of the host government, not to industry. So the big winners from developing oil resources are countries, nations and – if properly used – the peoples of those countries. The question is: What do countries do with those revenues? What do they do to offset inflation, to offset corruption, to prevent

197

unequal income distribution? What do they do to avoid turning into a petrol state, where other economic activity is attenuated because of the magnetism of oil? What do they do with the great wave of money that flows in? It is a misconception that companies cart off the bulk of the revenues; they go to the governments. That's why governments encourage companies to spend money exploring and developing, to take the risk, and then – if successful – to provide a flow of revenue.

I was thinking more of the exploitation of the native populations; this is what many NGOs get upset about.

Here, too, the language is confusing – 'exploiting resources' is a technical term but 'exploiting people' is a political one. The question is whether this huge source of revenue is being spent on health, education and social development. The 'native population' question is often really an issue about how the revenues are split between the national government, regional government and local peoples. And the conflicts can be very intense.

Is there a model country, a country that does the right thing with its revenues?

It's hard to point to one because the differences are so great. The countries involved are very different: Nigeria, Mexico, Kuwait, Norway, Russia, Abu Dhabi, and potentially Sao Tome. Some are very big; others like Sao Tome are very small. There are countries with tiny populations that possess huge sums of money. At present, there is considerable interest being shown by many countries in the idea of setting up an oil fund in order to 'sterilize' the revenues somewhat so they don't stimulate inflation and overwhelm the rest of the economy; it would also ensure that they can be tracked. Norway has such a fund, Alaska has one as does Alberta. Some Central Asian countries are in the process of establishing funds. Certainly, for a small population, the money can be quite overwhelming. Again, it's a matter of how that money is invested and then put to use.

Which, I suppose, depends on the good governance that already exists in the country?

Yes. In a larger country, of course, even though oil is rather important, it is only one of the major macroeconomic actors. In Mexico, the oil share of exports has dropped considerably over the past 10 to 15 years, but oil still provides about 35 percent of government revenues. For the most part, governments are better off with high oil revenues, but the oil business is highly competitive. Countries assume that companies have unlimited capital budgets and can spend money wherever they want. But this isn't the case. Companies locate in those countries that offer the best terms for their investors. And investors want a predictable, transparent legal system. They want a system of arbitration, a system contract, a stable fiscal regime. Those who invest in oil want a system in which the rules of the game are clear and are not subject to arbitrary change.

Will this change in any way when there is there a shift in emphasis from oil to natural gas?

We're at a stage now where we are witnessing the emergence of another global energy industry. Until recently, natural gas was a big regional business: Germany looks to Russia for the bulk of its gas; Japan looks to Indonesia and South East Asia. We're now moving from a market with rigid, 25-year contracts to a far more global market in which something like 200 billion dollars of investment will be required. This is the LNG business in which gas is turned into a liquid at very low temperatures, transported in special tankers, and then 'regasified' in consuming countries. The pattern of supply and demand is changing. Gas has become readily mobile; it is 'on

199

the move'. It can respond very quickly to changes in the market. Thus, we are witnessing the birth of a business in which gas tankers, like oil tankers, can alter direction on the high seas in response to changes in demand, price signals, or whatever. For example, if New England suffered an unexpected cold spell, a tanker bound for Europe could turn round and head for the east coast of the United States.

There are a number of factors driving this energy revolution. First, many countries have what is called stranded gas, i.e. gas that can't be pipelined to markets, that they would like to turn into revenue. Secondly, more and more, gas is becoming the favored fuel in the generation of electricity around the world. And thirdly, gas is economical. The costs have come down. Finally, North America is becoming more dependent on imported fuel. This is what happened with oil 30 years ago, when the US went from being largely self-sufficient to being an oil importer. Today, North America – Canada, the US and Mexico – needs more gas and no longer produces enough to be self-sufficient. By 2020, the US could well be importing more than 25 percent of its total gas in the form of LNG. But this development can only take place if there is sufficient investment – and we're talking about hundreds of billions of dollars. Without this investment, there will be serious consequences: lower economic growth and loss of jobs. Moreover, the environment will suffer because gas is an environmentally friendly fuel. It's clear that to attract investors, good governance rules have to be in place. There have to be stable 'rules of the game' for the gas business. Producers need to know that they have markets. Consumers want to know that the gas supply is guaranteed and not subject to interruptions and disruptions.

These concepts sometimes become very high-minded and abstract, but we have a new kind of global network in the making. This involves getting the technology right, the politics right, and the environmental policy right. It also involves getting the financial architecture right, i.e. the interaction between governments, financial organizations and companies. It's all part of the governance structure. It's not only national governments that make the rules – the fact is that regulating anything now is much more complicated than it used to be because there are a lot more participants and considerably more transparency. 'Rules' cover everything from international agreements to laws and regulations to norms and standards and values.

I've often heard it said that we are depleting the Earth's natural resources and this can only go on for so long. Will using natural gas make a difference?

For as long as I can remember, there's been talk of an imminent shortage of resources, especially oil. One of my professors used to relate how his teachers in the 1920s warned that oil sources would be depleted in 10 years. The subject has come to the fore again more recently. The projected time period often seems to be about 20 to 30 years. The reality is that world oil reserves have doubled since the 1970s. Of course there is an eventual physical limit to natural resources, but we don't know when this will happen. The issues raised about the future of oil are more political than geological. Gas certainly expands the supply of fuel we have. Technology is becoming ever more efficient. Moreover, we have learned to be more energy efficient and we use our resources more rationally. In fact, we now think of energy conservation as an energy source, and that's turned out to be profoundly important. Renewable energy sources are certainly more competitive than they were 20 years ago; wind energy is being actively supported and subsidized in both the European Union and the US.

Several years ago, I directed a task force for the US Department of Energy on energy research and development. Billions are spent on it every year, and I have no doubt that such R&D will eventually bring innovations. Some of them may

201

be related to consumption, i.e. in increased efficiencies. Today, Japan and the US use only half as much energy for a unit of GDP as they did in the 1970s. Europe uses about 40 percent less. It's possible that we would still be using a lot more energy had we not embarked on the conservation drive in the 1970s. Climate concerns have made a difference and speeded up technology. A new car in the US emits less than five percent of the pollution than that emitted by a car in 1973. That's pretty amazing. So you see there are many ways to look at sustainable development.

In terms of demographics, the world population is not growing as fast as expected, but the range is very great. In Germany today, only 17 percent of the population is under the age of 15; in the US, it's 21 percent, while in China, only 22 percent. In Mexico it's 35 percent. But in many countries in the Middle East it's 45–50 percent. That is an indication of future turbulence within the societies of the Middle East.

One thing that is becoming crucial in practical terms is China's integration in the world economy and how its role will change. Since reform began, well in excess of 300 million people have been lifted out of poverty – an extraordinary development. Now there's an important Chinese middle class.

Altogether, the reduction in poverty will be one of the great tests of globalization. If you look at the record, it becomes pretty clear that those countries that figure out an intelligent, reasonable way to engage with the world economy – that build the right institutions, that invest in education – do much better than those that don't. Four decades ago, the poorest continent in the world was Asia, not Africa. One of the biggest surprises now is India's involvement in the world economy; its growth currently stands around eight percent. This was driven partly by what the Indians saw happening in Korea and Taiwan. They asked themselves why South Korea's per capita income was the same as theirs in 1960 but then grew to become 10 times higher. I believe that the future will be heavily dependent on the new 'globalizers' – China, India, Brazil – and they will play a greater part in the rule-setting process. With so many participants in the world community, it won't be easy. But we need to have a common frame of reference, a common understanding, a common vocabulary.

How do you see the future of globalization?

We have our own scenarios for the future, and one of them is called 'Globality'. This describes a pretty well-run world economy and community, in which people cooperate within a framework. But it's equally possible to envisage something we call 'Fragmentation', where there is constant collision, disagreements and disputes, because we live in a world that, at one and the same time, is increasingly becoming a global marketplace but is still composed of nation-states. We have identified a series of tests to estimate how the world economy will work in this new, more interdependent world, to what degree people will recognize the value of such a world and to what degree they will reject it. The answer will revolve around key questions: What does globalization mean in terms of economic performance and jobs and standard of living? What does it mean in terms of the environment? What does it mean in terms of national identity and demographics? These are the issues that will determine whether people embrace globalization or rebel against it. Is it fair in terms of incomes? At the end of the day, it will be judged by the quality of the rules that apply to the system, whether they're seen as fair, moral and workable. We know the system won't be perfect, but will it do the job? We need to work out a framework over the next 10 to 15 years for this new era of globalization. That's where we need to focus our effort and energies.

Thank you.

The conversation was conducted by Susan Stern   **203**

Daniel Yergin

Daniel Yergin was born in Los Angeles in 1947. BA from Yale University and doctorate from Cambridge University. Chairman of Cambridge Energy Research Associates; a trustee of the Brookings Institution; a director of the Atlantic Partnership. A Pulitzer Prize-winning author, his publications include: *The Prize: The Epic Quest for Oil, Money and Power* and *The Commanding Heights: The Battle for the World Economy.*

Jeffrey D. Sachs

Getting Priorities Right

An Interview

You are a passionate crusader in trying to alleviate global poverty and fight disease. There are mechanisms, resolutions, institutions, funds already in place, but somehow, not enough happens. Why?

If everything is in place, then the main objective should be to ensure, at least with respect to the poorest countries, that they have the money they need to carry out programs. The crisis for many of the world's poor today is that even when they know what to do, how to do it, and they are eager to do it, they can't do it because they're too poor. For example, governments and major non-governmental organizations (NGOs) throughout the world all agree that education in poor countries should be extended to ensure that all children attend school. They'll say, 'we've even written up specific programs, we've done what the UN has told us to do and established so-called Education for All programs, but now we can't get them funded because the donors tell us they don't have the money'. It's my experience that much of the solution for the world's poorest people – the world's most desperate people, people dying of hunger, dying of disease, with no access to water and sanitation, with children who can't go to school – lies in bringing together clear goals, clear strategies and adequate financing.

The problem has been that typically, those three things have not come together. Frequently the problem lies with us, not with the poor countries. The rich countries aren't doing what they've promised to do because of their own budgets or other priorities. Of course, there are other parts of the world where the problems are not our fault, but the fault of poor government or a lack of seriousness. I don't think we can solve all the problems in the world ourselves, but we should make sure that we are not the obstacle. So we should work with any government ready to carry out good policies and when they're too poor to do it by themselves, we must ensure that they have our backing. This should not be hard to accomplish. We have established many new and sensible programs in recent years. For instance, the Education for All initiative of UNESCO and UNICEF, the Global Fund to Fight AIDS, Tuberculosis and Malaria, and the World Health Organization's new program to get three million HIV-infected individuals on antiretroviral treatment by the end of the 2005, called the Three by Five Initiative. So we have clear goals. Even more broadly, we've all adopted the Millennium Development Goals, which are specific targets to the year 2015. Many countries have already developed plans to meet these objectives and to these countries I want developed countries to say: 'Yes, you can go ahead, because we're going to give you the support you need. You've given us a serious budget and we're going to give you that amount of help so that you can carry out the plans.' Nothing more complicated than that. The reason I think this can be done is that the amount of help needed by these countries is quite small compared to the income of the rich world. So far we've chosen not to make these countries a priority. Instead of following through on our promises, we come up with lots of excuses. Germany and the United States, for example, have some way to go to achieve the international objective of 0.7 of

1 percent of GNP in donor assistance. The US is by far the worst donor in the world – it gives only one-tenth of 1 percent of GNP – and Germany also falls far short of the objective (0.27 of 1 percent of GNP). Both Germany and the US claim they are facing a budget crisis, but that is nonsense. If a government spends 40 percent of its GNP on public expenditure, it simply has to prioritize so the poor of the world fit into that range. The US is like the child who kills his parents and then asks the judge for mercy because he's an orphan. The Bush administration cancelled over two trillion dollars of taxes over the next decade, and then complains it has no money to help the poor.

The fact is: the president doesn't trust multilateral initiatives. We've now lived with three years of US unilateralism, and it is a disaster for the US and for the rest of the world that this government has been unwilling to form partnerships. That really hurts the poor because the value of a US AIDS project is very much less than the value of a truly international AIDS project. The White House is so aggressively unilateral in its thinking that not just Iraq, but even AIDS comes under this rubric. But on an optimistic note, I think the US is going to learn that this is such an expensive, ineffective way of operating that it is possible that even this present White House will change path. This kind of unilateralism is not only offensive, it's impractical.

I think the Bush administration's reluctance to form partnerships with other countries has to do with a lack of knowledge of the world. The current US government did not understand anything when it came in; it certainly knew nothing about AIDS. It wants to run the world agenda, but doesn't know anything about the world or its institutions. It doesn't know anything about economic development issues. Many mistakes are being made repeatedly because the Bush government operates more on ideology than on knowledge. However, even if you don't believe the truth, the truth is still there, and so eventually you're forced to confront reality. **207**

This is what is happening with this administration on one issue after another. It has taken three years, but it is now starting to fight AIDS, for instance.

What role does business play in the fight?

Business is not in the business of improving the world; it's in the business of making money. That is a kind of division of labor, and I think that's fine. It means two things, though. One is that the rules of the game need to be understood so that business doesn't have an adverse affect on the situation while pursuing its private interests. We need effective regulation against environmental damage for example. If we provide appropriate incentives, a company will even take care of these other issues – not because it is compassionate, but because it has business sense. Companies, I find, are most socially responsible when there's a clear framework of action. It's not their job to figure out what to do. But if the UN Secretary-General asks the business community to do more for AIDS and tells them how, he will usually get a pretty good response. We need more clarity here: the business community should understand that we have international goals, the Millennium Development Goals. Most big businesses work in very poor countries as well as rich countries, and they have the same kind of social responsibilities in both – not to be charities but to help make the local environment in which they operate productive and stable, so that they make money and the community prospers. When big business operates on home turf, it demonstrates social responsibility by sponsoring cultural events, giving money to universities and so on. When it operates in poor countries, it forgets those principles; it's far more negligent about the local social environment, political environment, and economic needs. However, with some guidance and some specific suggestions, businesses can become important participants in achieving these poverty reduction goals. It will require them to think more creatively about what they do, but we in the public policy community have to be more explicit. Rather than simply asking a business to improve its practices, it's much better to say: 'Here are five specific things you can do where you are working to help in the control of AIDS.' This approach usually gets a good response.

What role does civil society have to play?

There's a big difference between civil society and government. Government creates the legal framework which civil society can try to shape – but in the end, government has unique responsibilities. That's where political legitimacy needs to reside. However, that said, civil society has a critical role to play because I believe in open societies and I believe that although no particular organization is guaranteed a voice at the table, civil society organizations represent real, albeit often particular, constituencies, Although they may claim to represent the general good of the public, this has to be proved, not simply accepted. But their right to represent their own members, their right to speak up, and their right to try to shape the agenda can be accepted absolutely. By having a free society, we give space to these groups to try to earn their way by representing particular viewpoints in the public debate. For example, the Global Fund to Fight AIDS, Tuberculosis and Malaria, which I helped to design a few years ago with the Secretary-General of the UN, calls explicitly on each nation to ensure that government and civil society institutions put forward their proposals; governments cannot deny access to major civil society groups. Now in practice, that means that on any given national proposal, there may be eight or nine organizations on the list of the so-called country coordination mechanism. Why those particular eight or nine as opposed to some other eight or nine is somewhat arbitrary, but what is important is that the list can no longer include only one organization. And if a major group is denied access for political reasons, it can protest to the Global Fund. This has happened, the Fund looked into the matter and protested to the government of the country concerned.

Another area in which a similar procedure operates is the Poverty Reduction Strategy Process of the World Bank and the International Monetary Fund (IMF). Neither institution has been very participatory in the past. Now, as countries pursue their poverty reduction strategies, the IMF and the World Bank will, in principle, entertain documents and plans only if they are based on national consultations. At the beginning, the NGOs protested that the national consultations were a sham. Their protests were heard. Today, there is far more genuine participation and governments dare not object because they know that some of these groups have enough power in Washington, London, and Paris to stop the process by claiming it's a fake. So step by step, the process is opening up. There is some question as to legitimacy, but it's my feeling that we should just accept that tension. Not everyone will be represented, not everyone deserves to be represented; the groups that were represented last year may not be there this year or next year. It is partly a question of successfully mobilizing your constituency. This is politics, but that's okay.

The US is a hegemon – it usually gets its way, and it isn't too hot on the UN. What do you see as the future of the UN?

First, the US is not a hegemon. It's a country with an overgrown military, an overgrown military appetite, but it's made up of only five percent of the world's population. It's wealthy, generally economically dynamic, but it spends far too much on its military. It launched an unprovoked war – but it is not a hegemon. The world needs to know this and to treat the US as just one country of many. Europe should continue to do what it did over Iraq and say, 'we don't want to be part of this particular adventure'. Germany and France deserve huge applause for doing that. The US calls the shots because most everyone else is quiet. The rest of the world should say, 'The war on terror is one thing but it's not the entire agenda of the whole world. We can't forget issues of the environment, of poverty, of disease, just because the White House wants to talk about terrorism. There are other agendas and they're even more important for many people. Moreover, terrorism can't be defeated unless we make great progress on reducing poverty, on stopping environmental degradation, on controlling disease and so on.' So we need the rest of the world to speak up, and then we'll have a much more balanced agenda. When talking about the US agenda recently, George Soros called it the 'bubble of American supremacy', like a stock market bubble, and I think he's right.

As for the UN, it is not perfect, but it's the only international setting we have, or that we're going to have for quite a while, that can address the needs of global governance. So I'm a huge believer in it, and I devote a tremendous amount of my own time to trying to help make it work. And I think that it does work very well in many ways, and not so well in others. On the good side: there is tremendous expertise in the specialized UN agencies such as the World Health Organization, the Food and Agriculture Organization, the UN Environment Program, and the UN Industrial Development Organization. These are often mocked or even worse, ignored in the US, but they have tremendous technical knowledge and capacity to really understand the problems in poor countries and to help them solve their problems. That's what works very well. We also have the best Secretary-General imaginable, a person who can hold this world together even under present circumstances. But on the down side there is the problem of implementation. The UN is not designed to be an implementing agency – not because it's incompetent, but because it has not been in the interests of powerful countries such as the US that it should be able to implement. So the US deliberately weakens the UN and then makes fun of it for being weak. This is pure theatre. **211**

The US does not want the competition of global executive power from the UN, but the fact of the matter is that we need executive authority on a global scale; we need to find cooperative ways to actually implement our goals. And that requires multilateral, not unilateral approaches. So I believe we need to move from a UN that simply states goals and monitors them to an organization that can actually implement. Now strangely, George W. Bush has said the same thing. He has asked why the Security Council doesn't implement its resolutions. Well, I'd like to know why George W. Bush doesn't implement some of the resolutions the US has committed itself to, for instance the Millennium Development Goals. The US is a signatory, Germany is a signatory, 191 member governments are signatories – so let's get those goals implemented, not just monitored. And that means a complete change in our procedures as donor countries. A change in the way the IMF and the World Bank work, so that rather than simply squeezing poor countries to pay their debts, or to get their budgets under control, we help them to fight disease and invest more in children's education and so on. Implementation would be a terrific thing in those areas. But it would take the US and the European Union and the other powerful countries to say, 'Yes, we want the UN to be a genuine implementing agency.' This is how the poor are going to escape poverty, and how the global environment can be protected. If more countries wanted that to happen, it could happen.

Thank you.

The conversation was conducted by Susan Stern

Jeffrey D. Sachs

Jeffrey D. Sachs was born in Detroit, Michigan, in 1954. PhD from Harvard University (where he taught until 2002). Director of the Earth Institute, Quetelet Professor of Sustainable Development, Professor of Health Policy and Management at Columbia University; research associate of the National Bureau of Economic Research. Serves as special advisor to UN Secretary-General Kofi Annan on the Millennium Development Goals.

Mark Malloch Brown

Partnering with the Private Sector in Development

The private sector has a critical role to play in helping meet the challenges of development. Partnership and enlightened self-interest can help to guide the way.

The private sector and the modern challenges of development

The world of development has undergone a seismic shift over the last several years reflecting a response to global events such as September 11th, and a new consensus around the challenges the world urgently needs to address. The universally agreed Millennium Development Goals (MDGs), an ambitious agenda to halve the proportion of people living in extreme poverty and hunger by 2015, represents an unprecedented declaration of determination by the world to make the fight against extreme poverty the central theme of the global development agenda.

But make no mistake; while the goals are achievable, they present a phenomenal challenge. Take the example of sanitation. Currently, over 1.5 billion people lack access to proper sanitation. One of the most successful non-governmental organisations (NGOs), Sulabh in India, has provided 10 million people with safe and effective sanitation over the last 30 years. However, to achieve our goal in sanitation means connecting 10 million people *every 30 days* – a rate substantially greater than previously achieved in the developing world. The magnitude of this challenge underscores the fact that these goals cannot be achieved by the public sector alone, but will require private sector know-how, technology and capital.

The explicit endorsement by world leaders at the 2002 World Summit on Sustainable Development (WSSD) in Johannesburg on the role of public–private partnerships in sustainable development and achieving the MDGs was a significant breakthrough. At the same time, businesses are recognising the value of becoming active participants in development issues as they face increased consumer and investor pressure for corporate social responsibility and feel the impact of global disease and global conflict on business operations. Companies are also beginning to see enlightened self-interest in opening up new markets in the developing world and the knock-on benefits of developing new business models that can serve poor populations at the 'bottom of the economic pyramid'.

But international corporations are not, however, the only part of the private sector that we must consider. The local private sector in developing countries is where much of our focus is going to have to be to meet the overarching challenges of poverty reduction, economic growth and sustainable development. Growth, jobs and opportunity belong there – with the small and medium size enterprises (SMEs) that represent the bulk of employment and economic activity in the world's poorest nations. And as the development community has come to recognise, the development agenda must be driven by developing countries themselves; local economic development is the only way that self-sustainability can be achieved. As Senegal's president Abdoulaye Wade has noted, 'No country we know has succeeded in being salvaged from its underdevelopment through aid, loans, or both.' While we can point to some areas of development progress over the last few decades, we need to accept that we have not yet begun to ignite a real private sector economy over much of the South.

So where does this leave us? What exactly should the role of the private sector be in the post-Johannesburg context? **215**

And is there real scope for public and private sectors to work together in addressing the challenges of meeting the MDGs? Events since the WSSD can guide our thinking about how public–private partnerships can work in order to achieve our twin goals: taking advantage of the support the international private sector has to offer and creating the conditions for the private sector in developing economies to flourish.

High impact roles for the private sector in development

Much has been made of the gap between rhetoric and reality in the debate over public–private partnerships since the WSSD. I would argue that, rhetoric aside, there are very real, high impact opportunities for partnership with the private sector in meeting the challenges of development. Critical to the debate, however, is understanding where high impact opportunities lie, as well as the incentives that drive private sector participation. I outline some of these opportunities below. While not exhaustive, I hope they will highlight actions that will enable the corner to be turned in terms of transforming developing countries' economies and the lives of millions of poor people.

Filling service delivery gaps
Public–private partnerships have great potential to fill critical gaps in service delivery that can make a substantial difference to the world's poorest people.

Take energy for example. There are nearly two billion people in the world who do not have access to electricity and almost as many again who have very erratic access. National grids are not reaching out to the rural or urban poor fast enough, triggering repercussions from environmental degradation to health problems. Lack of access to electricity is also one of the crucial barriers to economic development and improved productivity. It is clear that the public sector in developing countries will simply not be able to tackle this problem alone. Decentralised local power generation solutions will require private know-how, technology and capital in partnership with a public regulatory environment and public capital, to make these ventures viable. And civil society must have a role in managing local distribution and energy conservation and ensuring affordable pricing.

Similar arguments exist for water, sanitation, telecommunications and other capital-intensive services. To meet the MDGs, the private sector must be involved. For the private sector to be involved, the public sector must be receptive to its needs: it is in business to make money. Thus, in order to make these partnerships work several elements must be recognised – by all partners. The private sector must be able to make risk adjusted returns on their investment. This is an important factor that will be crucial to the potential success and scalability of these partnerships. Public–private partnerships can play a key role by reducing the risk inherent in such activities and by engaging the government and local communities; public capital will often be needed in order to make the risk-reward ratios workable. Some may question why public resources should help a private entity earn profits. The simple reality is that markets are not working in developing countries to fill the supply gap for services critical to human development. The risks common to developing countries, which include capital risk, currency risk and security risk, have proved too great. Either we need to lower the risk – by engaging public capital and key stakeholders – or we need to subsidise higher prices in order to attract private sector partners.

At the same time, public sector partners must ensure that proper regulatory schemes are in place, that these partnerships clearly address national priorities and meet the needs of the intended beneficiaries, and that knowledge transfer and domestic capacity-building are part and parcel of the arrangement. Some emerging examples in this area are beginning to show the potential that exists.

The e7, a group of nine leading global electrical companies, has successfully launched some innovative projects in rural electrification. The projects demonstrate the viability of new technology applications in developing countries and ensure that projects achieve financial sustainability and long-term management. In Indonesia, a rural electrification project using solar and mini-hydro technology supplies power to 4,000 people in eight rural villages. The project combined public and private investment and created a host of small, locally run 'micro-utilities' to manage the facilities and take responsibility for operation, maintenance and financial sustainability. NGOs and user groups were engaged to train micro-utility entrepreneurs as well as raise awareness among users in local communities. The technology and strategy used in this project allowed for a sustainable financial model that made it possible for power to be supplied at low cost, and four years later, more than 80 percent of customers continue to pay their electricity bills.

Another interesting example comes from the Congo. An initial cooperative venture involved 185 families in Butembo who pay $10 a month to fund a turbine that provides power to homes and small businesses. Based on the success of this arrangement, 25 of Butembo's businessmen each invested $15,000 to form a joint venture with a South African engineering firm to harness turbine power from a large river. The power generated will be used to supply power to more homes, businesses and also make the local airport safer.

Increasing transparency

Another area where the private sector has an important role to play in development is by changing its own engagement in developing countries and making a commitment to be more transparent about investments made and royalties paid

through contracts and other routes. This is critical so the

public can see where money is going and demand greater accountability from governments, thereby blocking opportunities for corruption.

This is especially important in areas such as West Africa, which is currently poised to benefit from increased oil exploration and production. The countries in the region are expected to receive $10 billion in new investment annually for the next 20 years as well as billions in additional oil revenues from increased extraction. Chad, for example, is expected to receive $80 m a year for the next 25 years, a 50 percent boost to its annual budget. That is a large amount of money and potentially very beneficial or very destabilising.

The vision of greater transparency is a central element of recent broader initiatives such as the Extractive Industries Transparency Initiative and the 'Publish What You Pay' movement. This route may be most effectively and appropriately pursued by companies working in partnership with public bodies such as the United Nations Development Programme (UNDP) or the World Bank. The new model of revenue management related to the Chad–Cameroon pipeline may serve as an effective example for future public–private cooperation on this issue.

Applying global technology to local challenges

The use of technology has the potential to make vast improvements in development. In many developing markets, technology can allow countries to leapfrog deficiencies in infrastructure that could take decades to address. We are seeing cellular technology that can service villages without access to fixed-line telephone networks, and tele-medicine applications that can fill gaps in healthcare provision. There is enormous scope for innovative public–private partnerships in this area – partnerships that can draw on global skills and expertise, but then apply them to local challenges. These applications can embrace a variety of important development sectors – health, education, agriculture and financial services

219

are among those areas where technology can make a difference.

There are some notable examples of global technology adapted to developing countries. The I-Communities Program developed by Hewlett-Packard adapts technology products to both create entrepreneurs and deliver important services to rural populations, all on a financially sustainable basis. The *e-choupal* initiative in India makes use of Internet kiosks to improve the income of soya bean farmers by facilitating access to information on world market prices for their product. The ICICI bank in India uses technology across the board to deliver banking services in small urban/rural markets to better monitor the progress of loans to SMEs and smaller borrowers, and to reduce the cost of lending. In Chile, low-tech solutions have made no-frills banking accessible to poorer segments of the market.

Making partnership work

While much was promised at Johannesburg, it is clear that expectations have not been met, causing many in the development community to re-examine the legitimacy and potential contribution business can play in development. It has forced us all to examine how to make this partnership work better and how to ensure it has a meaningful impact on development, instead of delivering small gains that fail to address underlying systemic problems. Making the partnership work will require that some core principles are observed.

First, development impact will not be maximised unless partnerships are integrated into national poverty reduction and economic competitiveness strategies. This requires that public sector partners in development help to shape the agenda to ensure that partnerships are 'demand-driven' and respond to the highest priority needs. Secondly, the incentives for each party joining the partnership will clearly be different and this must be recognised. The private sector will focus on delivering shareholder value over the long term and acting with an eye to the bottom line. While some may find this incompatible with development, I would propose instead that we adopt a vision that does not abdicate the profit motive, but rather seeks to harness that motive for development. By doing so, it can make available a fuller extent of the unique resources that business can bring, motivated by its enlightened self-interest. And by harnessing the profit motive, we can engage all private sector actors, including the SMEs that are the critical link in the 'last mile' of service delivery.

The private sector's role in development is not, however, solely limited to partnerships. There are many activities where the private sector, acting alone and driven by market incentives, can have substantial development impact. However, for a variety of reasons these market-based mechanisms have not yet materialised on a large scale in the developing world. Within this context, the use of partnership can be a valuable route to reducing risk, resolving information asymmetries, increasing confidence in making investments and laying the groundwork for future market mechanisms to work. It can also be critical in ensuring that social value is maximised.

Making things work will require overcoming mental barriers. While public sector actors must come to terms with the fact that the private sector will ultimately be acting with a view to the bottom line, the private sector must also factor in differences in capacity and resources of their public sector partners and be willing to invest in seeking benefits that can ensue from serving these new markets.

Getting the equation right is of utmost importance because the quantum leap in development impact will be taking the most successful innovations and scaling them up. For this to occur, the conditions and incentives must be right otherwise these efforts risk being reduced to one-off phenomena.

UNDP's commitment to private sector partnership

One of the welcome advances at the UN in recent years has been the steadily growing engagement with the business community. This was revitalised four years ago by the launch of the Global Compact, which currently has over 1200 companies participating. And at UNDP we have established a specialist unit, the Division for Business Partnerships, to develop and promote our partnership agenda with the private sector.

Within this context, there are two special initiatives that I would like to flag as part of our commitment to partnership with the private sector: the Growing Sustainable Business initiative (GSB) and the Commission on the Private Sector in Development. The GSB initiative, initially championed by Sir Mark Moody Stuart, promotes new investments in developing countries that can deliver both profits and address poverty alleviation. Active in Ethiopia, Tanzania and Madagascar with plans for expansion to more countries this year, the projects include several innovative approaches in service delivery, including water, energy and the telecoms sectors, and have put SME development, multi-stakeholder engagement and integration with national development priorities at the heart of the equation. It is a unique vision of public–private partnership that marries the profit motive with development impact; a vision we hope can be a model for the future.

The second initiative is UNDP's Commission on the Private Sector and Development. Launched by the UN Secretary-General in July 2003 and led by Paul Martin, Prime Minister of Canada, and Ernesto Zedillo, former President of Mexico, the Commission published its report on its findings this spring. In it, the Commission outlined strategic recommendations on how to promote strong domestic private sectors in developing countries: how to build markets, provide access to affordable capital, use foreign direct investment (FDI) to stimulate investment and create a simplified regulatory environment that brings companies into the formal economy.

Conclusion

It is clear that the potential benefits from engagement of the private sector in addressing the challenges of development are vast; we have only just begun to scratch the surface. Making the partnership of public and private sectors work productively will take a great deal of work and understanding from all sides, as well as an appreciation of the different incentives and capacities each actor brings to the table. But only if we tackle the kind of issues I have highlighted here can we help create the kind of business class, job creation and hence tax revenue base that is indispensable to boosting the economic growth needed to meet the MDGs and the underlying goal of development itself: helping developing countries to map out their own exit strategies from aid and stand firmly on their own feet, meeting the needs of their own citizens from their own resources.

Mark Malloch Brown

Mark Malloch Brown was born in London in 1953. Administrator of the United Nations Development Programme (UNDP) since July 1999. Chair of the United Nations Development Group; currently working to develop a strategy to support the achievement of the Millennium Development Goals. Vice President for External Affairs and United Nations Affairs at the World Bank (1994–1999).

Rupert Neudeck

Development Aid –
The Real Story

At times of global crisis, nation-states often appear to be powerless to deal with the issues that have become so much a part of our everyday lives – poverty, war, terror, starvation, human rights violations and forced migration. And yet this perception is based on a very European premise. In the continents inhabited by the poorest of the poor, the issue presents itself differently: Can any nation-state find solutions to the problems experienced by millions of people who are only gradually starting to constitute a 'nation'? If supranational and international solutions are to be found at all, states first have to function as such – that is, find their feet as states. This is no straightforward matter. Alliances and working relations between states can only be built on the foundation of governments exercising legal responsibility within the state context.

Even in the era of globalisation and the so-called *global village,* we are still faced first and foremost with the task of guaranteeing and exercising nation-state responsibility. The shocking consequences of *bad governance* are glaring in many parts of Africa and Latin America, and to a lesser extent in South and South East Asia. Most people still have little awareness of the global structure of the world; they know only the United Nations. Yet when pushed, the rulers of this world always develop a supranational bias whenever difficulties arise.

The existence of an institution charged with taking major global responsibility is a great step forward in the history of humanity. Throughout the world, UN special agencies work

wherever need manifests itself by taking care of refugees,

attempting to alleviate hunger, looking after children and promoting people's health. These organisations are the only resort for many around the globe, but over the last 20 years their operational capacity has been considerably curtailed and many are little more than coordinating agencies based in the major towns of the countries concerned.

Still severely lacking are regional federations and alliances, even though the organic and organisational preconditions for such forms of international collaboration certainly exist in most affected regions. The Africans, for example, have not yet formed a pan-African corps to act as blue helmet troops for the UN. Military deployments in Sierra Leone and Liberia organised by Economic Cooperation of West African States (ECOWAS), under the leadership of Nigeria, are best quietly glossed over. The abbreviation of the West African blue helmet troops, ECOMOG, was translated by the civilian population in both countries into: Every Car Or Mobile Gone.

The Asians, on the other hand, have thus far been unable to create joint forms of cooperation or a peacekeeping force capable of intervening in emergency situations due to their isolation from one another as sovereign states. The wars in Korea, Cambodia, Kashmir, Afghanistan, Tajikistan and, finally, the terrible first Gulf War, all took place without any scrutiny on the part of the broader Asian public or the ASEAN states.

In the case of North Korea, too, efforts have failed to mobilise the appropriate forces, either outside or inside the country, to intervene in their internal conflicts. It is the people who suffer as a result. According to estimates by international organisations, two million North Korean citizens have already died from starvation. Nothing was done by the rest of the world to prevent this tragedy reaching such horrendous proportions.

However, it is we Europeans who bear the greatest responsibility. The issues of global responsibility and human rights have semantic significance but otherwise they don't affect us. We secretly cling to the notion that welfare provision for the First World and the welfare provision for the Third World are two entirely different things. We have no difficulty whatsoever in modestly claiming our health, superannuation, pension and holiday rights, while remaining impassive to the problems and needs of people in the Third World.

Thirty years ago, we in Europe and North America persuaded ourselves that the states of the Third World would recover with the help of our structural, technological and financial aid. These hopes and expectations have proved to be false because our aid has been a sham. We sent a multitude of experts to as many countries without actually making a difference. We acted as though we wanted to help, whereas in fact there was no real desire to do so. The Germans surpassed everyone else on this score. Over a period of decades they used their development aid in more than 100 countries in order to enforce their political 'Hallstein' doctrine: if, say, a country in Africa, Latin America or Asia recognised the second German state, the GDR, as an actually existing political entity, that country was penalised by the FRG through the withdrawal of development funding. If the country dutifully returned to the fold of those who recognised only the FRG, however, it was richly rewarded.

This led to a deep-seated atrophy within the German development aid system which, in my opinion, will not improve in the near future. The German ministry for economic cooperation and development (BMZ) and the state development aid organisations have whole battalions of experts; to my mind, these battalions should all be demobilised and aid concentrated on five or six countries. But getting rid of these apparatuses and changing direction in development policy makes people very uneasy; they prefer to stick to ineffective policies.

One answer would be for non-governmental organisations (NGOs) to develop in their stead. NGOs are particularly suited to intervening in crisis situations and helping the people affected. In order to do this, however, they really do need to be NGOs in the truest sense of the word – in other words, independent of states and governments.

In reality, far too many of the organisations that proudly call themselves NGOs have long since ceased being such. Almost 90 percent of the funding received by many NGOs to cover their projects and general expenditure is government money. I know of NGOs which depend on government money for up to 100 percent of their funding that still unashamedly call themselves NGOs. The temptation to become an NGO in name only and receive subsidies in the form of government funding is even greater now due to the casual way the European Union dispenses subsidies. EU funding extends beyond pure project financing. On top of the total amount approved for a project, it pays the organisation concerned another seven percent of this total towards its structural costs. As a consequence, these so-called NGOs no longer require donations and support from the general public.

NGOs now face a major challenge. They need to determine to which camp they belong: those that are truly committed to the old model of a social organisation and are keen to convince the citizens in their own country to support a campaign with private donations ('pure'), and those that prefer to take the easy route of government subsidies and are now defined solely according to the government projects they undertake ('impure').

So far, the very effective character of NGOs has prevented the international community from taking a critical look at this division between 'pure' and 'impure' organisations. German development aid researcher Professor Franz Nuscheler, in his 1995 book *Lern- und Arbeitsbuch Entwicklungspolitik* (Textbook of Development Policy), was the first to call on the NGOs to purge their own ranks. According to Nuscheler, the NGOs have long since realised the possible negative effects of allowing their activities to be financed in part by the state:

227

there is a danger that they could be misused as a humanitarian fig leaf to conceal a development policy of which they are actually critical. In 1993, for example, the church-based aid organisations alone received grants amounting to 296 million deutschmarks, while the other NGOs received 126 million. Government guidelines view such subsidies in the following light: 'Cooperation between the state and non-state organizations contributes towards raising awareness among the German public of the range of work undertaken through development aid, reducing people's reservations against development policy and reinforcing it as an area of politics in its own right.'

These kinds of conditions, says Nuscheler, place the so-called NGOs in a precarious position because they require them to mobilise support for state development policy in return for state subsidies. The NGOs thus run the risk of gambling away by stealth a chunk of their independence by accepting state subsidies. This in turn changes NGOs into quasi-non-governmental organisations (quangos) or perhaps even governmental non-governmental organisations (gongos).

However, if NGOs remain true to their role as a critical counterpart to the state and government, there is much they can achieve. They can do this, for example, through their unremitting pointed critique of governments in the countries in which they operate, as well as by reinforcing what has somewhat too frequently – and thus at times erroneously – been called 'civil society'.

'Prevention' has also become a politically correct call to battle. Political parties, foundations and institutions are constantly talking prevention, yet hardly anyone has the courage to say outright that our societies, the way they are presently constituted, see no cause to opt for any kind of prevention. Apparently the horse must have bolted before anyone attempted to lock the stable door.

One of the most striking examples of this was the genocide in Rwanda. The fighting that eventually cost 800,000 human lives in the East African country began during the night of 6 April 1994, following the shooting down of President Habyarimana's aircraft. On 11 January 1994 – i.e. about three months before the outbreak of the bloodiest, fastest genocide in modern-day history – the Canadian general in command of the UN's blue helmet troops, Romeo Dallaire, contacted the UN Secretary-General and demanded that the hideouts and caves being used by the perpetrators to conceal their weapons be eliminated. Dallaire was convinced that he would be permitted to do this once it had been approved by the UN Secretary-General: prevention was still an option at that point. But the incumbent under-Secretary-General responsible for blue helmet operations, none other than Kofi Annan, refused to approve the operation because it would have changed the role of the 2700-strong troops of the UNAMIR from that of observers into that of combatants.

In retrospect, the urgent need for this kind of preventive action is obvious. But while the genocide in Rwanda was descending into a bloodbath, it did not occur to Europeans to think about prevention – they were too preoccupied with the task of evacuating those deemed to be 'more valuable' from the scene of civil war and genocide.

In a word, NGOs themselves have very little, if any, room for manoeuvre once they have made themselves comfortable within the cosy confines of legality; when they don't realise, for example, that so much more work is involved in preventing genocide in the first place. NGOs must abandon the boundaries of legality, whatever the cost. They need to practise disobedience internationally on land, in the air and in the water – just as organisations such as Greenpeace have been doing for years. And NGO activists must also be prepared to risk their lives to help people whose own lives are in danger.

NGOs do not receive legitimisation through democratic elections. They are legitimised, however, by the money that millions of supporters donate in what may be seen as a secret plebiscite. Moreover, NGOs are citizens' initiatives that

229

emerge from democratically organised societies. It is extremely hard to imagine NGOs being able to take root in the unpromising conditions of dictatorial and authoritarian regimes.

What range of responsibilities and authority should 'stateless' organisations have in order to make them equal to the global challenges they face and to make the world governable again? By this I don't mean the actual areas of responsibility allotted to us by governments or large intergovernmental bodies. Legitimisation can only be given by one's own population, civil society – governments can only ever have an abstract, derived form of responsibility.

The following episode may help to illustrate this point. On 13 December 1999, I landed at Nairobi's Jomo Kenyatta International Airport together with Norbert Blüm and Heiner Geissler. Waiting for us at the exit was the German ambassador to Kenya, Jürgen Werth, who asked to speak with us. The three of us were intending to set off the following morning on a ridiculously dangerous journey across the border between Kenya and Sudan and into the Nuba mountains in Central Sudan. More than 350,000 people live there without any humanitarian or political aid, or any support from their own government. Cap Anamur, an NGO, has been running a hospital concealed in the side of a mountain there since 1997.

We met the ambassador in the sports club of the hotel in Nairobi where we were due to spend the night. He had the task of advising the two elected members of the German parliament from the CDU party in the strongest possible terms not to undertake their trip into the Sudan. This he dutifully did, without making any attempt whatsoever to prevent me, the representative of an NGO, from embarking on my expedition, in the full knowledge that he would not succeed in any case. What he did succeed in doing, however, was to considerably frighten the two MPs on the evening before our departure.

Cap Anamur was working illegally in the Nuba mountains – without government financing they had no choice. To us in central Europe, acting illegally means doing something that is against the law. But this is not the real obstacle. What most of us lack is the courage to spend time living with the have-nots and the street urchins, to share their work and to make new friends, such as those among whom a stranger can quite happily live in the Nuba mountains.

What then is required of those who take on responsibility, who want to help? What skills and characteristics do they need to have to make this world governable, i.e. 'better'? First, they need the ability to detach themselves from their 'Euro worship', from the congenital arrogance that many Europeans have. At the next level, they need practical and intellectual skills. Taking on responsibility requires sound professional training and on-the-job experience. And they should enjoy their chosen jobs, because the conditions in the countries needing help will be much more difficult than those at home – being passionate about what you are doing can help to make the hard times more bearable.

Anyone who wants to take on responsibility for others has to have an affinity for the people they are helping. It is important to avoid committing the cardinal sin of development aid. Towards the end of the 1960s, so-called helpers were able to earn quite a tidy sum: after spending a period of two or three years abroad they didn't need to work again for some time. Supplements added to salaries that were already inflated, along with perks such as the 'risk bonus', etc. effectively meant that this line of work promised better-paid and the most secure jobs available at the time. In the meantime, the countries we were supposed to be helping went to rack and ruin.

The success of development work stands and falls with the amount of respect and acceptance helpers demonstrate towards the cultures, different ways of life, communal modes of living and religions they encounter, and on their ability to

231

adapt to these living conditions. The organisations that will survive are those which are able to escape the orientation of societies based on a division of labour; they must be able to detach themselves from European standards regarding luxury, working conditions and insurance. They will be sensitive to the fact that it is not appropriate to impose or force anything on other people, societies and countries. Only when a whole new generation of helpers has decided to take responsibility on the basis of these premises will large parts of the world become governable.

Rupert Neudeck

Rupert Neudeck was born in Danzig in 1939. Studied law and theology. In 1979 founded Komitee Cap Anamur Deutsche Not-Ärzte e.V., an organisation that provides humanitarian aid. In 2003 he founded the aid organisation Grünhelme e.V. (Green Helmets). Author of numerous publications.

Human Rights

Irene Khan

The Good Fight

An Interview

What role does the global human rights debate between NGOs, governments and business play today and how do you see the position of Amnesty International in it – as an ally or an adversary?

I think the global debate on human rights and common values has become very important because of the way in which our world is being divided. Whether through globalisation or the new global security doctrine – people are increasingly being split into 'ins' and 'outs', into accusers and the accused.

Our world is becoming fractured. What will be the glue that will keep us together? It has to be common values and I believe that human rights issues offer some common ground. Human rights are about justice and despite cultural differences I believe that every civilisation and every culture shares a basic common understanding of what justice is about. It's about people being treated fairly, it's about restoring human dignity, and it's about a higher state of what it means to be human. These basic ideas are more valid today than ever.

Amnesty's mission is to improve observance of human rights, so our task is to conduct a dialogue with anyone who can make a difference. We're a membership-based organisation with 1.8 million members in more than 100 countries around the world. And we use a range of techniques to conduct a dialogue with our partners. We prefer working *with* them on issues that matter to us, but we shall use whatever means we believe necessary in order to get our message across to companies or governments.

We recognise, for instance, that companies are important actors when it comes to improving a human rights situation, so we need to work with them rather than against them through boycotts and sanctions. Only recently our members gave us the authority to call for a boycott if we considered it necessary but this has never been Amnesty's way of working. I think it is much more important to convince businesses – or governments – to change their behaviour rather than force them to do so.

When you talk to businesses, how do you present a human rights issue – as a business case or as a moral case?

I think a human rights issue is both a business and a moral case. A couple of years ago, I was at a meeting where the head of Cisco Systems was talking about human rights. When one of the journalists asked him, 'The business of business is business – why are you talking about human rights?' he replied: 'There are more than a billion people in the world today who earn less than a dollar a day. That means there are a billion people who can't use Cisco Systems software and it's my business to increase my market. And I am going to bring more of those people into a position where they can access it.' So it depends on whether your view is long term or short term.

In most cases, the best way is to match your moral case to your business case. There are situations where this is not possible, but I think it is happening much more often than not. These days it's not always clear who's an investor and a shareholder, who's an employee and who's a manager in a company – the more those lines get blurred, the more pressure is put on the company to behave ethically. This is why public opinion is becoming so important.

How has the human rights issue changed over the years that you have been involved with it?

The most marked changes have taken place in three areas: the agenda, actors and answers. As far as the agenda is concerned, I think the discussion on human rights has broadened and there is a much greater acceptance of the validity of economic, social and cultural rights as part of the human rights issue, the so-called second generation human rights. We started moving into this area only in the last two years. The issues of poverty and social inequity are becoming a greater part of the human rights debate than has ever been the case.

As the agenda is expanding, we're beginning to realise that we also need to address other, different actors who bear responsibility: companies, armed groups, women, religious institutions, community leaders, to name just a few. This is probably the biggest challenge to the human rights movement because traditionally, the human rights issue has developed as the relationship between the state and the citizen, regulated through international treaties. We are beginning to vary our approach to different actors to deliver the human rights agenda. As the power of local NGOs, grass-roots organisations and community groups has grown, so has our alliance with them. Since the real test of human rights implementation takes place locally, large NGOs such as Amnesty and Human Rights Watch have to learn to work with the people on the ground.

And, finally, we are now setting up groups in Russia, Central Europe and Central Asia, where the issues are quite different and the circumstances in which our new members are working make it much harder for human rights defenders. Other social movements are emerging in these countries such as environmental and women's rights groups, and development networks. So we have to ask ourselves: What relevance

235

does the human rights issue have for their agendas? What new answers can we provide? What new value can we bring to their discussions?

We see Amnesty adding new value to the local debate by providing a global reach – through the combined power of our 77 national chapters – that local groups would be unable to achieve otherwise. Historically, Amnesty's strongest achievements have been promoting the adoption of international treaties and working with international institutions – such as the International Criminal Court, the office of the High Commissioner for Human Rights and Convention Against Torture – primarily through its global span.

The leverage we can achieve in this way plays a key role in our internal strategy of working with local groups: we call it 'giving space to the voiceless'. As an example of this; in early December I went to Brazil to meet with a number of local human rights groups – women, landless farmers and indigenous people among others. At a press conference to launch our report about what was happening to social activists in Latin America, we invited the local Brazilian activists to the podium and gave them space and an opportunity to talk, something they had not been offered by their own government or media.

Another positive example comes from Mexico. We have taken up the case of several hundred women killed in the city of Ciudad Juarez on the Mexican–Texan border in the past 7–10 years. Working with women's groups and with the mothers of the murdered women, we have been able to bring the case to the attention of Mexican President Vicente Fox and to put pressure on him to intensify government investigations into the killings.

In what direction do you see the activities of Amnesty and other NGOs moving?

In the past couple of years we have been making a much greater effort to build up our accountability and transparency to the broader human rights community. We see ourselves as social citizens in this broader community. We remain, of course, accountable to our own members and to our donors within whatever legal framework we are working, but we are looking into engaging more with other human rights groups, letting them know what we're doing and why we are doing it, and changing our reporting systems in order to be part of the community. This is an evolving process because until recently most NGOs – certainly Amnesty and others – didn't quite understand that relationship.

Amnesty's philosophy has always been that it is a collective that works with individuals who suffer from human rights violations. Traditionally, we adopted the issue of wrongful imprisonment and worked for prisoners' release. But our relationship with them was more of a saviour and the saved – we came to those who were in prison and we got them out of prison. However, the human rights situation is moving away from that type of individual work. We'll certainly continue doing that kind of work, but our emphasis is now on systemic change. So, if you're talking about violence against women, then saving one woman is not the answer. If you're talking about child labour, then getting one child out is not the issue. The issue is changing the systems which allow human rights abuses to happen and that means working together with other groups that are affected by these systems to bring about the necessary changes.

How do you find the balance in a situation where correcting a human rights violation may lead to further harm such as the ban on child labour in Bangladesh that considerably worsened the economic situation of children there?

I think the balance has to be worked out on a case by case basis. Each specific case redefines issues so a comprehensive approach is required. Take the situation with Iraq, for example. On the one hand, there was the question of overthrowing or removing the regime that was obviously despicable and harmful to human rights. On the other hand, we faced the problem of how to remove that regime and cope with the inevitable consequences of that action. And it's very clear from the Iraq experience that there are no simple answers to this problem.

Amnesty's approach to the Iraq crisis was to focus on the situation of the people and our position throughout this crisis right up to the military intervention was that it was necessary to protect the rights of the Iraqi people. If a decision was made to attack Iraq militarily, the decision-makers had to make sure civilians didn't suffer. And it was just as important to us to know what kind of systems would be put in place to protect people after the military intervention and to allow them to have a voice in their government.

So I think we've got to look at such situations from the perspective of a human rights impact. Of course, there are other issues that come into play – security and weapons of mass destruction and so on – but we would like governments, companies and other responsible actors to focus on a more comprehensive approach because in the human rights scene there are fewer and fewer cost-free answers.

When last year Washington and London justified their military plans in Iraq with the need to protect human rights of the Iraqi people, Amnesty issued a statement saying the plans weren't about human rights, and human rights shouldn't be used as a pretext. However, you're now saying human rights were also the issue in Iraq.

True, those military plans were also about human rights, but Saddam Hussein's appalling human rights record didn't just emerge in 2003. Amnesty published reports about the gassing of the Kurds in 1988, but then the British and American administrations said they didn't believe us. Therefore, our statement was effectively saying that you can't ignore the human rights record for 15 years and then bring it up when it suits your own security strategy or foreign policy objective. That kind of a selective approach – using human rights issues as an excuse to pursue specific political goals – may be the way governments work, but it brings the human rights system into disrepute because it reduces people's confidence in the validity of the issue if they see human rights used as a way of justifying political and military reaction.

Michael Ignatieff said recently that governments are 'real political animals' and will act only in their own interest, using a human rights issue if it furthers their own cause. According to this view, it wasn't in the interests of London and Washington to intervene in 1988, but it was in 2003. Do you see it the same way?

I agree with Michael Ignatieff that governments are political animals and that they will pursue their political goals whatever way they can, including using human rights to justify their actions. That's why I believe that we need to make sure no one undermines the framework and the rule of international law and international human rights. Once that is allowed to happen then basically the entire human rights system will be demolished. So I would argue that while governments will try to manipulate the system to their advantage, there has to be some means of containing their behaviour. This is what we're advocating through public opinion, it's what the UN is trying to do through its human rights machinery. Otherwise, if we allow human rights to simply become a foreign policy tool, then the value-based approach to human rights will be destroyed.

Thank you.

The conversation was conducted by Igor Reichlin

Irene Khan

Irene Khan was born in Dhaka, Bangladesh, in 1958. Currently Secretary-General of Amnesty International (since August 2001). Led the UNHCR team in former Yugoslav Republic of Macedonia (1999); appointed Deputy Director of International Protection (1999). UNHCR Chief of Mission in India (1995); headed the UNHCR Centre for Research and Documentation (1998). Recipient of a Ford Foundation Fellowship and Pilkington Woman of the Year Award 2002.

Mary Robinson

Strange Times for Human Rights

An Interview

How has the issue of human rights changed over the past 30 years?

I see the focus moving now from writing laws to implementing them. It's also increasingly shifting to holding governments and other responsible parties accountable and to finding effective ways to do that. What really drives me is seeing the victims of violations or those suffering due to the non-implementation of human rights laws – seeing people living in absolute poverty or dying of AIDS.

The issue itself is changing too. Until fairly recently, we had a warped development that had grown out of the Cold War. This resulted in two international covenants: one on civil and political rights, which the West took seriously, and the other on economic, social and cultural rights. The latter approach was favoured at the time by the Soviet Union and many developing countries, who took the attitude: we will feed our population, we will look at things like education and health, and only then, maybe, will we consider the issue of political rights. This way it could avoid having to address the issues of fair trial, freedom of expression and freedom of political activity. So we had a standoff.

I was hoping we could get over that problem after the fall of the Berlin Wall, but economic, social and cultural rights still haven't attained their true significance, although I think the European Union is increasingly recognising their importance for Europe and especially for developing countries.

Merging these two sets of human rights is incredibly important, and that is how I saw my job as High Commissioner when I started in September 1997. I was very conscious of the need for a balanced broad agenda that put equal emphasis on civil, political, economic, social and cultural rights. But I wanted to bolster both sets of rights in different ways: first by protecting and promoting civil and political rights, and, as my ultimate goal, by enforcing the prohibition of torture and guaranteeing freedom of expression. The second way involved enforcing the implementation of economic, social and cultural rights and ensuring that the responsible parties were kept accountable. I feel it is extremely important to vary the ways in which the latter is achieved. You can look at budgets or bring court cases, as in South Africa and India, or accountability can be built into the reporting process to the treaty bodies in which civil society is increasingly participating. So when governments say to the UN Committee on the Rights of the Child: 'We're doing X or Y', civil society has a role and can say 'No, they're not. In fact, on the ground, they're not doing that at all.' And the UN Committee will weigh the matter and come up with its report. It's still not a perfect system but it's the beginnings of accountability.

What about the framework of the human rights policy? Is that also changing to fit the issue?

What has changed, in some respects anyway, is an increasing awareness by groups working on local issues at the grassroots level – on children's rights, women's rights and on combating poverty. There is a useful international dimension that allows them to argue locally with their governments and then if that fails, shame their governments via Geneva, through the inter-American system or the European Court for Human Rights in Strasbourg. This is also increasingly happening in Africa too. The new African dimension, the optional Protocol to the African Charter on Human and People's Rights on the Rights of Women in Africa is now a tool for women's groups there. If this protocol is ratified it will make a huge difference to women's rights in African countries.

All these systems are helping to improve accountability. They aren't perfect but because of the networking by civil society groups – particularly on economic, social and cultural rights – these systems are now becoming more useful as tools. Good practices are increasingly being shared; a greater knowledge of case law in courts in some countries is triggering similar cases being taken elsewhere, while the experience of going to Strasbourg is particularly valuable.

For example, those working on children's rights and on economic and social rights, are learning that if a government delays its reporting to the UN, they can bring in an alternative report. If a government produces a report with which they disagree, they can submit a parallel report that will be considered by the UN Human Rights mechanisms. At the same time, we have a maturing system of treaties through which the office of High Commissioner supports the five key committees: the Committee on the Rights of the Child, the Human Rights Committee for the International Covenant of Civil and Political Rights, the Committee on Economic, Social and Cultural Rights, the Committee against Torture and the Committee for the Elimination of Racial Discrimination.

The UN's Division for the Advancement of Women in New York supports the Convention for the Elimination of Discrimination against Women (CEDAW) Committee, where a lot of experience is being shared. What these committees lack are the resources: they're chronically underfunded because some governments don't want them to be effective. While at the UN, I tried very hard to resource those five committees, but whenever I raised the subject of their extra-budget funding, even developed European countries responded with 'Oh, this should be funded from the regular budget' – and then made sure that the funding wasn't forthcoming.

I was able to secure some additional funds outside the membership albeit with difficulty. It's a major struggle to get adequate resources for those committees in order to give them what they need to be rigorous, to be able to carry out limited research and to engage in proper discussion of the reports received from different countries. They need to be able to process those reports faster – delay in dealing with reporting results in a filed report that is in some cases still being considered by the committee five years later.

Now if we talk about public–private partnership, would you say that the best form of partnership is at the local, regional or intergovernmental level?

I suppose it depends. It is very important to try to engage a wider range of partners. I have already mentioned how grass-roots organisations can use regional tools, if they exist, as well as UN or intergovernmental tools. I also see business communities increasingly being responsible for exercising power. While the primary responsibility remains with governments, globalisation in part means deregulation and reduced activity by governments on a whole range of services such as education and health – even prisons and other aspects of the justice system. But governments must remain ultimately accountable – even if they are not in fact providing the services – to ensure that these services are carried out in a way that progressively implements economic, social and cultural rights. At the same time, if the business community is delivering those services as part of public–private partnerships, then it is responsible for making sure that it's not complicit in any violations of human rights. It must be increasingly proactive in supporting people's rights to health, to education, to freedom from torture and to freedom of expression.

There has been criticism of the International Monetary Fund (IMF), whose policies sometimes force national governments to cut budgeted programmes in order to improve their governance. How do you see these problems being resolved?

Let's take education in developing countries as an example. I would prefer to have a strong government involved in the education system because its responsibilities guarantee that there will be access to education in the poorest/rural areas. But the reality is that the IMF policies have focused on structural adjustment which has resulted in weakening public access to education.

At the same time, the elites in these developing countries have privileged access to education and private schools, so it is vital that governments take responsibility for implementing anti-discrimination measures. Many countries end up with a two-tier system consisting of private schooling for the elites and a public education system which has been weakened by structural adjustment policies. So, on the one hand, there is the government which is responsible for providing access to public education and ensuring there is no discrimination in the elite school system, and on the other there are the IMF policies that are weakening access to education and hindering the capability of countries to implement their legal commitments to progressively implement economic, social and cultural rights.

The project which I am now leading – the Ethical Globalization Initiative (EGI) – seeks to focus on this issue of accountability. The wide majority of the world's governments have by and large ratified the various human rights treaties, therefore they have a responsibility, whether in the context of the IMF, the World Bank or the WTO, to ensure that policies do not undermine progressive implementation of economic,

245

social and cultural rights. Regrettably, the IMF's current structural adjustment policies and its approach to the debt problem very often undermine – and even prevent – human rights implementation.

How will EGI deal with this issue? By confronting the IMF?

No, we are not seeking to be confrontational – we want to raise awareness and catalyse new thinking and new partnerships which recognise the links between human rights, human development and human security. EGI is a very small initiative that has three institutional partners: the Aspen Institute, Columbia University and the International Council on Human Rights Policy. We see ourselves as a facilitator and communicator. We aim to catalyse ideas on bringing a human rights perspective into trade and development, taking a human rights approach to migration, addressing the right to health as a human right, and bringing that into the whole debate on access to drugs and treatment in the context of combating HIV/AIDS.

We seek to communicate at different levels: government leadership, business, civil society and academic. We're linking academic resources at Columbia with Trinity College, Dublin and with other European universities as well as the University of Pretoria – bringing them all together with a particular focus on Africa.

We're talking about public–private partnerships, i.e. NGOs and business in the private sector and government agencies or international organisations in the public realm. For such partnerships to work well there must be mutual trust and mutual accountability. Do you see problems with that equation?

I find it hard to describe as a partnership the interaction on tougher issues – ensuring that police forces do not use torture and that judges are independent, securing freedom of expression and freedom of religion. Rather, this is an act of insisting on government's accountability since it bears the primary responsibility. Understandably, this is a more tension-filled approach – it requires great strength and determination on the part of local human rights defenders to carry out the difficult task of pressing their governments into implementing human rights treaties. As a last resort, international human rights groups can intervene to provide support.

Defending human rights is a struggle and it is this struggle that has helped to carve out the agenda for their defenders: fighting violence against women, opposition to the smuggling of human beings, and giving voice to those without political rights. But it's much easier to talk about partnerships in a development context, such as the implementation of the UN's Millennium Development Goals which are extremely important for the realisation of economic, social and cultural rights.

Such a partnership is now developing between the UN and the business community. Last year, the UN Sub-Commission on the Promotion and Protection of Human Rights launched a draft of a normative framework for businesses: Norms on the Responsibilities of Transnational Corporations and Other Business Enterprises with Regard to Human Rights. It aims to apply the norms to businesses at every level and to bring clarity to the human rights principles in the UN's Global Compact initiative.

Companies that have adopted the Global Compact have undertaken to support the Universal Declaration of Human Rights and to ensure non-complicity in its violations as well as to support core environmental and labour standards. But actually, the compliance bar has been set very low in my view – companies which sign up have not been required to demonstrate in a rigorous enough way how they are implementing the commitments they have made. We come back again to the issue of accountability. The new UN norms will raise the bar; if we can persuade businesses to have confidence **247** in the value of the norms for making progress, they can be helpful in addressing concerns about the Global Compact.

Monitoring compliance is, of course, a key issue. We need an objective system of monitoring; civil society could monitor companies, businesses could carry out peer reviews, maybe an NGO watchdog will be needed. But I think it's too early for the Commission on Human Rights to engage in this monitoring because businesses are very much divided on the issue. So I'd rather hasten slowly here to be on the wise side.

If you were to make a forecast, in what direction do you see the human rights issue moving?

I think the implementation of economic, social and cultural rights will become considerably more sophisticated, government accountability will increase, the trend towards international governance in this area will accelerate and businesses will be increasingly expected to behave as partners rather than as transgressors.

But in general, it's a strange time for human rights. I'm half-pessimistic when I'm looking at their future. In some respects the situation is much more difficult, but there is an incredible vibrancy apparent in current efforts to implement economic, social and cultural rights – even the US is sitting up and taking note.

Thank you.

The conversation was conducted by Igor Reichlin

Mary Robinson
Mary Robinson was born in Ballina, Ireland, in 1944. Executive Director of the Ethical Globalization Initiative. Founding member and now Chair of the Council of Women World Leaders; Honorary President of Oxfam International; Pro-

fessor at the School of International and Public Affairs at Columbia University. President of Ireland (1990–1997); UN High Commissioner for Human Rights (1997–2002). Recipient of UN's Global Leadership Award, the J. William Fulbright Prize for International Understanding and the Indira Gandhi Peace Prize.

Security and Peace

Jean-Marie Guéhenno

Peacekeeping Today

A blue-helmeted battalion from Pakistan works alongside troops from Bangladesh, Nepal and Uruguay in the volatile Ituri region of the Democratic Republic of the Congo, to keep the militias from fighting and the population from being victimised. Civilian advisors are in Dili transferring skills in information technology, management and administration to the nascent Timorese government. In Kosovo, seasoned police officers from Berlin and Buenos Aires, from Cairo and Kathmandu, are training, advising and monitoring a new police force, while judicial and corrections experts help to develop effective courts and prisons to ensure the architecture necessary for the rule of law. Humanitarian workers in Liberia are providing guidance and support to newly disarmed and demobilised combatants and their families, including child soldiers as young as nine. Military observers from Jordan and Kenya monitor compliance with the ceasefire agreement between Ethiopia and Eritrea.

This is a snapshot of United Nations peacekeeping today. In late 2003, 13 UN peacekeeping operations were on the ground around the world, varying greatly both in size and function ranging from around 50 military observers stationed between India and Pakistan to 15,000 troops authorised to deploy to Liberia and carry out a variety of tasks from relatively straightforward monitoring of ceasefire lines to implementing comprehensive peace agreements and even administering entire territories. Earlier predictions to the contrary notwithstanding, the demand for peacekeeping continues to grow. This is particularly true in Africa, where the deadliness of the conflicts and the desperate humanitarian need they create are not matched by the efforts of the international community to prevent, manage and resolve these man-made catastrophes. UN peacekeeping remains the main if not the only tool to address this critical need.

A great distance has been travelled since Ralph Bunche first developed the outlines of what would become peacekeeping 55 years ago, but the main character of this unique activity remains the same. Although not specifically mentioned in the UN Charter, peacekeeping is a concrete tool used by the Security Council to exercise its primary responsibilities in the maintenance of international peace and security. Peacekeeping places on the ground between hostile parties a physical and credible manifestation of the will of the international community, as expressed in the unique legitimacy of the universal organisation that is the UN. In 1956, Ralph Bunche wrote a message for the Secretary-General, Dag Hammarskjöld, to send to the UN emergency force when it arrived in the Suez Canal area, describing the troops as the 'frontline of a moral force which extends around the world'.

While UN peacekeeping has since then developed into a more flexible instrument, fulfilling a broad range of political, military, administrative and socio-economic functions, it continues to be based on the principles that Ralph Bunche developed to supervise the Middle East truce in 1948 and which formed the basis for the first UN peacekeeping force sent to the Suez Canal in 1956. These principles require that the parties to the conflict consent to the deployment of the operation, which will act impartially between them and not use force except in self-defence. If these conditions are absent it simply is not peacekeeping.

251

Perhaps the most important lesson learned from the UN's intervention in Bosnia and Herzegovina in the early 1990s is that peacekeeping cannot be a substitute for facing aggression. The other lesson also learned in Bosnia and Rwanda during the same period is that neutrality is not impartiality and, if adopted as a stance in the face of murderous violence against civilians, is tantamount to complicity with its perpetrators.

There are clearly situations when UN peacekeeping cannot be effective because the parties fail to reach a point where peace is at least possible. In these cases the Security Council must not send in peacekeepers – a 'thin blue line' can do little when faced with an advancing armoured column and may even do more harm by raising expectations among the population that the international community, represented by the peacekeepers, is committed to their safety and security.

UN peacekeeping has evolved as conflicts have become more complex. Although interstate conflicts have not disappeared, the UN now mostly faces the formidable challenges posed by civil wars in failed or failing states that pit multiple armed militias against each other, wreaking havoc and death among civilian populations. In these circumstances, peacekeeping has proved it can still be an effective instrument. But such situations are fraught with danger, and risk failure for the international community and further tragedy for the affected civilian population if the UN is not given (i) a clear mandate, specifying not only the goals to be achieved but also the means for achieving them as well as (ii) the human, material and financial resources to undertake the operation effectively.

An essential lesson learned by the UN from its peacekeeping experiences in the 1990s is that the goals set by the mandate must be clear. The precise role of the UN operation must be spelled out by the Security Council in its resolutions, which must have realistic and practicable objectives. The political exigencies of the Security Council must not put at risk either the mission or its personnel. First and foremost, the Council has to be acutely aware of the situation on the ground. Early and accurate information about the conflict is as essential as the means to analyse the information and develop effective peace strategies. The Council can only then make clear what the UN is to achieve.

Most of the tasks of peacekeeping operations today – supporting the implementation of a peace agreement, assisting political processes and institution building, training new police forces, supporting humanitarian assistance, facilitating the return of refugees and displaced persons, monitoring respect for human rights, assisting in the implementation of constitutional, judicial and electoral reforms, supporting economic rehabilitation and reconstruction – cannot be carried out in a non-permissive environment. The civilian personnel who perform these functions are not soldiers and they cannot do their job from behind concrete walls and barbed wire. That is why, before sending in a UN peacekeeping operation, the Security Council must be certain of the commitment of the parties to peace and of their consent to the involvement of the UN.

The adjunct to clear goals is a consensus on what means can be used to achieve them. This is an important issue that has implications for the underlying principles of peacekeeping. Although about a third of Security Council resolutions since the end of the Cold War have invoked Chapter VII of the UN Charter – those articles that govern the use of force – it has often not been clear how much force can actually be used in peacekeeping operations. While the use of force in self-defence remains one of the bedrock principles, peacekeeping today operates in environments where this principle, as well as the formal consent by the parties to the deployment of UN personnel, means little to the rogue militias, the spoilers of the peace process and the ordinary bandits who seek to exploit post-conflict situations, especially during their volatile early

253

stages. Under these circumstances, UN peacekeepers must arrive ready to withstand any challenge to their authority. They have to respond firmly to tests of strength and send a clear message that they will defend both themselves and the peace process that they are deployed to support.

For a peacekeeping mission to succeed in challenging environments, there must be a shared understanding of the need for a robust operation, deployed and configured not only to be able to use force but also to keep the initiative and, if challenged, to defend itself and the mandate. Such an escalation capability is essential to project credibility: the more force it is clear you have, the less you will need to use it.

Successful peacekeeping requires, above all, troops, police and other personnel from the member states of the UN. This is the other basic premise of UN peacekeeping, i.e. that countries will provide the necessary personnel for duty under the auspices of the blue UN flag – there is no standing UN army. Without these national contributions, UN peacekeeping would not exist.

The multinational forces in Bosnia, Kosovo and Afghanistan, authorised by the Security Council, are undoubtedly critical contributions in the efforts to maintain international peace and security. The UN operation in Kosovo, for example, could not be effective without the security environment provided by the NATO-led KFOR multinational force. The importance of these operations mandated by the Security Council but carried out by other organisations such as NATO, the European Union or by a coalition of member states, is considerable. The downside, however, is that there are fewer contributions by these same countries to UN-led peacekeeping operations; contributions that are particularly important for the UN operations in Africa, where most UN peacekeepers serve.

The international community may well be moved by the crises in Africa but the actual effort it expends on that continent does not match the needs and certainly pales into insignificance in comparison to efforts elsewhere. For Kosovo alone, KFOR fielded as many as 50,000 troops at full strength in a territory one-third the size of Belgium. Today in Africa, there are around 40,000 troops in all the UN peace-keeping operations, including the mission in the Democratic Republic of the Congo, where just over 10,000 UN troops are deployed in a country the size of Western Europe.

We have seen certain efforts outside the framework of a UN operation – such as those of the EU in Bunia, in the Democratic Republic of the Congo, and of Great Britain in Sierra Leone – to provide military force in situations of inse-curity in Africa. These efforts are vital and have saved many lives, but the question still remains as to whether such efforts would have been necessary had the UN operations in Sierra Leone and the Democratic Republic of the Congo been configured and equipped from the very beginning with the necessary resources to accomplish their respective mandates, including a rapid military response capability.

If the UN is to succeed in its indispensable peacekeeping duties today, it must be able to count on the different person-nel contributions needed for effective implementation of a mandate. The robustness of a peacekeeping operation, which is essential to its success, relies not only on the worthy infantry battalions that cover the terrain but also on those critical logistical and technical capabilities that ensure the flexibility and effectiveness of the operation. A small group of air traffic controllers can keep the airports and landing strips of the Congo open and working, for example, but such a capability is to be found principally in the armed forces of developed countries. It is this sort of specialised support the UN cannot do without. If it cannot come under the UN blue flag then we must continue to find ways – as the EU did in the Congo – to ensure that it comes somehow.

The realities facing the UN are those of a continent – Africa – that has more than its fair share of conflicts, which **255** combine with other factors to produce massive humanitarian crises that must be addressed urgently. The reality is a case such as that of the extremely tentative, volatile but hopeful peace process in the Democratic Republic of the Congo. The reality is that of a Liberia, which would have descended into chaos and extreme violence had the Economic Community of West African States and the UN not brought the promise of peacekeeping. The reality is that when faced with these crises, and despite the admirable willingness but ultimately limited capacity of African states and regional organisations to take on these challenges, it ultimately falls to the UN to take the lead.

Such is the case today. The prospects for the longer term, however, may be more encouraging. Africans are bringing the biggest civil wars to an end. A pragmatic optimism, based on experience and increasingly resilient, is taking hold in African politics. Post-colonial African diplomacy has developed under some of the worst imaginable conditions, yet it has developed and continues to improve. We should also see an increased and strengthened African peacekeeping capacity, able to contribute to the global requirements of UN peace-keeping. The African Union is developing a standby force based on the formation of multinational brigades organised on a sub-regional basis. These and other multilateral and bilateral efforts to strengthen African peacemaking and peacekeeping capacities need the critical support of the international community.

For peacekeeping to succeed, we have to be absolutely clear about what we are doing and to what end. There must be a peace to keep and on which to build. We must have the necessary resources to do the job – no one should be expected to accomplish a task as complex as peacekeeping without the necessary political, military, financial and human resources. And yet, that is what has happened in the past. UN peace-keeping may not always be the right tool, but sometimes it is the only tool. It must be made to work.

Jean-Marie Guéhenno

Jean-Marie Guéhenno was born in France in 1949. Currently UN Under-Secretary-General for Peacekeeping Operations. French Ministry of Foreign Affairs, Policy Planning Staff (1979–1981); Head of Cultural Affairs of the French Embassy in the US (1982–1986); Director of the Policy Planning Staff (1989–1993); Ambassador to the Western European Union (1993–1995). Mr. Guéhenno is Chevalier de la légion d'honneur.

Mary Kaldor

An Era of Repressive Globalism

Before 9/11, there was a lot of optimism about global governance. As early as 1795, Immanuel Kant pointed out that the world had shrunk to the point at which a right violated in one part of the world was felt everywhere. Growing interconnectedness in all fields of social endeavour and the increased speed of communication and travel over the last decade seemed to have made this observation a reality. After the end of the Cold War, many hoped that a multilateral system of rules would supplant an international system based on military power and that such a system would provide security for individuals and not just states. Global security, moreover, would provide a basis for legitimacy, allowing the newly emerging institutions of global governance to tackle a range of global problems including poverty, combating disease, saving the environment and so on. In such a system, states would continue to act as the repositories of sovereignty but this would be pooled in relation to certain key issues, most notably security; in effect, sovereignty would become increasingly conditional, dependent on respect for human rights.

Unfortunately, the attack on the World Trade Center marked instead the beginning of an era of 'regressive globalisation', a term coined by Martin Shaw to refer to the rise of groups who favour globalisation when it serves their particular interest and who promote a backward-looking ideology within a global framework. By backward-looking, I mean an ideology that celebrates the past and cannot offer a viable project for the future. In particular, I mean groups who still cling to an old-fashioned notion of sovereignty. Both the Bush administration and the various religious and nationalist militant networks that have emerged over the past decade represent, in different ways, examples of 'regressive globalisation.'

The Bush administration starts from the premise that the United States represents 'good'. America is a cause not a nation, involved in a powerful moral crusade to spread the American model of 'free market democracy' and to promote this ideal in the face of all kinds of threats that represent 'evil'. Central to this idea is the belief that this can be done through military power. It is a way of reminding the world of the American victory in 1945. This victory, it is argued, this moment of triumph, brought democracy to Europe. As a senior official in the Bush administration said during an interview: 'I know this will shock you. But there are moments in history when the world needs a violent onslaught. You would never have got your democracies in Europe had it not been for two world wars.' This notion that America spreads democracy through military power held sway during the Cold War years. Many of the members of the current Bush administration were also members of the Reagan administration – Bush's 'axis of evil' echoes Reagan's 'evil empire'. The search for new enemies began long before 9/11 – rogue states who sponsor terrorism or who acquire weapons of mass destruction were being discussed in the late 1990s. Since 9/11, the enemy has been extended to those we don't necessarily know, hence Donald Rumsfeld's famous remark about the 'unknown unknowns'.[1] The new national security doctrine claims an extraordinarily wide mandate to deal with these 'unknowns' through pre-emption instead of deterrence.

Central to this vision is reliance on high technology. It was American know-how that is thought to have been responsible for the victory in the Second World War, in particular the American capacity for mass production. Now it is argued, the US has to demonstrate its ability to make use of the new information technologies. The so-called revolution in military affairs (RMA) is supposed to be as path-breaking as was the invention of the stirrup or gunpowder. As Elliott A. Cohen put it in 'A tale of two secretaries':

> However jerky the transmission belt, the qualities of the modern American economy – its adventurousness, spontaneity and willingness to share information – eventually reach the American military. Just as the teenager who grew up tinkering with automobile engines helped to make the motorised armies of WWII work, so do the sergeants accustomed to playing video games, surfing web pages and creating spread sheets make the information-age military of to-day effective.

In fact the military tactics have not changed much since the Second World War – the American armed forces still emphasise aerial bombardment and rapid offensive manoeuvres. Accuracy has greatly improved as has battlefield knowledge, but these technological advances have been grafted onto existing structures and strategies enabling the military to stage ever more spectacular performances along the lines of past battles.

This theory is 'regressive' because it is aimed mainly at Americans and because it rests on a celebration of past victories. It can be understood as an attempt to preserve the institutional structures of the Cold War period and impose them on a very different world. American sovereignty remains paramount in this vision and the US reserves the right to decide what rules it will accept or reject; hence the rejection of treaties such as the Kyoto protocol on climate change, the Landmines Convention, the Biological Weapons Convention and, above all, the International Criminal Court. On the other hand, the sovereignty of other countries is conditional dependent on whether states conform to the American definition of 'good' – a definition that is clearly subjective since some states such as Iran are classified as 'evil' whereas other equally authoritarian states such as Saudi Arabia or Uzbekistan are considered to be 'good'.

Unlike the Second World War, however, exercise of military power in today's world is limited. One reason is the decline in American willingness to participate in war. During the Second World War, there were massive increases in taxation and thousands of Americans lost their lives. Moreover, the world was hungry for dollars so that large-scale aid through lend-lease served to mobilise the American economy. Nowadays, Americans do not have to pay anything; on the contrary taxes are cut and the administration takes great care not to risk American lives. Currently, due to huge budget and current account deficits, the US is dependent on borrowing from abroad to pay for its wars, i.e. on non-Americans. The only involvement most Americans have with war is simply watching it on television.

Another reason for the limits on military power is the difficulty of winning wars given the constraints of participation and the growing acquisition of weapons by unconventional enemies. Undoubtedly, the US has a big advantage in conventional warfare, but the growing accuracy and destructiveness of all weapons – including small arms, grenades, hand-held rockets etc. – means that unconventional enemies, or what the Americans call 'asymmetric threats', can nullify that advantage. Conventional military power can be used with much greater precision and with more lethal results than in the past, but it is much more difficult to impose order and to defeat an enemy. In Afghanistan and Iraq, governments were toppled with dramatic speed, yet in both cases the remnants of the regime remain underground. Saddam Hussein has thankfully been captured but Osama Bin Laden remains at large. Both countries, characterised by continuing violence and insecurity, are still far from being models of 'free market democracy'. Continuing reprisals against suspected enemies in both Afghanistan and Iraq, in which many civilians are killed,

261

creates resentment against the US and contributes to the kind of polarisation in society that benefits the unconventional forces.

But these limitations may not matter; they need not result in a questioning of the overall strategy. If the financial world fears the collapse of the American economy, it will continue to lend to the US regardless of its reservations about American wars. Provided American victories are reported in the US media, the negative post-victory consequences may only be of concern outside the US. If Bush can stand on an aircraft carrier announcing 'mission accomplished' and bring turkeys to cheering troops in Baghdad on Thanksgiving, the wars will have served their purposes. As long as Americans believe in their moral crusade, the effect on the rest of the world is unimportant – indeed the continuing activities of terrorists may serve further to legitimise their belief in the rightness of their cause.

Although extremist religious and nationalist groups are not new – many groups have their origins in the 1920s and 1930s – a new combination of political extremism (exclusivism or fundamentalism[2]), violence against civilians and criminality has largely come about in the last two decades. Because of attacks on Western targets, the Western media tend to focus on global Islam. Yet similar regressive ideological groupings can be found in all major world religions (Christian, Jewish, Hindu, Sikh and Buddhist) as well as among many national or ethnic groups. It is sometimes difficult to distinguish between religious and nationalist groups since national identity is often equated with religion, e.g. Catholics and Protestants in Ireland or Hindu and Sikh nationalists.

This emerging phenomenon can be explained partly in terms of the decline in secular left ideologies, particularly socialism and post-colonial nationalism, and partly in terms of the growing economic and social insecurity associated with globalisation. Typical recruits to these movements are unemployed young men, often migrants, either from countryside to town or from South to West, who have experienced the loss of ties to their places of origin and yet do not feel integrated in their new homes, and who lack sufficient income to marry. Membership in militant groups provides a source of security (through associated NGOs or local religious centres) and a source of income (through criminal or semi-criminal activities) as well as a sense of moral worth, purpose and adventure.

Nearly all these groups aspire to state power in the name of religion or ethnicity. They have an old-fashioned view of state power – they still believe in an absolutist notion of sovereignty and reject the conditionality that has accompanied globalisation. They believe that other religions or ethnicities can somehow be excluded from their bordered territory. The global Islamic groups, often connected to al-Qaeda, tend to favour regional Islamic states. Thus al-Qaeda favours a Muslim caliphate for the whole of the Middle East, while Jemaah Islamiya, a network spread across Indonesia, Malaysia, the Philippines and Singapore favours an Asian Muslim caliphate. The South Asian organisation Jamaat-e-Islami similarly wants to unite Muslims.

They also all tend to be nostalgic for some imagined past, a 'golden age' when they are believed to have controlled their states. And they all share a deep belief in the notion of struggle. All of these groups have a clearly defined notion of 'us' and 'them', 'good' and 'evil', of *jihad,* cosmic war or Armageddon, and they often celebrate epic battles and heroic warriors. But despite their backward-looking ideology, these are groups that make use of globalisation. They often consist of transnational networks with partners in many different countries; nearly all have important diasporas that are a source of money, techniques and ideas. They finance themselves through transnational organised crime – trade in drugs, human trafficking, smuggling of alcohol or cigarettes – the growing darker side of globalisation. They spread their ideol-

263

ogy through the new media; for al-Qaeda, videocassettes, for example, have been critical in sending messages and in planning actions.

For these groups violence can be best understood as a form of political mobilisation. Unlike earlier terrorists, who attacked strategic targets such as important officials or key installations, the new groups deliberately target civilians, often using the most macabre and spectacular violence. The attack on the World Trade Center must have been the most spectacular act of violence in history. Such attacks confirm the notion of struggle and of grand conflict. They generate further insecurity, which helps to mobilise extremist sentiment. As Osama Bin Laden said in a video-taped interview with Al Jazeera in December 2001: 'Regardless of whether Osama is killed or survives, the awakening has started, praise be to God.'

There is the risk that these various forms of regressive globalisation will feed off each other, squeezing the space for debate and deliberation, for forward-looking projects more in tune with the current context. In Iraq, the Americans confront an unsavoury alliance of the remnants of the former regime and Jihadists. Far from defeating terrorism in Iraq, the war brought these groups together and has been followed by a wave of terrorist violence in Saudi Arabia, Morocco and Turkey. American support for local 'wars on terror' in Russia or Israel and for undemocratic regimes provides further fuel for the terrorists' arguments. The Americans insist that unlike the terrorists they try to minimise civilian casualties and by the standards of past wars, the civilian casualties in Afghanistan and Iraq were relatively low – around 3,000 in Afghanistan and 8,000 in Iraq although this figure excludes the number of military casualties (not even counted) and the number of people who fled their homes or who died from the associated humanitarian crisis. But by the standards of human rights, these numbers are very high – certainly higher than the numbers usually killed in terrorist attacks. And these numbers add to the perception of double standards, of a privileging of America vis-à-vis the rest of the world.

Could the Iraq and Afghan models spread? Both the Bush administration and the new militant nationalist and religious groups thrive on struggle. They cannot defeat each other, but they can sustain a long-term conflict. After all, Rumsfeld has already stated that like the Cold War, the war on terror will last 50 years. A parallel might be drawn with the Israeli–Palestinian conflict. Suicide bombers who kill large numbers of Israeli civilians do not help the cause of building a Palestinian state. Likewise, Israeli reprisals and attacks on suspected terrorists, in which many civilian Palestinians are killed, make sense in terms of Israeli security. But both types of violence increase polarisation and support for extremists – both Hamas and right-wing Zionism – making the conflict ever harder to resolve.

What then are the prospects for progressive globalisation? Can liberal Americans and moderate Muslims build an alternative alliance together with majority opinion? Fifteen million people demonstrated worldwide on 15 February 2003, expressing an emerging global norm that nowadays war is illegitimate. Can a divided United Nations, a divided European Union and other international organisations build on that expression of global opinion to provide an alternative, forward-looking plan that offers real security? In Iraq, international agencies such as the UN, the EU and the NGOs, which do provide some protection for individuals in conflicts even when they do not have military forces at their disposal, are noticeable by their absence. Is this the likely direction for the future?

Proposals and ideas abound – 'The Responsibility to Protect', the Ogata-Sen Commission on Human Security, the concept of global public goods and the Millennium Development Goals. The problem is how to put these ideas into practice in the face of growing regression. Regressive globalisation cannot be reversed but it can be contained if progressive

265

globalisers have sufficient political will. At the root of these new dangerous tendencies is insecurity, both physical and material. We need to develop the capacity to protect individuals and to arrest criminals; we need global redistribution; and we need to support genuine efforts to construct democracy. This requires resources that, at least in financial terms, are commensurate with what people were willing to pay during and after the Second World War. And it requires a human commitment not to risk lives in the crazy way that lives are risked in war to kill others but in the way that human rights groups and aid agencies, policemen and firefighters, are ready to risk lives to save others. In other words, the regressive spectacle needs to be supplanted by a progressive reality.

Notes

1 'There are things we know that we know. There are known unknowns. That is to say, things we know we don't know. But there are also unknown unknowns. There are things we don't know we don't know ... Each year, we discover a few more of these unknown unknowns.' Quoted in G. John Ikenberry 'America's imperial ambitions', *Foreign Affairs* September/October 2002, p. 50.
2 By exclusivism, I mean groups that want to exclude others of a different nationality or religion. By fundamentalism, I mean groups that are inflexible about their doctrines and want to impose them on others.

Mary Kaldor
Currently Director of the Program on Global Civil Society at the London School of Economics; Co-founder of European Nuclear Disarmament (END); co-chaired the Helsinki Citizen's Assembly; member of the Independent International Commission to Investigate the Kosovo Crisis. Author of many publications.

Robert Kagan

The Unraveling of the Transatlantic Partnership

An Interview

Your follow-up to Of Paradise and Power *is on legitimacy. How legitimate is America's power in a global world?*

Legitimacy has taken on new significance since the end of the Cold War. Of course legitimacy is going to be questioned now that America has become the superpower in a unipolar world. However, there is no doubt that America needs allies. Not so much in a material sense; America may want assistance, but I doubt that Europe is going to be able to provide a great deal of military assistance on most of the issues with which the United States is involved. America probably won't get much in the way of economic assistance either. However, that still leaves psychological assistance – that's what America needs most from its allies. I think that what we've seen happen over Iraq – the psychological abandoning of the US – is a warning sign to us all of the dangers that lie ahead. What we used to call the West is going through a crisis of legitimacy because America has enormous power and a substantial number of its Western partners no longer consider its actions legitimate. This questioning of America's legitimacy is difficult for the American people, because contrary to mythology, they do care what the rest of the world thinks about them – particularly what the rest of the Western liberal world thinks – and if their closest philosophical brethren are constantly telling them they're acting illegitimately, illegally, immorally, they are not unmoved. And so somehow or other, we're going to have to find a new way to place American power in a legitimate context.

Until the end of the Cold War, America had a natural legitimacy. Everybody agreed on what the threat was, everybody agreed the threat needed to be deterred and that only the US had the power to deal with the threat. Therefore, through force of circumstance, the US leadership was considered legitimate. There was an ideological divide between democracy and totalitarianism, and that in itself gave the US legitimacy. The world was bipolar: American power was great, but so too was the power of the Soviet Union. When the Cold War went out of the door, all those elements of legitimacy went with it. So of course we now have to find some new grounding and I think that this can be found only in our common liberal values, our shared Western principles. Having said that, I do wonder whether our strategic visions have become so different that we will be unable to find that sense of common interest, common community, and common principles. That's my main concern after Iraq ...

Before the Iraq war, my view was that although Europe and America lacked a common strategic vision, there were many other ties that bound them – from political philosophy to economics – so that although the two continents might go their own way on certain strategic issues, we would manage to agree on a division of labor. Europe would concentrate on Europe – which is what Europe is mostly interested in now anyway – and the US would concentrate on the rest of the world, and that would be fine. But now it's clearer to me that this isn't going to happen. I think we have something approaching a schism in the West, and that our strategic differences are affecting all other issues.

Do you see any way to close the schism on strategic issues?

I can be very pessimistic about that. Both sides would have to agree to a grand bargain: America would have to be willing to allow its allies to have genuine influence over the way in which it, the sole superpower, wields that superpower, and Europe would have to accept the American perception of the nature of what threatens us and agree that its own way of dealing with the threat is inadequate. The US would have to defer, or at least make concessions, to its liberal democratic allies, and they would have to take far more seriously the threats that America perceives as such – and recognize that force is needed to deal with these threats on occasion. Now, I have no idea why the Europeans would ever accept that view. At the same time, it is very clear that we have little choice but to come up with a new kind of transatlantic bargain that recognizes what the real transatlantic differences are. As I said, I'm pessimistic. I'm worried because I think that we're entering one of the most dangerous periods in modern history. Not just the threats from al-Qaeda and terrorism – I think East Asia is a heartbeat away from major crises caused by North Korea, or China and Taiwan, etc. We do have a proliferation of weapons of mass destruction; that's an indisputable fact. We could wake up five years from now and another 10 countries will have nuclear and other such weapons. Right now, we're going into this period of crisis with the West divided, and that means that the sum total of liberal democratic power and capability which could be mobilized against the threats is diminished. I can only hope that the leaders on both sides of the Atlantic refuse to let this situation continue.

When I wrote *Of Paradise and Power*, one of my intentions in bringing to the fore the gap in values between the US and Europe was to make people think seriously about the value or perception differences. I hoped that if we could all admit that we no longer look at the world the same way, we might be prodded into doing something constructive about the situation. Unfortunately, I now have the feeling that we've become frozen in this disagreement and I'm not sure anybody has the will to move ahead to a resolution.

269

The US and much of Europe view security issues rather differently. On other issues – sustainable development, the fight against diseases such as AIDS – there is also transatlantic disagreement. America boycotted Kyoto, the International Criminal Court ... how unilateralist is the US?

These issues operate on discrete plains. The US can behave unilaterally in some areas and multilaterally in others, and by and large it is no more unilateral on trade, for example, than any other free trade-professing nation, including the countries of Europe. We do agree on most issues, we do have common principles; it's only on strategic issues that we seriously differ, or at least, that we lack common principles.

While George W. Bush is in power – or at least as long as Bush keeps his present cabinet – America may continue to follow its own path without too much regard for the rest of the world. But I think many Americans have learned a lesson from the gratuitous unilateralism of the first years of the Bush administration. They have realized that America is paying a high price in terms of global respect: not because Bush was opposed to Kyoto, but because of the way he handled Kyoto; not because Bush was opposed to the International Criminal Court, but because of the way he handled it. I think it's unlikely that the next president is going to make that kind of mistake. Frankly, I've always argued there are times when the US has no choice but to behave unilaterally – particularly on security issues – because no other country has the military power. But for the rest, I see no point in gratuitously offending everybody in areas where we do have a choice. There were legitimate objections to Kyoto, objections which European leaders would eventually have recognized, but there was a regrettable lack of diplomacy on the part of the administration. But this, unlike global poverty, for example, is a problem we can deal with – it needn't be a problem in the future. We can deal in partnership with many of the world's problems – AIDS, for example. The US under Bush, pushed probably by Colin Powell, actually has a good record on AIDS. What I'm saying is that a lot of Europeans – and indeed, many Americans – have over-interpreted the way the Bush administration has gone about things and concluded that the US will act unilaterally in every area of global concern. The fact is the US is not by nature a big hegemonic bully which has to have its own way on every single issue of international concern.

So you see the apparent unilateralism and lack of diplomacy on the part of the US as a passing phase?

In some respects, I believe we have a uniquely inept administration which was completely unprepared to deal with what turned out to be a problem that it never intended to deal with. This administration came to office expecting that since the Cold War was over, everyone could relax and the US could afford to pull back a little bit. The whole idea of exercising global leadership was not high on the agenda because it didn't appear to be necessary. The Bush administration came to power in 2000 with vaguely minimalist, realist, neo-isolationist tendencies. Then came September 11th, and all of a sudden, the US was back in the global business. What the Bush administration failed to take into account is that when you get into the global business, there are certain rules to the game. You have to try to win friends and influence people. The Bush administration forgot the lessons of the Cold War, during which we listened respectfully to various international concerns that weren't of particular interest to us, but which made everybody else happy and softened the blow of our hegemonic power. That is something President Reagan knew how to do: he knew how to soften the edges even as he stuck to his basic principles. Reagan took the transatlantic partnership seriously and forged excellent relationships with Margaret Thatcher and Helmut Kohl, for example. But

271

George W. lacks Reagan's interpersonal skills and what we got after September 11th was naked hegemonic power. I'm glossing over other problems such as major structural differences between the erstwhile allies, but I do think that some of the worst mistakes were caused by the character of the administration.

So you think the problems boil down to a failure to communicate?

A failure to communicate all round, and this brings me back to my primary concern. The Europeans, the people of Europe, don't see the same terrorist danger the Americans see. They don't see an international terrorism danger – they see a domestic terrorism danger. According to a recent poll, they even see the US as a danger. Most Europeans seem to consider immigration to be the biggest threat they face. They don't feel threatened by al-Qaeda, they didn't feel threatened by Saddam, they don't feel threatened by the Iranians and they don't feel threatened by North Korea, because heaven knows, North Korea has nothing to do with their lives ... and since they don't feel threatened by international terrorism, they don't feel they need the security blanket offered by the US. There are undoubtedly some wise European leaders, the Joschka Fischers of this world, who do understand where the real dangers lie. I would say that the strategic leadership of Europe, including France, is fairly aware of the dangers, but the problem is that they spend very little time explaining them to their own people and their own people just don't see them.

Thank you.

The conversation was conducted by Susan Stern

Robert Kagan

Robert Kagan is currently senior associate at the Carnegie Endowment for International Peace, where he specializes in US leadership and foreign policy. Contributing editor to the *Weekly Standard* and the *New Republic*, monthly columnist for the *Washington Post*. Publications include: *Of Paradise and Power* and *American Power and the Crisis of Legitimacy*.

Luis Moreno-Ocampo

States, the Private Sector and the International Criminal Court

For the international community, the establishment of the International Criminal Court (ICC) is comparable to the evolution of national criminal justice systems, a process which spanned over 10 centuries. The involvement of the national state in the solution of conflicts between private citizens and in defence of the victims of crimes was a revolutionary step. Similarly, the Rome Statute has made it possible for the international community to assume responsibility for the protection of the citizens of individual countries.

The creation of a permanent international criminal court proved elusive for the international community for over a century. Although this goal has now been realised, the global system of justice which entered into force in 2002 requires the decisive action of numerous actors if it is to attain the objectives it has set for itself. The role played by states in this system remains crucial. Additionally, for the system to be truly effective, the involvement of other actors – including civil society and the private sector – is crucial.

This chapter briefly explains the origins of the ICC and the way in which it interacts with states. It then presents some thoughts on the possible impact of the Court's activity on the private sector. It also assesses the potential for the private sector to help the Court fulfil its long-term goals merely by taking advantage of the opportunities for economic development likely to be created by the work of the Court.

Developing a global system of justice: an historical perspective

On 17 July 1998, the international community took a decisive step for the protection of citizens around the world when it adopted the Rome Statute creating the International Criminal Court.[1] The Rome Treaty creates a global system for the prevention, investigation, prosecution and eventual punishment of the most horrendous crimes. It gives the Court jurisdiction over genocide, crimes against humanity and war crimes committed on or after 1 July 2002.

The establishment of a permanent court with global reach was a major accomplishment and one that, remarkably, came about during times of peace, not war. In this sense it is entirely unique, as all of its predecessors – whether successful or not – were created as responses to specific international crises. The motivation for such action by the international community during peacetime is substantially harder to inspire, as Robert Jackson, Chief US Prosecutor at Nuremberg, noted in his personal memoir of the trials: 'In untroubled times progress toward an effective rule of law in the international community is slow indeed. Inertia rests more heavily upon the society of nations than upon any other society.[2]

As stated above, past examples of international justice mechanisms were all direct responses to war or armed conflict. One of the earliest (and ultimately unsuccessful) examples dates back to the Allied attempts after the First World War to try German citizens allegedly guilty of war crimes before tribunals constituted by the victorious armies.[3] Nuremberg, similarly, was a response to the Second World War. The advent of the Cold War had a chilling effect on international justice – and on idealism-based international institutions in a more general sense – which stretched over the next four decades. But even in the post-Cold War era, great strides made in the field of international justice – as exemplified by the Security Council's creation of the International

275

Criminal Tribunal for the former Yugoslavia (ICTY) in 1993 and the International Criminal Tribunal for Rwanda (ICTR) in 1994 – were direct responses to specific armed conflicts. It was not until the adoption of the Rome Statute in 1998 that the world community was spurred into action based on ideals and prevention.

Actors in the global system of justice

Working with national states

The principle of complementarity enshrined in the Rome Statute attempts to resolve the tension between national sovereignty and the realisation of international justice for the victims of the most egregious crimes. This principle establishes that the ICC acts as a court of last resort for cases in which national states are unable or unwilling to act. The primary responsibility to prevent, control and prosecute atrocious crimes remains with the states in whose jurisdictions they are committed. National investigations and prosecutions, where they can properly be undertaken, will normally be the most effective and efficient means of bringing offenders to justice; states themselves will usually have the best access to evidence and witnesses.

The genius of the principle of complementarity is that it permits states, paradoxically, to serve the cause of international justice by asserting their sovereign right to prosecute genocide, war crimes and crimes against humanity in their own domestic systems. Thus, complementarity ensures an international rule of law while still affirming the rights and sovereignty of nations. It creates a truly interdependent, mutually reinforcing system.

International cooperation is crucial. The ICC is called upon to act when the national state is *unable* to take action, for example, in situations of violence over which state authorities have no control, or when it is *unwilling* to act, for example, in situations where those who have the monopoly of force in a state themselves commit the crimes. It goes without saying that in such cases, national enforcement authorities will not be at the Prosecutor's disposal. These are not matters which need normally trouble a domestic prosecutor, but they are all relevant to an ICC prosecution and they all underline the necessity of state support for the Office of the Prosecutor in the bringing of any investigation. In other words, the ICC Prosecutor will need international support in order to investigate his cases.

Both by its statutory design and by the practical realities facing global institutions which operate without a global state, the Court is bound to work with national states if it is to achieve success. Whether cases are tried in national court systems or whether they land in the ICC's own courtrooms, the realisation of justice will be dependent upon a healthy, vigorous relationship between states and the ICC. Therefore, the Prosecutor will encourage states to take ownership of the Court.

In sum, states are crucial actors in the fulfilment of the ICC's mission. They are not, however, the only ones who can have an impact on the attainment of the objectives of the Rome Statute: civil society has also played a major role in the development of the international justice system and continues to do so; and the private sector, which in the past has often been left out of the equation, can begin to play a greater role in the realisation of peace and security than it has in the past. For the purposes of this chapter, I will focus on the role of the private sector.

The private sector

Judicial action by the ICC, while vital to long-term stability and restoration of justice in war-torn societies, cannot itself realise the goals of lasting peace and respect for international justice envisioned in the Rome Statute. For the attainment of these goals, the action of states, the private sector and other

277

actors is necessary. This section is concerned with the ways in which the ICC will, as a natural by-product of its operations, reduce risks for the private sector to become involved in the economies of regions in which the ICC helps to restore peace. The actions of the private sector will in turn contribute to long-term goals of global stability and prosperity.

As Goldsmith and Krasner have argued, international institutions relying solely on ideals cannot be effective:

> We believe that normative ideals can provide a hope for progress, an emotional appeal, and a ground for international action. But ... ideals can be pursued effectively only if decision-makers are alert to the distribution of power, national interests, and the consequences of their policies.[4]

In other words, institutions must successfully align values, power and interests if they are to attain their objectives. Goldsmith and Krasner cite the European Union as an example of an institution whose creation was motivated by ideals but which successfully aligned these other factors, thereby creating incentives for cooperation beyond pure altruism or moral purpose. As they point out, it worked 'because each nation benefited from the institution and had an interest in complying with its terms'.[5]

This point is certainly well taken and has implications for the effective functioning of the ICC. The type of internationalist idealism mentioned by Goldsmith and Krasner motivated the creation of the Court and is now enshrined in its Statute. However, to ensure successful operation of the Court, the mere advocacy of such ideals will not be enough; they alone cannot bring about peace, security and the well-being of the world.

We at the Office of the Prosecutor must be conscious of the impact our work has on the interests of others. We see tremendous opportunities for development in regions of the world in which the ICC will work. ICC prosecutions contribute to the pacifying of violent regions in which it is currently impossible to invest. In that sense, the private sector has an interest in our work. And the decisive action of the private sector – through investment in regions reclaimed from violence by the ICC and others – is crucial if the work of the Court is to have lasting effects. The creation of jobs and the healthy exchange of goods can act as incentives against violence. We believe that, in this sense, ideals and interests are aligned.

The link between instability and private sector investment

The ICC is likely to intervene in regions in which the presence of rich natural resources is not coincidental but, in fact, a primary cause leading to the intervention. Businesses, especially in the extractive industry, know well how the commodities they mine often become war spoils in civil and tribal war-torn areas. Such industries have often invested resources in those regions only to be forced to scale them back as conditions worsened. Entire local communities suffer in those retreats, built as they are around long-term projects in remote locations.

Projects in these industries are speculative enough without the added risks of life-threatening environments and the disruptions of violence. They are usually long-term and capital-intensive and, therefore, require significant upfront investment for the construction of tailor-made equipment and infrastructure at early exploration phases when results are not quite certain. To optimise returns, they are typically financed, at least in part, by outside creditors who must feel comfortable with the risks assumed. The due diligence process surrounding third-party financings relies on the reports of experts, such as engineers and commodity price forecasters, who perform stress tests and project results under different scenarios for potential creditors to evaluate the attractiveness of the investment. Financiers and underwriters are under stringent legal requirements to ensure that the risks are disclosed fully and fairly to the ultimate creditors.

279

Yet, while certain kinds of country or regional risks (usually macroeconomic and occasionally legislative or regulatory in character) are palatable to specialised investors, others fall outside any level of investor comfort. Risks such as hostilities and persistent violence threatening life and property, while quite normal in situations where the ICC might intervene, are precisely the subject of 'major adverse change' clauses that typically excuse financiers from performing under their contractual obligations in worst case scenarios.

Furthermore, to operate in such situations, private enterprises must often engage in graft and other practices that subject them to significant litigation, regulatory and long-term reputational risks in their own countries. Statutes, rules and conventions, such as the US Alien Tort Claims Act, the Foreign Corrupt Practices Act and the Organization for Economic Cooperation and Development Convention on Bribery have been used to expand the jurisdictional reach of courts in those countries to enhance corporate accountability for conduct abroad. The private sector has acknowledged that valuable opportunities are being lost and that collective action is necessary. Recently, it has begun to engage in voluntary compliance initiatives, such as the UN Global Compact and the UN Norms on the Responsibilities of Transnational Corporations and Other Business Enterprises with Regard to Human Rights.

How the private sector can support the work of the ICC

The crimes over which the Court has jurisdiction typically involve the massive and systematic destruction of human lives. In addition, these crimes also have profoundly long-lasting, destabilising effects on the societies against which they are perpetrated. In such tragic circumstances, states are usually either unable to control the crimes or they are themselves responsible for the atrocities.

Furthermore, although many war-torn regions are rich in resources – and, as pointed out above, the conflicts are often waged over resources – the average citizen tends to be extremely impoverished and the economic infrastructure rarely functions satisfactorily. The economic instability is both an exacerbating cause for conflict, because citizens who are mired in poverty live without hope and can be driven into conflicts over resources, and a tragic outcome of protracted fighting, because violence and political instability quash economic productivity. At the most basic level, these conflicts destroy lives, but in doing so they also destroy possibilities for economic development and a viable future.

The ideals of justice served by the ICC cannot endure without a reduction of conflict and without fostering institutions. Peace, fairness, stability, development and economic opportunity are integral to the mission of the ICC. This mission cannot be accomplished without the collaboration of all actors that share a stake in it. But those actors need not be motivated by merely idealistic or moral calls to action – legitimate businesses stand to gain considerably by this collaboration because if the ICC can help to stabilise violent regions, the impact on local economies is likely to be significant. It is therefore in the interests of the private sector to support the work of the ICC. The involvement of the private sector, in turn, is indispensable if the work of the Court is to have lasting consequences.

In the immediate term, the economy must be able to accommodate those who are no longer involved in the committing of atrocities as a result of prosecutions. Child soldiers who have been demobilised by the prosecutions of their generals and commanders, for example, must have educational opportunities and, later, the possibility to join the productive sector of society. The private sector can generate employment opportunities for them and for other individuals no longer involved in hostilities. In a more long-term sense, through investments and financial attention, it can also help

281

to connect regions previously disconnected from world markets and thus help to reintroduce pariah states, formerly embroiled in violent conflict, to the world community.

While the rich resources of these regions present attractive extractive and investment opportunities for businesses, the risks and constraints are often an impediment to action. The pacifying effects of justice mechanisms in conflict-ridden societies, exemplified by this new International Criminal Court, can help usher in a new era that will allow businesses to legitimately invest, create jobs and introduce a flow of goods. By taking advantage of new business opportunities, the private sector will become an integral and pragmatic contributor to an institution founded on idealism.

Conclusion

The existence of the ICC represents a valuable opportunity for collective action in the eradication of organised and mass crime. With the cooperation of states, the Court can progress towards this goal. But the lasting effects of its work will depend partly on the extent to which the private sector takes advantage of the opportunities for development created by the Court.

Notes

1 The Court was established on 17 July 1998 through a treaty that was signed by 139 states. Despite the open opposition of some states, the 60 ratifications required for the Statute's entry into force were obtained in less than four years. By December 2003, 92 countries had ratified the Statute, thereby becoming States Parties.

2 Telford Taylor, *The Anatomy of the Nuremberg Trials, A Personal Memoir.* New York 1992, p. 55.

3 Although the Versailles Treaty required Germany to surrender its own citizens for trial to these tribunals, the Allies were forced to reconsider once it became clear that public sentiment in Germany was defiant and threatened

to destabilize the peace. Germany proposed holding the trials before the Supreme Court in Leipzig, and this solution was accepted, resulting in trials in which many defendants were exonerated and from which countries such as Belgium and France withdrew in protest. Ibid, p. 17.

4 Jack Goldsmith and Stephen D. Krasner (2003), 'The limits of idealism', *Dædalus, Journal of the American Academy of Arts and Sciences,* Vol. 132, No. 1, p. 48.

5 Ibid, p. 62.

Luis Moreno-Ocampo

Luis Moreno-Ocampo was born in Buenos Aires in 1952. Chief Prosecutor of the International Criminal Court (elected April 2003). In 1985, served as Deputy Prosecutor in the trials of the military juntas that ruled Argentina between 1976 and 1983. Founded a private law firm in Buenos Aires (1992). Member of the Board of Transparency International in 2002/2003.

Shashi Tharoor

Saving Humanity from Hell

At the beginning of March this year, as the debates were raging in the Security Council over Iraq, a BBC interviewer rather glibly asked me, 'So how does the UN feel about being seen as the "i" word – irrelevant?' He was about to go on when I interrupted him. 'As far as we're concerned,' I retorted, 'the "i" word is indispensable.'

It wasn't just a debating point. Those of us who toil every day at the headquarters of the United Nations – and in particular our colleagues on the front lines in the field – have become a little exasperated at seeing our institutional obituaries in the press. The contretemps with the United States over Iraq has led some to evoke a parallel to the League of Nations, a body founded on great hopes at the end of the First World War which was reduced to debating the standardisation of European railway gauges the day the Germans marched into Poland. Such comparisons are grossly overstated. As Mark Twain put it when he saw his own obituary in the newspaper, reports of the UN's demise are exaggerated.

On the principle that the best crystal ball is a rear-view mirror, let me first venture back into history. The UN was founded during a period when the world had known almost nothing but war and strife, sandwiched between two savage world wars that began within 25 years of each other. Horror succeeded horror, until, in 1945, the world was brought face to face with the terrible tragedies wrought by war, fascism, attempted genocide and nuclear bombing. Had things gone on like that, the future of the human race would have been bleak indeed. Fortunately, the great statesmen of that era found an alternative way of ordering human affairs. Despite local eruptions of conflict and outrages against human rights, the world was spared another global conflagration. International cooperation and collective agreement on global norms superseded the use of force time after time. The peoples of the so-called Third World threw off the yoke of colonialism, and those of the Soviet bloc won political freedom. Democracy and human rights are not yet universal, but they are now much more the norm than the exception.

None of this was accidental. It was the direct result of a conscious decision by a group of far-sighted leaders, in and after 1945, to make the second half of the 20th century different from the first. They drew up rules to govern international behaviour, and they founded institutions in which different nations could come together for the common good, functioning on the basis of international cooperation, the elaboration of consensual global norms and the establishment of predictable, universally applicable rules, to the benefit of all.

The keystone of the arch, charged with keeping the peace between all the nations and bringing them all together in the quest for freedom and prosperity, was the UN itself. Visionaries such as former US President Franklin Delano Roosevelt saw the UN (as he stated in his historic speech to the two Houses of Congress after the Yalta Conference) as the alternative to the arms races, military alliances and balance-of-power politics which had led to war so often in the past.

In the view of people like FDR, the UN stood for a world in which citizens of different nations and cultures regarded each other not as enemies but as potential partners, able to exchange goods and ideas to their mutual benefit. His successor, President Harry Truman, stated it clearly: 'You have created a great instrument for peace and security and human progress in the world', he declared to the assembled signatories of the UN Charter in San Francisco on 26 June 1945. 'If we fail to use it, we shall betray all those who have died in order that we might meet here in freedom and safety to create it. If we seek to use it selfishly – for the advantage of any one

285

nation or any small group of nations – we shall be equally guilty of that betrayal.'

That was then, of course, and this, 59 years later, is now. How many of today's American critics of the UN, who have rushed to proclaim its irrelevance (and even, in a few cases, to celebrate its alleged demise) would recognise the voice of an American president in Truman's speech that historic day? 'We all have to recognise,' he declared, 'no matter how great our strength, that we must deny ourselves the licence to do always as we please. No one nation ... can or should expect any special privilege which harms any other nation ... Unless we are all willing to pay that price, no organisation for world peace can accomplish its purpose. And what a reasonable price that is!'

Few in Washington today would agree now that that is indeed a reasonable price for the world's only superpower to pay in the interests of something as amorphous as 'world peace', especially in an era of terrorism. It is in the US, above all, that the organisation has suffered most. The notion has gained ground of late, particularly in the wake of Robert Kagan's *Of Paradise and Power*, that the elemental issue in world affairs today is the incompatibility of the American and 'European' diagnoses of our contemporary geopolitical condition. In this view, the US sees a Hobbesian world, rife with menace and disorder, that requires the imposition of order and stability by a Leviathan, while Europe (and much of the rest of the world) imagines a Kantian world of peace and rationality which can be managed by reasonable-minded leaders coming to sensible arrangements through institutions such as the UN. Since the latter view is a fantasy, such analysts suggest, the institutions underpinning it are equally impractical and ineffectual. In the real world, a Hobbesian Leviathan could not possibly function if he were to be tied down by a system of rules designed to serve smaller states: he would be a Gulliver restrained by, in Charles Krauthammer's words, the 'myriad strings' of the Lilliputians 'that diminish his overweening power'. Hence the answer lies in disregarding the UN and, as Michael J. Glennon argued in *Foreign Affairs,* restoring might to its rightful place in world affairs.

There are many flaws in this argument, but the key one lies in its central premise. For the UN was not created by Kantians; it was established as a response to a Hobbesian world. Indeed, it is important to remember that it is the UN that won the Second World War: the countries which the media called 'the Allies' called themselves 'the United Nations' from 1943 on. The Charter, in other words, was the work of the victorious Allies of the Second World War converting their wartime alliance into a peacetime organisation. They saw the Hobbesian world of the preceding three decades, which had inflicted upon humanity two savage world wars, several brutal civil wars, the atrocities perpetrated by totalitarianism and the horrors of the Holocaust and Hiroshima, and vowed 'never again'. But the Leviathan imagined by the visionary statesmen of that era (notably FDR himself) was not that of a single colossus; instead it was made up of a system of laws that would ensure that the world of the second half of the 20th century would be a better place than the one that had barely survived the first half.

So great was the perceived American stake in such a system that the US became its principal financial contributor, paying up to 50 percent of the UN's regular budget in the first years of the organisation (a figure astonishing to recall at a time when so much American diplomatic energy was recently invested in reducing its current share from 25 percent to 22 percent). Gulliver was to lead the Lilliputians, not feel tied down by them; they provided him with a springboard, not a rack.

And so the world of which FDR and Truman spoke was a world for which they and all the Allies had fought – a world of increasing openness, of imperial contraction making way for the expansion of freedom, of growing mutual confidence and above all, a world of hope. But that hope seems to have faded around the world – a recent Pew Poll in 20 countries

287

shows that the UN has suffered a great deal of collateral damage over Iraq. The UN's credibility has been dented in the US because it did not support the war and in 19 other countries because it did not prevent the war. Does that mean that the UN is finished?

Far from it. First of all, the US is back at the UN on Iraq. The Security Council unanimously adopted three post-war resolutions (1483, 1500 and 1511) governing the arrangements under which the victorious coalition should run that country. Although these actions did not put the UN 'in charge' of Iraq, they again confirmed Washington's increasing need, not just for international support, but for the imprimatur of the world body. Without 1483, the occupation forces could not have sold a drop of Iraqi oil as they would not have had a title to it under international law; potential buyers would have feared a lawsuit from companies claiming to hold prior contracts with the deposed (but once legal) Iraqi authorities.

Indeed, the very submission of these resolutions by the US to the Security Council was an acknowledgement by Washington that there is, in Secretary-General Kofi Annan's words, no substitute for the unique legitimacy provided by the UN. And the acceptance of the resolutions by other Council members, even those who led the demarche against the US intervention, demonstrated their understanding of the importance of collective action.

Similarly, the key message of President Bush's appearance before the UN General Assembly in September last year should not be forgotten. In calling on the Security Council to take action against Iraq, he framed the problem not as one of unilateral US wishes but as an issue of the implementation of UN Security Council resolutions. The UN and the earlier decisions of its Security Council remained at the heart of the US case against Iraq.

Secondly, the League of Nations analogy simply does not apply. By the late 1930s, two of the three most powerful countries in the world at the time – the US and Germany (the third being Great Britain) – did not belong to the League, which therefore had no influence on their actions. The League ceased to exist because it had become truly irrelevant to the global geopolitics of the era. By contrast, almost every country on earth belongs to the UN, including the world's only superpower, the US. Every newly independent state seeks entry virtually as its first order of governmental business; its seat at the UN is the most fundamental confirmation of its membership in the community of nations. The UN is now seen as so essential to the future of the world that Switzerland, long an outsider because of its fierce neutrality, decided by referendum in 2002 to join. No club that attracts every eligible member can easily be described as irrelevant.

Thirdly, the authorisation (or not) of war in Iraq is not the only gauge of the Security Council's relevance to that situation. Just four years ago, the NATO alliance bombed Yugoslavia over its government's conduct in Kosovo without the approval of, or even reference to, the Security Council. My interviewer's 'i' word was heard widely in those days – Kosovo, it was said, had demonstrated the UN's irrelevance. But the issue of Kosovo returned to the Security Council, not just when an attempt to condemn the bombing failed, but over the administration of Kosovo after the war. Only the Security Council could approve administrative arrangements in a way that conferred international legitimacy upon them and encouraged all nations to extend support and resources to the enterprise. And only one body could be entrusted with the responsibility to run the civilian administration of Kosovo: the UN. Whatever tasks the UN ultimately takes on in a post-war Iraq, it is important to remember that this is not the first time the UN has been written off during a war only to be found essential to the ensuing peace.

The UN offers a legitimacy that no ad hoc coalition can muster for itself. When the government of India declined a

US request to participate militarily in Iraq because it needed the protective shield of a UN mandate before it could deploy troops under American command, it underscored this message. Many other countries, in Europe as well as Asia, require UN resolutions before they commit troops abroad. Washington is discovering in Iraq that the US is better able to win wars alone than to construct peace alone: military strength has its limitations in the area of nation-building (as Talleyrand said, the one thing you cannot do with a bayonet is to sit on it). I am convinced we will see the increasing inter-nationalisation of the rebuilding of Iraq in the months to come.

But whatever happens in Iraq, let us not forget in penning the premature epitaphs for the UN that its relevance does not stand or fall on its conduct on one issue alone. When this crisis has passed, the world will still be facing (to use Secre-tary-General Kofi Annan's phrase) innumerable 'problems without passports' – problems that cross all frontiers unin-vited, problems of the proliferation of weapons of mass destruction, of the degradation of our common environment, of contagious disease and chronic starvation, of human rights and human wrongs, of mass illiteracy and massive displace-ment. Robert Kagan's famous, if fatuous, proposition that Americans are from Mars and Europeans are from Venus has gained wide currency these days in the US. If that is so, where are Africans from – Pluto? The tragic confluence of AIDS, famine and drought in parts of Africa threatens more human lives than the crisis in Iraq ever did. These are problems that no one country, however powerful, can solve on its own and yet which are the shared responsibility of humankind. They cry out for solutions that, like the problems themselves, also cross frontiers. The UN exists to find these solutions through the common endeavour of all states. It is the one indispensa-ble global organisation in our globalising world.

And no, it is not perfect. It has acted unwisely at times, and failed to act at others: one need only think of the 'safe areas' in Bosnia and the genocide in Rwanda for instances of each. It has sometimes been too divided to succeed, as was the case over Iraq. And all too often, member states have passed resolutions they had no intention of implementing themselves. But the UN, at its best, is a mirror of the world: it reflects our divisions and disagreements as well as our hopes and convictions. Sometimes it only muddles through. As Dag Hammarskjöld, the UN's great second Secretary-General, put it, the UN was not created to take humanity to heaven, but to save it from hell.

And that it has, innumerable times. How quickly we forget that during the Cold War, the UN played a vital role in preventing regional crises and conflicts from igniting a superpower conflagration. And even while they were disagreeing on Iraq, the members of the Security Council were agreeing, at the very same time, on a host of other vital issues – from the Congo to Cote d'Ivoire, from Cyprus to Afghanistan. Let us not distort the record by seeing the UN's work on international peace and security only through the prism of one issue, Iraq.

And let us also remember that the UN is both a stage and an actor. It is a stage on which the member states play their parts, declaiming their differences and their convergences, and it is an actor (particularly in the form of the Secretary-General, his staff, agencies and operations) executing the policies made on that stage. The general public usually fails to see this distinction; to most people 'the UN' is a shapeless aggregation in which the sins of omission or commission of individual governments on the 'stage' are routinely blamed on the organisation (and so discredit the 'actor'). When American officials blame the UN for failing to prevent genocide in Rwanda, overlooking the role of the US in ensuring inaction by the Security Council on that issue, the point could not be clearer.

As it attempts to face the 'post-post-Cold War' world of the early 21st century, the UN provides an indispensable forum for bringing states together to tackle the great problems of our time. Some say the Security Council is too much in thrall to its most powerful member. The debates over Iraq have proved that this is not always the case; but even if it were, it is far better to have a world organisation that is anchored in geopolitical reality than one that is too detached from the verities of global power to be effective. A UN that provides the vital political and diplomatic framework for the actions of its most powerful member, while casting them in the context of international law and legitimacy (and bringing to bear upon them the perspectives and concerns of its universal membership) is a UN that cannot be anything but relevant to the world in which we live.

This is why I am proud to use the other 'i' word and to affirm the UN's indispensability – as the only effective instrument the world has available to confront the challenges that will remain when Iraq has faded from the headlines.

Shashi Tharoor
Shashi Tharoor was born in London in 1956. Studied history in New Delhi, law and diplomacy in the US (PhD Fletcher School). Has served the UN since 1978 and is currently UN Under-Secretary-General for Communications and Public Information. Author of eight books, including *The Great Indian Novel, India: From Midnight to the Millennium* and, most recently, *Nehru: The Invention of India.* (The opinions expressed above are his personal views.)

Fareed Zakaria

On Illiberal Democracy and the Power of a Hegemon

An Interview

What do you see as the greatest challenges facing the world?

There are two imperatives right now. The first is to create greater democracy, by this I mean broadening participation, allowing more people to have a say. The trend is unstoppable. It's very powerful and healthy and it has one great virtue: it legitimizes processes and outcomes.

The second imperative is for effective governance. Globalization and demographic change are causing new problems. In Europe, for example, major demographic shifts are forcing the continent to deal with immigration and to change the social market, which has to be rescaled and reduced. In the United States, entitlements must also be changed. In the Third World, governments have to take economic steps that are painful in the short term but yield long-term benefits. In all these areas, democracies tend to do badly because they naturally gear themselves towards short-term solutions for existing constituents. The imperative for effective governance therefore requires some level of insulation from the democratic decision-making process. And this is exactly what is happening, even if most people don't recognize it.

The world is no longer the same as it was 30 years ago. Take the example of central banks. Nobody would have predicted or believed possible that the most important economic lever in advanced industrial societies would be wielded by unelected, essentially unaccountable bankers.

Such a development would have been considered a travesty of democracy. In fact, it has happened, it has proved to be successful – indeed it is widely regarded as one of the stabilizing pillars of societies. Nobody would have believed that all trade legislation would be effectively carried out in an entirely insulated process where people like Pascal Lamy and Robert Zoellick would have enormous authority shielded from democracy. If you look at the nitty-gritty of international life, you see a powerful trend toward delegation to organizations such as the World Trade Organization (WTO), to central banks, to antitrust authorities. None of these is democratically elected. But what we lack is a process that links democracy to delegation – a bargain, a partnership.

We need a democratic system, but within that system we need a mechanism whereby certain areas are delegated to non-elected bodies that are overviewed and checked, of course. This mechanism will provide both the needed legitimacy and effectiveness. Right now we have the one but not the other. Europe is a good example. Brussels is by and large effective at deregulation, at antitrust, at economic coordination, but it is widely viewed as illegitimate. The national governments are essentially viewed as legitimate, but are increasingly unable to make any of the tough decisions that are required, which is why we are witnessing the rise of radical parties. The mainstream political system is unable to tackle the major problems people are concerned about: the rise of immigration, the future of the welfare state etc. The danger is that whenever European politicians are faced with a difficult decision to make, they find it too easy to simply shove it off to Brussels and let Brussels take the bad publicity. In the bargain or partnership I'm proposing, both sides have to live up to their roles and responsibilities. Elected politicians must explain the importance of delegating certain decisions; explain why it is in the long-term interests of society that pension reform or immigration reform should be dealt with in a way that does not pander to a short-term political constituency. For their part, the Brussels bureaucrats, the appointed delegates, must create a process that is open and transparent so that people can understand what is going on. I believe that this is a happy bargain. I would find it more dangerous if we kept moving towards a more democratic process which ended up being totally irrelevant and with everything being run by unidentifiable and unaccountable cliques.

What role will non-governmental organizations play in your bargain?

I don't think enough people have given sufficient thought to the nature of NGO activity. There is a tendency to believe all NGO activity is good, because it is somehow grass roots. NGOs play an important role – they can act as eyes and ears. They do what we in the media ought to be doing: watching, looking, observing, and reporting. But NGOs also have their own agendas: they are often very narrowly based with narrow interests and a particular point of view. They can use evidence in a somewhat selective way because they are entirely unaccountable to the public. Of course they should exist and flourish, but they should be placed in proper perspective. They are interest groups – some are good, some are bad, some behave honorably, others don't. They are not a substitute for governance or for government. Moral authority should lie with democratic governments, not interest groups. Of course it's good to have checks, of course it's good to have eyes and ears and it's good to have citizen activity. But there is another form of citizen activity, and that's called voting. The governments so often criticized by NGOs have been tested by that form of citizen activity. So while I welcome NGOs, we should not fall into the easy trap of assuming that they are all moral and that democratic governments are immoral. At the end of the day, the power of the government, the power of the state is the dominant force shaping societies in today's world. So it

295

makes sense for NGOs to work together as partners with democratic governments. After spending his life and fortune supporting and funding NGOs, George Soros has come to the realization that if he really wants to make a difference, he has to influence the US government.

What role do you think that business has to play in good global governance? Business is no more legitimate or democratic than NGOs.

I believe that business is a great force for good in the world. Not because a particular business is a good corporate citizen, but because private businesses, i.e. Western capitalism, create wealth, they employ people, they create work habits, and they create a bourgeoisie – all tremendously positive in a society. There is no doubt too that NGOs have pushed business to live up to certain standards, helping to produce a capitalism which is both efficient and humane. This has been achieved through partnership. Whenever there is a combative, legalistic attitude between business and either the state or NGOs, nobody gets anywhere. But when the state or NGOs try to shame business into being humane, it usually works. Take the Sullivan Principles in South Africa – they have been effective through shame. Or companies like Nike which has been shamed into changing its policies. In my opinion, business is probably the single most important actor outside the government and what we really need to achieve is a partnership between business, government and society – a triangle. Business can bring tremendous benefits to the Third World. It can open up countries to modern ideas, to modern trade, to modern communications, to a modern work ethic.

Of course business can also be terribly exploitive – in countries with huge natural resources, for example – so there is a flip side. But in general, business has the potential to achieve a balance that works for everybody. It pays for a company like Microsoft to train people in Third World countries – it makes sense for such companies to have an educated population. And again, the best way to maintain high standards is through constant vigilance and pressure, not regulation. We tend to hold Western companies to Western standards even when they operate in a non-Western country. This is fine in the case of human rights, but not when it comes to wage levels. It's absurd to say, 'Well you're paying people only six dollars a day.' If they were making three dollars a day before you came along, you've just doubled their wages. You can't look at Bangladesh from the viewpoint of New York City.

What do you see as the role of the US in world governance?

I think we are only beginning to see the outlines of a new world order. I believe that American power is no passing phenomenon as many have assumed: I think it is likely to be a permanent feature of the new world – and my time horizon is the next 50 years. There are some reliable indicators for future trends – demography, for example. Europe and Japan, which are the principal economic rivals to the US, will both be ageing societies 25 to 50 years hence. The US will be young and virile thanks to immigration and our natural reproduction rates. In terms of spending on research and technology, key indicators of future growth, America is now in a league of its own. All the leading research universities, with perhaps the one exception of Cambridge in the UK, are located in the US. The gap is growing: already 45 percent of all biomedical research in the world is being performed here, a country with just five percent of the world's population. As far as military power goes, the US is again in a league by itself, and the gap is growing much faster. So I think we live in a world which is going to be shaped primarily by what this one country does. The crucial issue will be how the US chooses to exercise this hegemony. Will it be through institutions and consensus, or will it try to do it in a more ad-hoc fashion? There is little danger that the US will try to act entirely unilaterally – this is a caricature of reality. The question is more whether the US will try to work through ad-hoc coalitions or through institutions. I hope very much that it will be through institutions, because they provide a greater degree of predictability and stability in the world.

What institutions do you have in mind?

Existing institutions such as the United Nations, the World Bank, the International Monetary Fund (IMF) and NATO. However, we should be thinking creatively about whether new institutions are needed. In order to successfully prosecute the war on terrorism, I believe we may need a new global agreement, dare I call it an institution, so that we end up with a truly united front against the terrorists, so that we can share data efficiently and coordinate activities throughout the world. You may argue that people and populations don't always agree on the nature of a threat and how to combat it. But it's too easy to say that simply because people perceive threats differently, we'll never get our global act together. We have to go through the difficult process of talking, bargaining, and cooperating. Europe and the US have often disagreed, but on many issues – trade for example – there is less disagreement than there was in the past. The US and Europe have differing views on Iran, but we have managed to present a reasonably united front which is putting very productive pressure on the Iranians. This cooperation has dramatically increased their joint power. If we had that kind of cooperation in the Middle East, we could achieve far more. However, the need for compromise and cooperation goes far beyond the US and Europe. An international order requires cooperation between all the major powers, certainly including China, Russia and India. Integrating these three countries into the global framework is crucial. These powers need to feel that they have a stake in creating a new international order otherwise there's a real risk that they will engage in their own version of unilateralism. Should this happen, and should the US and Europe find themselves having to ally on an ad-hoc basis with just one of the other powers, the world will be fragmented and unstable. So we need rules of the road, agreement to consult and collaborate, agreement to disagree at times, and these rules need to be applied at first to relatively simple issues such as trade. But at least there would be deference paid to the forums and to the processes. Such an international order is a far more powerful vision than that of the US operating not *through* an international system, but rather *as* that international system.

Isn't there a danger that the rules will be set aside whenever they happen to be inconvenient? Take the Stability Pact in Europe: the countries that designed it are now ignoring it. And the US is highly selective as to which rules or international conventions it signs.

Structures have to adapt, they have to be flexible. I believe that much of what is happening in Europe is an entirely healthy process. People and countries are recognizing that the Union they had envisaged is not going to materialize. What they want is actually what they already have: a Union which deals effectively with trade and social matters. However, this is not about to translate into a superstate, it never will. This is all to the good. As for the UN, there's a lot about it that doesn't work. The US is asking itself on a case-by-case basis whether there are benefits to channeling its power through the UN. If the answer is negative, it won't. But then, other countries – France, for example – have acted no differently in the past. Nevertheless, I would argue that there are powerful advantages to legitimizing the process. When it comes to conventions such as Kyoto, I regret the way the Bush administration handled this, but Kyoto was dead to begin with. Almost none of the European countries are meeting their targets under Kyoto. It is an irrelevant treaty because it does not take China and India into account. There's no way global warming can be tackled if the two largest, fastest-growing countries in the world are not included in the agreement. The US cares about the environment – it was the first country in the world to really get serious about producing cars with catalytic converters, cleaning up the air and increasing the water supply – but it felt that Kyoto was unworkable. But when you are the richest and most powerful nation in the history of the world, you must signal your intentions to the world. You should not crudely say, 'Kyoto is dead', but explain why and invite people to restart the negotiations. The world needs to be reassured that the US is not an 8000 lb gorilla on the loose. It's not a style versus substance issue. In this case, style *is* substance.

People must bear in mind that the US is the oldest constitutional democracy in the world. It has a very lively media and a greater proliferation of NGOs than anywhere else in the world. The government does not operate a rogue regime. But undoubtedly, America could do a better job partnering with the rest of the world and the rest of the world could do a better job partnering with America. It is all well and good to talk about American unilateralism, but there is also a problem of European delusion, a delusion that you can somehow be above power politics, and that you can despise the country that is engaged in it. To build the kind of world I'm talking about, the US and Europe have to be on the same page, because between us we produce well over half of the world's GDP. Together, we can create a kind of nucleus which draws in countries like Russia, China and India and provides the true beginnings of a stable world order.

The fact is that America has the power and if that power is not harnessed, America will go ahead and do what it wants. And the rest of the world will face the very awkward situation of having to deal with the reality of a successful America. If the US had gone into Iraq alone and been successful, it would have been strengthened in its conviction that it had no need for any partners or alliances. And that would have been destructive.

So the message is that the world has no choice but to team up with the US because it's too dangerous to let it go it alone?

Well, I think that international politics are determined in large part by the realities of power. And you cannot get away from the reality that we live in a unipolar world. The question to the rest of the world boils down to this: Do you want to try to tame, harness and influence that single pole, or do you want to try in a futile manner to set yourself up as a competing pole? By working with the US, Europe can help further a common vision of a better world.

Thank you.

The conversation was conducted by Susan Stern

Fareed Zakaria
Fareed Zakaria was born in Mumbai, India, in 1964. Editor of *Newsweek International,* regular columnist for the domestic edition of *Newsweek,* political analyst for ABC News. Received a BA from Yale and a PhD from Harvard. His latest book is *The Future of Freedom: Illiberal Democracy at Home and Abroad.*

The Internet

Zoë Baird and Stefaan Verhulst

Rethinking Global Internet Governance

It came and went quietly, but the recently concluded World Summit on the Information Society (WSIS) in Geneva may represent something of a watershed moment in the history of the Internet. For all their differences, governments coalesced around the need to define and develop some form of global governance for the Internet. The Declaration of Principles, agreed upon on the final day of the meeting, refers to the need for 'management of the Internet'. In addition, it envisions a major role for governments in this management. 'Policy authority for Internet-related public policy issues is the sovereign right of States', the Declaration affirms. 'They have rights and responsibilities for international Internet-related public policy issues.'

It was not so long ago that the Internet was cherished precisely for its lack of rules and for the absence of anything that could be called 'governance'. As John Perry Barlow famously put it in his 1996 *Declaration of the Independence of Cyberspace*: 'Governments of the Industrial World, you weary giants of flesh and steel, I come from Cyberspace ... You have no sovereignty where we gather ... We have no elected government, nor are we likely to have one.' Yet the residents of cyberspace did not rise up in protest at the declaration of the WSIS.

Calls for a new system of rules are signs of growing complexities and the mainstream reach of the network. The fact is that the former system, which emphasised self-regulation and laissez-faire, is not adequate for the task. The growing commercialisation of the Internet, the proliferation of spam, identity (ID) theft, viruses, the violation of intellectual property rights and the remaining imbalance of access and connectivity are challenging the tremendous potential of the network. The creativity and innovation of the Internet need to be protected from those who would take advantage of chaos and abuse. In short, we are facing a worldwide crisis of governance on the Internet.

There are many underlying reasons for this crisis, of course. But we believe that the main reasons comprise the international decentralised nature of the Internet and the resulting insufficiency of traditional systems of regulation. The Internet clearly needs some rules. But attempts to develop a new system of governance are unlikely to succeed if they look for answers only to the nation-state, which by definition is limited in its centralised authority and effectiveness to the borders of a single nation or the parties to treaties.

The purpose of this chapter is therefore to argue that we not only need Internet governance, but that we need a new paradigm of rule-making. The crisis of governance forces us to develop a new model of governance. Some essential components of this model are that: it must be international, capable of operating across borders; it must be multi-sectoral, including a wide variety of voices and participants; and finally, in this search for multi-sectoral governance, civil society must be accorded an equal voice alongside governments and industry.

Of course these three components are only preliminary and represent just the outlines of a new model. We are only now beginning to understand what it will take to govern the Internet – to balance innovation with rules, and to reach the necessary compromise between order and creative chaos. **303**

This process of generating new forms of Internet governance is, moreover, part of a more general search around the world for new, international models of governance to manage trade, immigration, security, development and other pressing global concerns. Existing forums of global governance – the World Trade Organization (WTO), for instance, or the World Intellectual Property Organization – have both something to teach emerging models of Internet governance and something to learn from them. The discussion here can therefore be seen as a contribution to a broader and still evolving conversation.

The need for a new model of governance

In order to understand Internet governance, it is helpful to briefly consider the history of the network. Created by the United States Department of Defense in the 1960s, the Internet was initially a creature of government. Nonetheless, a large part of its early success can be attributed to the absence of anything that could be called governance. From its inception, the network thrived on a culture of openness and of collaboration between industry, civil society and users. Deregulation and privatisation emerged as dominant tropes; the attendant notion of 'self-regulation' was supposed to offer a more flexible and adaptable form of control.

Early on, the results of this culture were impressive. They included the consensus-based standards, including TCP/IP and HTML, which fuelled the Internet's growth and popularity. But as the Internet grew in complexity and as the number of users (and interests) on the network increased exponentially, cracks began appearing in the surface of Internet self-governance. The newly apparent commercial value of the Internet, in particular, began complicating matters. As the dot-com economy boomed, companies had less incentive to collaborate with their competitors and more incentive to steer the development of the network in a direction that served their own commercial purposes. As Lawrence Lessig observed so astutely in his 1999 book, *Code and Other Laws of Cyberspace,* the absence of government control of the Internet did not mean that there would be no control at all; it simply meant that others could exert control, primarily through the code and software programs they wrote. In addition, and partly as a result of this growing commercialisation, the network became increasingly clogged with various forms of 'abuse': some analysts estimate, for example, that up to 50 percent of traffic on the network today consists of unwanted emails and other forms of communication (spam), while paedophilia websites rose by 70 percent in 2003; also in that year approximately seven million people in the US alone became victims of identity theft.

These problems have not gone unnoticed (as, indeed, is illustrated by the WSIS Declaration). Around the world, governments have woken up to the dangers posed by an unregulated Internet and have stepped up their efforts to respond. The US, for example, enacted an anti-spam law (CAN-SPAM Act) that contains punitive and other measures designed to limit unwanted emails. The European Union, too, has enacted a series of strict directives regarding privacy and electronic communications. More generally, recent months and years have witnessed a slew of laws to uphold (and update) intellectual property rights, to limit the proliferation of viruses, and to regulate online gambling, ID theft, piracy and pornography.

The limits of the state

Such laws are no doubt well intentioned. They are unlikely, however, to prove sufficient to address the Internet's crisis of governance for at least two reasons. First, because freedom from state regulation has in fact been central to the Internet's success; regulation always poses the danger of overregulation, which could stifle the entrepreneurial and innovative spirit of the network, and mission-creep. Purely technological solu-

305

tions, however, have similar problems. While vigorous filtering, for instance, will purge spam from inboxes, it can also act as an unintended censor by suppressing any mention of the typical spam themes – and even references to spam itself – in legitimate personal emails. It is therefore essential that any attempt to impose order on the Internet sees government (and technology) as just part of the solution among many actors.

Second, and perhaps even more fundamentally, government control is not the answer for the simple reason that it is unlikely to work. The Internet is too dispersed, too decentralised and too international. It truly is beyond the reach of any single nation-state. This means that it is resistant to traditional forms of regulation. It requires us not only to exert some control, but also to develop a whole new method of control.

Consider, to begin with, recent attempts by the record industry to limit the flow of copyrighted material on peer-to-peer file-sharing networks. While several countries (including the US) have ruled in favour of the record industry, such rulings have little practical effect when the networks themselves transcend national boundaries and legal jurisdictions. One new file-sharing network, Earth Station 5 (ES5), vividly illustrates the point: currently operated from the West Bank and Gaza, the network operates in a legal no-man's land, safely beyond the reach of most state authorities.

Such difficulties can be found across a range of issues. But the difficulties, it is worth noting, are not just limited to challenges of enforcement: the international nature of the Internet also raises questions regarding cross-jurisdictional harmonisation. Not every country has the same legal standards regarding free speech; likewise, not every country has the same protections for privacy. This means that even when nation-states (or groups of nation-states) are capable of exerting control, their efforts may be undermined by colliding legal norms and standards, leading to a possible Balkanisation of the Internet.

A notable – and notorious – instance of such collision occurred in 2000, when a French court, citing that country's anti-hate speech laws, ordered Yahoo! to block the auctioning of Nazi memorabilia on its site. The order, which would have affected all users of the Yahoo! network, was inconsistent with American free speech traditions and laws. A French court was in effect assuming the right to dictate what Americans (or Indians, or Russians or Brazilians) could view on the network. A similar collision of legal standards occurred last year, when an Australian court ruled that a Melbourne businessman could sue Dow Jones for libel in Australia even though the content in question originated from the US. Both cases shed light on the weaknesses of existing, state-led systems of governance: it is difficult (even impossible) to govern a global resource such as the Internet when the global community disagrees on the legal (or other) norms that should form the basis for governance.

Towards a new model and the importance of civil society

Taken together, these examples effectively demonstrate the challenges of governance on the Internet. It is now clear that the absence or Balkanisation of rules can challenge the potential of the network; but the nation-state, it should be equally clear, is not capable of realising that potential on its own. What we need, as we have argued, is an altogether new model of governance – one that is capable of governing across borders, and capable of supplementing (although not replacing) the powers of the state.

Lessons from other attempts at governance

Fortunately, we can turn to (and build on) some existing examples of international, non-traditional regulation. The Internet Corporation for Assigned Names and Numbers (ICANN), for instance, provides one innovative model of decision-making. Although ICANN has had many teething problems, its management of the Domain Name System (DNS) nonetheless provides a valuable illustration of how an international resource can be managed by a multi-sectoral, non-governmental organisation (NGO). Likewise, the Digital Opportunity Task Force (DOT Force), initiated by the leaders of the Group of Eight (G8) nations in 2000, provides an interesting experiment of cross-sectoral engagement. Government-created and endorsed, but led by a mix of government, business and NGOs from the developed and developing world, the DOT Force successfully managed to create a global action and implementation plan to use information and communications technologies to support economic and social development. Its governance structure and multi-sectoral processes have since been applied to the UN-ICT Taskforce.

Of course none of these organisations is perfect and their scope is limited. Their failings have as much to teach us as their successes. ICANN's many problems, for example, offer a useful set of lessons in developing a more effective system of rule-making for the Internet. Although the organisation's recent reforms may have put it on a new path, ICANN remains dogged by perceptions that it has been insufficiently participatory and open. Developing countries and civil society groups, in particular, have felt left out of the decision-making process. This sense of exclusion has undermined ICANN's legitimacy and authority, and therefore limited its effectiveness: it provides a cautionary reminder that any system of international rule-making needs to include as wide a range of voices as possible. That is why, as we have repeatedly argued, Internet governance must be based on a principle of multi-sectoral participation.

This principle, as much as the need for international solutions, is essential for successful governance. Traditional regulation relies primarily on the coercive and punitive powers of the state. But effective Internet governance is likely to rely on a culture of mutual interest and deference. Its authority will therefore depend crucially on its legitimacy and that, in turn, will rely on perceptions of inclusiveness, a sense that actors representing various sectors and regions have a voice at the table of Internet rule-making.

The role of civil society

Certainly, governments and the private sector must be among these actors: each represents an essential pillar upon which Internet governance rests. But an equally important, if often overlooked, pillar is represented by civil society. Indeed, civil society – in the form of NGOs and public interest groups – has an equally important role to play in multi-sectoral Internet governance.

Representing the public interest
First, civil society is an important actor because it is often best placed to represent the public interest. As noted above, many of the problems we are facing on the Internet stem from its growing commercialisation. But this is not necessarily against the public interest: indeed, commercialisation is at the root of much of the innovation and creativity on the network. Inevitably, however, there are times when private and public interests collide; and at such times, civil society groups are ideally placed to represent the latter and to defend individual rights against the state.

Trust

Part of the reason that civil society can play this role is because it possesses significant capital in the form of trust. Unaffiliated with the state and the commercial sectors, civil society groups are often able to articulate an independent and reliable point of view. Indeed, a recent survey on trust, conducted with 36,000 people by the World Economic Forum, found that civil society, i.e. NGOs and advocacy groups, had the second highest ratings as trusted parties (after the armed forces); the institutions that were least trusted were governments (at the very bottom) and private companies. Another survey on Internet accountability conducted by the Markle Foundation showed similar results, with respondents reacting positively to the idea of NGOs having a role in developing rules for the Internet. The public assigns a positive score to this idea (a rating of 7.1) – a far more favourable rating than those received by technical experts (6.6), individuals (6.3) or state governments (5.0). Given the widely recognised importance of trust in facilitating economic, social and other interactions, such figures point to the important role played by civil society in promoting the health of the online environment.

International

Finally, civil society can play an effective role because it often is truly global (and increasingly so) in its reach. Given that Internet governance requires international coordination, it is of course essential that it should include groups with global reach. Transnational NGOs and other civil society groups, which have grown rapidly throughout the world in recent decades, are ideally placed to fill the role of an international actor representing all segments of the global community. Indeed, a significant proportion of international aid is already channelled through international NGOs, and they have also been at the forefront of international advocacy and rule-making for a range of issues.

Such advocacy, it is worth adding, is particularly important as a means of including developing countries in Internet governance. The early failures of ICANN, as well as the recent problems encountered by the WTO at Cancun, clearly demonstrate the perils of multilateral governance mechanisms that fail to address the needs of the developing world. Without an inclusive process, international rule-making institutions will lack legitimacy and thus authority. Perhaps even more importantly, the failure to include developing nations in rule-making processes will lead to an imbalance in those rules, a systemic exclusion of nations and populations that will only become more pronounced as the network evolves. Ultimately, such imbalances will not only harm developing nations; they will also undermine the network itself, stunting its growth and limiting the number of new, innovative applications that may emerge from the user community.

Conclusion

We remain fundamentally optimistic that we can develop new models of governance that will help us overcome current difficulties with the network and allow people to benefit from its tremendous potential. The model we have argued for must have three essential components: it must be international in its reach and authority; it must be based on multi-sectoral and geographically inclusive participation; and it needs to include representatives of civil society.

If each of these three conditions is fulfilled, we believe that the benefits will extend beyond the health of the Internet. Certainly, we will see the network flourish. But in addition, and partly as a result of this flourishing, the Internet can also become an instrument for greater global cooperation and harmony. At a time when so many of our conflicts are being driven by competing ideologies and ideas, a global and inclusive Internet can play an essential role in encouraging healthy

311

(and peaceful) debate and discussion of those ideas. So much is at stake – for the Internet itself, and more generally for the global community.

Zoë Baird

Zoë Baird is President of the Markle Foundation, New York. Baird's career spans business, government (Carter and Clinton administrations) and academia (Yale University). Currently a member of the Secretary of Defense's Technology and Privacy Advisory Committee. Serves as a director of the Chubb Corporation, the Brookings Institution, and the James A. Baker III Institute for Public Policy among others.

Stefaan Verhulst

Stefaan Verhulst was born in Belgium in 1966. Currently Chief of Research at the Markle Foundation, New York. Previously Founder and Director of the Programme in Comparative Media Law and Policy (PCMLP) at Oxford University. Has served as consultant to various international and national organisations including the Council of Europe, European Commission, UNESCO, UNDP, USAID and DFID. Author of numerous books and articles.

Economics

Mario Monti

Governing EU Economic Space

Political leaders throughout Europe are facing a paradox. On the one hand, Europeans want them to find solutions to the major problems confronting our societies. People expect the European Union to take the lead in seizing the opportunities provided by globalisation for economic and human development, and in responding to environmental challenges, unemployment, concerns over food safety, crime and regional conflicts. On the other hand, people increasingly distrust institutions and politics or are simply not interested in them. The problem is particularly acute at the EU level. Many people are losing confidence in a poorly understood and complex system to deliver the policies that they want. The EU is often seen as remote and at the same time too intrusive.

New instruments for governance?

The European Commission has reflected on the different avenues to improve transparency and coherence of the way the EU is regulated. It has come to the conclusion, publicised in a White Paper on European Governance, that the EU must follow a less top-down approach, simplify existing rules and complement its policy tools more effectively with non-legislative instruments.

During the reflection on the art of governance, something described as co-regulation entered the debate. Co-regulation is a form of regulatory intervention, developed in consensus with the industry concerned, in areas where it is agreed that intervention is necessary. Indeed, the first question to be asked is: Should the EU intervene at all? If this is answered positively, the chosen form of an intervention should be one which is effective and guided by the common public interest – not just by the interest of the industry concerned.

At least with regard to competition law, I wonder whether we really need new forms of governance instead of improving the instruments we already have. The starting point for this reflection is that the competition rules of the EC Treaty have to be observed imperatively by all actors of any regulatory model and they have to be enforceable. For these reasons, the application of a consent-based process of establishing rules would not be appropriate in competition law legislation.

Implementation and enforcement of competition rules require in the first place an intelligent application of established regulatory tools. No co-regulatory agreement or concept of self-regulation or self-control could replace clear, enforceable rules of competitive market behaviour which guarantee all undertakings the same chances for success. If a need for regulation is identified, it should be developed, implemented and applied in a consistent and strict manner, with a view to avoiding unnecessary bureaucratic burdens. Pressure by interest groups ought to be resisted; this requires more courage than resorting to some form of partnership in government. The focus of regulatory reform in competition is therefore on better regulation, not on alternatives to it.

An integrated strategy for governing EU economy

An important objective of regulatory reform has an economic bias: to foster a competitive and dynamic economy, characterised by growth and employment. This objective, which was defined by the European Council of Lisbon in March 2000, can be achieved only if we make sure that all related government action becomes part of a coherent policy strategy. The Competitiveness Council, created by the European Council of Seville in June 2002, is now combining the Internal Market, the Industry and the Research Councils into a single body to ensure a coherent political strategy for competitiveness.

In view of the need to accelerate economic reform, the Competitiveness Council has been asked to assume a horizontal role of enhancing competitiveness and growth in the framework of an integrated strategy, reviewing on a regular basis both horizontal and sectoral issues. The Commission has contributed by developing an integrated strategy for competitiveness. I consider this initiative most useful for the improvement of European economic governance. To be effective, the proposed horizontal approach should lead to concrete policy decisions on the basis of identified weaknesses and focus attention on key competitiveness issues such as productivity growth, innovation and market reform. In March 2004, the Council will discuss a Commission communication on an integrated competitiveness approach.

Contribution of regulatory reform to competitiveness

How can regulatory reform in competition policy contribute to the objectives of Lisbon? The role of competition in this context, in my view, is obvious. A competitive economy is not conceivable without competition. Competition is the condition for innovation, efficiency improvements and necessary restructuring in a global market. Competition is a key instrument that not only enhances the competitiveness of our industry but also fosters growth and creates sustainable employment.

We need to adapt the competition rules to the realities of a modern, open economy. As in other areas, in the application of competition law, industry needs to be free from unnecessary regulatory burdens and enabled to react swiftly to the challenges posed by a rapidly changing global economic environment. For the third year in a row, the EU growth rate has been disappointing, and, indeed, during this period there have been calls for the relaxation of the competition rules. But a substantial relaxation would be a step in precisely the wrong direction. Without competition, the driving forces behind growth and employment would be lost. The direction in which we have to go is therefore clear: rather than having less competition we need, on the contrary, to introduce more competition in sectors still not open to the market. As far as the application of the competition rules of the Treaty is concerned, we certainly need less red tape and fewer unnecessary regulatory burdens for enterprises, while maintaining the standards.

Deregulation

Let's consider, for example, telecommunications, a sector that has undergone a thorough overhaul and has shown a tremendous increase in productivity. But despite liberalisation and the availability of competition law instruments, we have not yet reached market conditions in the electronic communications sector which would allow *ex ante* regulation to be abandoned. In fact, one could even wonder about the apparently unusual combination of regulation and competition which is embodied in the new regulatory framework – the Commission could be blamed for introducing new regulation instead of reducing the existing one. What really matters, however, is not abandoning regulation as an instrument altogether, but keeping the approach to regulation consistent with the approach to antitrust analysis and enforcement. The essential point is not whether there is more or less regulation, but that the right type of regulation is being used.

In the past, the sector-specific regulation was a fragmented set of norms which held back rather than supported the development of competition. Traditionally, in the electronic communications area – as much as in gas, electricity, railways, water, and terrestrial broadcasting – a member state not only had a different regulatory framework to another member state, but also a totally different framework from one sector of the economy to the other. This is changing radically. In the area of telecommunications, the EU has now firmly adopted an approach which envisages that regulation is essentially economic, based on the view that intervention in the market is still necessary to address certain sorts of market power, and, in particular, market failures which derive from formerly monopolistic market structures.

Regulation thus is increasingly determined by a competition policy perspective. Competition instruments and regulatory tools are complementary means – they deal with a common problem and try to achieve a common aim. This aim is no longer the protection of monopoly rights but the introduction of market mechanisms which work for the benefit of the consumer and the economy on the whole.

Modernisation of core competition rules

In its own administrative procedures the Commission has also made considerable progress towards efficiency. In late 2002, the Council adopted Regulation 1/2003 in the area of antitrust policy which lays down a new framework for applying Articles 81 and 82 of the EC Treaty. This regulation, which enters into force on 1 May 2004, opens a new chapter in the application of the EU antitrust rules by the Commission, national competition authorities and national courts throughout Europe.

With regard to antitrust policy, our system has in the past been characterised by the fact that exemptions from the prohibition of restrictive agreements could only be obtained from the Commission upon notification. This led to a centralisation of the handling of antitrust cases in Brussels. Consequently, it had a negative impact on the Commission's ability to set its own enforcement priorities and severely limited the potential of national competition authorities to contribute to the enforcement of EU antitrust rules.

Some years ago, the Commission acknowledged the need to reform the old antitrust enforcement system and increase its overall performance. The main feature of the new system for the enforcement of Articles 81 and 82 EC is that it abolishes the exemption notifications to the Commission, thereby allowing the Commission to concentrate fully on the pursuit of serious infringements of competition law in *ex officio* and complaint procedures. At the same time, business is relieved from burdensome notification requirements.

The second central element of the reform is that it levels the playing field for undertakings in the internal market. Under the new regulation, agreements between undertakings will be assessed against a single competition law standard, the standard of Article 81 EC. The reform also enables national competition authorities and courts to enforce the EU antitrust rules. They will be able to directly apply the prohibition of restrictive agreements, and the exemptions thereto. Cases will be dealt with by the authority closest to the companies concerned and best placed to restore competition to the marketplace.

In the area of merger control, the challenge is to ensure the continuing effectiveness of our system in the face of increasingly complex cases and closer scrutiny by the European courts. With that objective in mind, in 2000 the Commission launched a comprehensive review of its merger control system. To be clear, merger control is less interventionist than it may seem at first glance – it is certainly not the Commission's intention to impede the evolution of market structures. Mergers are often necessary to deal with the challenges of a changing economy. Therefore, the Commission has very rarely blocked a proposed merger – only 18 out of more than 2200 cases reported to it since 1990 – but of course, the blocking of mergers receives much more public attention than their authorisation.

The new regulation introduces some flexibility into the investigation time frames and reinforces the 'one-stop shop' concept. The improved system of allocation of cases between the Commission and national competition authorities will ensure that the case is dealt with by the most appropriate authority while at the same time avoiding the need for multiple filing. The new regulation allows the notifying parties to request referrals at the pre-notification stage. Notably, parties may request that cases without an EU dimension be referred to the Commission if the concentration would have to be notified in at least three member states.

The reform also clarifies that the substantive test contained in the regulation covers all types of harmful scenarios, whether dominance by a single firm or effects stemming from a situation of oligopoly that might harm the interests of European consumers. This clarification creates an improved legal security as the new test clearly defines the assessment criteria. It covers all forms of concentration that could be harmful for the consumer and clearly defines the limits of the Commission's scope for intervention.

Finally, in the area of state aid, the Council has rightly insisted on several occasions that the overall amount of state aid should be reduced and more focused on supporting horizontal objectives instead of certain sectors or even single undertakings. These selective subsidies are extremely distort-

319

ing. In state aid matters, it is not always easy for the Commission to defend its line, particularly when big enterprises of national importance are calling for public support. Aid for rescue and restructuring operations gave rise to some of the most controversial state aid cases in the past and is possibly the most distortive type of state aid.

This is a sensitive area due to the potential conflict between the way a member state wishes to pursue its industrial and structural policy and the Commission's role, which is to protect and maintain a level playing field for industry throughout the EU. The Commission is often confronted with the argument that the EU state aid policy leads to loss of jobs. The Commission must firmly resist any undue pressure of this kind. Each aid measure in favour of a single undertaking has a negative effect on competing companies who are managing to operate without public aid and, in turn, puts their employees' jobs at risk.

State aid control needs to strive for more effectiveness to allow the Commission to concentrate resources on important cases which present real competition concerns at the Community level. Work is most advanced in the area of procedural reform. A series of changes to simplify and modernise procedures has been identified and a regulation detailing provisions for the implementation of the state aid procedural regulation (Council Regulation No 659/1999 of 22 March 1999) is being prepared. It is also intended that new instruments will be developed to simplify procedures regarding those aspects of aid that do not give rise to significant competition concerns.

The international dimension

While tackling the challenges within the EU, we must not lose sight of the international dimension in competition matters. As the world already has about 100 countries with some form of competition regime, the Commission has placed particular emphasis on international cooperation at the multilateral level. It is certainly disappointing that work on a global policy regime within the World Trade Organization (WTO) suffered a major setback in the current Doha round. But this is mitigated by the huge success of the International Competition Network (ICN). This informal network of most of the world's existing competition authorities has the objective of fostering the policy dialogue and identifying best practices.

The second annual conference in Mérida in June 2003 brought together most of the 80 competition authorities that have joined the ICN. It confirmed the high priority that every authority must give to competition advocacy in order to increase public awareness of the benefits of competition and actively influence other policies from a competition perspective. The conference also discussed how to improve further global governance mechanisms for reviewing international mergers. It endorsed recommendations for the review of multi-jurisdictional mergers, aiming to identify the steps which competition authorities may usefully take to facilitate cooperation and convergence. This should help to make the review process more efficient thereby reducing the costs and burdens associated with international merger reviews.

Conclusion

Governance in competition policy has won the intellectual debate. Economists and lawyers throughout the EU recognise the benefits of competition to consumers and the economy. It is also winning the political support of the public – consumers are becoming more convinced of these benefits. Competition authorities are trusted, their actions are transparent and their objectives are generally accepted. This is rewarding and provides encouragement to the Commission to continue its work in this area.

321

Mario Monti

Mario Monti was born in Varese, Italy, in 1943. EC Commissioner in Brussels (since 1995); President of Bocconi University in Milan. In 1987–88, helped to draft the Italian Competition Act; member of the working party that prepared Italy for the single market in 1988–90.

C. Fred Bergsten

The G2: The Best Way to Go

In this chapter, I propose the creation of a 'G2' consultative mechanism through which the European Union and the United States would manage their own economic (and possibly some security) relations and informally steer the world economy. This mechanism would address a growing number of pressing governance issues through different groups of officials from different ministries on both sides of the Atlantic, loosely coordinated by an 'overview group'. I shall start with a brief rationale for the G2 and then turn to the key practical questions that would be involved in setting it up and operating it: What topics would it address? Who would address them?

I should stress at the outset that the G2, in playing its global management role, would be an informal process that would not replace any of the existing institutional mechanisms (including, for example, the G7/8). On the contrary, it would seek to energise those broader groups and greatly enhance their effectiveness by providing leadership within them from the only two entities – the EU and the US – that together can make them exercise their own responsibilities more successfully.

Conceptually, the new G2 would represent the innermost of a series of concentric decision-making circles. The next circle, moving outward from the G2 itself, would be the present 'inner circles' such as the 'finance G7' (of finance ministers and, sometimes, central bank governors) on macroeconomic and monetary matters and the 'quad' on trade issues. Beyond these groups lies the next ring, the 'executive committees' of the formal global institutions, including the International Monetary and Finance Committee (formerly the Interim Committee) of the International Monetary Fund (IMF) and (sometimes) the CG18 of the GATT/WTO, which are intended to streamline and improve the functioning of those nearly universal organisations. The multilateral organisations themselves, such as the IMF and WTO, would constitute the outermost of the concentric circles that make (or ratify) the final and formal decisions in their issue areas.

As the centrepiece of this proposed pattern of international decision-making, the G2 would be a totally informal operation. There would be no need to announce its creation or even confirm its existence publicly. The inherently diffuse (and probably uneven) nature of its operation across a wide range of issue areas, as described below, would facilitate (if not necessitate) such a 'stealth' existence.

The need for a G2

There are four basic reasons to create an informal G2. First, Europe and the US currently have no conceptual foundation on which to base their relationship. The Cold War provided such a foundation for four decades but no replacement has yet been found. Without such an intellectual basis, there will be constant risk of erosion or even rupture of transatlantic ties.

Second, a G2 would help to counter the chief foreign policy shortcomings of each transatlantic partner: America's tendency to unilateralism and Europe's tendency to insularity. Precisely because of its unquestioned superiority at this point in time, the US needs a trusted and reliable ally to protect it from the constant go-it-alone temptations of superpower hegemony. At the same time, given the present stage of its institutional evolution, the EU needs a globally oriented partner to overcome the powerful impetus to self-centred behaviour that derives from its enormous internal agenda.

Third, the world economy, like any political or social entity facing collective action problems, requires leadership from those of its members that have both the capacity and the will to provide it. This need is greater now than in the past due to the rapid growth in the total number of state actors (187 members of IMF, 144 of WTO), and even more so given the growth of the number that have a real impact on the world economy (probably 30–40). For the foreseeable future, only the US and the EU enjoy the ability to provide leadership in global economic governance. With the expansion of the EU, the population, economic output (especially at PPP exchange rates), per capita income, trade flows, openness ratios and most other economic indicators of the two are remarkably similar. Japan, once a member of a putative G3, is fading fast and will probably continue to do so if only for demographic reasons. China is the rising power and may need to be added to the leadership core in a decade or two, but it is still a very poor country with an inconvertible currency, only halfway to being a market economy and probably even further away from political democracy. Hence, only the G2 can steer the world economy for the foreseeable future.

Fourth, a G2 already exists in at least a few issue areas, demonstrating that the idea is feasible. It has been in place on trade policy for about 40 years, since the original European Economic Community centralised that function in the Commission, and has reached its zenith with the close current relationship between the US Trade Representative Robert Zoellick and EU Trade Commissioner Pascal Lamy. It exists in a sense in the military dimension through NATO, especially with the recent expansion of NATO initiatives outside the European theatre. A G2 is clearly a practical possibility.

What would a G2 do and how would it work?

A functional G2 would always be simultaneously pursuing two sets of objectives: a more effective relationship between Europe and the US and more effective global economic governance. These two objectives are almost always compatible and mutually reinforcing. Indeed, harmonious transatlantic relations are a necessary condition for global stability and the latter is in turn extremely valuable, in both economic and political terms, to the EU and the US.

Questions have legitimately been raised as to whether policy instruments exist that could be deployed effectively even by the most efficacious G2 mechanism. An exhaustive analysis of such instruments is beyond the scope of this short chapter, but I shall attempt to show the feasibility of new policy action if the transatlantic partners decide to embark on such a course.

There are two basic strategies for creating a G2. One would be 'top down', with a decision at the highest levels to develop intensive transatlantic consultation across a wide range of issues with *ex ante* determination of a large set of specific topics to pursue under that rubric. There might be an overall steering committee that would relate the separate issues to each other and provide overall political impetus. The alternative strategy would be a 'bottom up' and more evolutionary approach, with opportunistic development of consultative ties on individual issues, for example in the international monetary arena if sharp new instabilities in the dollar–euro exchange rate were to require much more active cooperation, or on environmental issues if the US agreed to work seriously with the EU on an acceptable successor to the Kyoto protocol.

Whichever of these paths were eventually chosen, or permitted to evolve, it is useful to consider the potential issue areas that might be amenable to G2 management. At least 10 possibilities come readily to mind: trade, competition policy, regulatory policy including corporate governance, macroeconomic policy, international monetary policy, international financial markets, energy, the environment, migration and global poverty. All of these areas would almost certainly benefit from more systemic and sustained attention from the responsible EU and US authorities working together within a new G2 framework. Trade, for example, already enjoys a high degree of G2 management and the benefits are obvious. Even here, however, there are key systemic issues that are not being addressed: the rapidly proliferating network of G2 bilateral trade agreements and the need for a more coordinated response to the critics of globalisation. There are two main issues: getting the members of the G2 to think of themselves primarily as stewards of the global trading system, rather than as mercantilist adversaries, and institutionalising the strong personal ties that fortunately now exist in this domain and that clearly have been important in preventing real trade conflict during this period of extensive and intensifying disputes.

This list of specific candidate issues for G2 management reveals immediately that any such process, if carried out on anything like the scale suggested, would engage very large numbers of people from a wide array of official (and perhaps some private) institutions on both sides of the Atlantic. There would have to be a great deal of flexibility and informality in the process or it would risk becoming hopelessly bureaucratised.

The process could be viewed as deepening and institutionalising, at the G2 level, the transnational coalitions that already function in some areas (central bankers, competition authorities and trade officials are well interconnected) and creating new coalitions where they are either non-existent or embryonic (energy and environmental officials do not communicate as well). Each responsible group could set out its own agenda and timetable, building on whatever practices were already in place. The mandate would be to establish or maintain a process of consultation on the key issues being faced in each issue area.

Wherever possible the G2 would build on existing mechanisms involving public officials, business leaders and civil society. An example is regulatory policy, where the Trans

Atlantic Business Dialogue (TABD) has tackled a number of critical issues, seeking mutual recognition agreements (MRAs) on some. Another is corporate governance, where cooperation between the American and European Business Roundtables could develop voluntary but useful codes to prevent future Enrons or Parmalats. More broadly, 'track II' diplomacy conducted by a variety of non-governmental organisations (NGOs) – which has become very popular in Asia and across the Pacific but curiously is less utilised across the Atlantic to date – could generate ideas for official G2 consideration and, even more importantly, help spread the concept underlying this new strategy, especially the vital changes in mindsets in both America and Europe that will be necessary to make it work.

Three types of exchanges should take place in each group. One would simply be **informational:** full briefings on the latest developments in each region in the respective issue areas so that future actions in the other could at least take account of the partner's decisions. The second could be on **policy interactions** or the international implications of pending policies on one of the respective partners, for example, the potential impact on international capital flows and exchange markets of large US tax cuts or reform of the Stability and Growth Pact. The third and most advanced exchange would be the possibility of occasional **cooperative or even coordinated action** to improve the prospects for effective response to a particular policy challenge.

A further operational element is the possible creation of a coordinating committee to maintain linkages and promote consistency between the (10? more?) issue-specific consultative groups. Such a committee is not absolutely essential but, operating as a small and very informal secretariat, could help to keep the various parts of the programme in sync and avoid overlaps or inconsistencies. The committee could also 'assign' topics to individual consultative groups that might be mandated by the transatlantic political leadership at their regular summits (which could now become much more meaningful by drawing on the work of the consultative groups). If it were staffed by close personal representatives of the political leaders, as would be essential at least at the outset of the operation, it could also infuse 'political will' and even do some trouble-shooting on its own should individual groups become bogged down by parochial problems peculiar to their topics.

Overlap with other international groups?

A final question that has been raised about the G2 idea is whether it would duplicate existing groupings. All the other 'Gs', certainly including the G7/8 and the formal international institutions such as the IMF and WTO, would continue to exist. To the extent that the G2 became an effective steering committee, the existing organisations would in fact become more significant in bringing the leadership decisions to the next circles of leadership and carrying out agreed policies.

However, with the decline of Japan and the irrelevance of Canada and Russia on most global economic issues, isn't it perhaps legitimate to ask whether the G7/8 is not already essentially a a G2, thus obviating the need for anything new?

The answer is a resounding 'No'. First, the G7/8 includes three countries that are of marginal relevance for most major international economic issues (Canada, Japan and Russia), which inherently complicates its discussions and makes agreement more difficult. Second, the presence of four European countries plus the Commission reduces rather than enhances the prospect of a common European position; the G7/8, as is its wont, has ducked rather than confronted that fundamental problem in achieving meaningful coordination. Third, the G7/8 summits have to a great extent become media shows rather than substantive meetings, and political rather than economic conclaves, where substance does not survive. Fourth, the 'finance G7', which escapes some of the shortcomings of the summits, has also become almost totally ineffective due largely to the pact among its members not to criticise each other and their resignation to inertia in the face of 'overwhelming market forces' as well as the independence of their central banks. Fifth, none of the G7/8 variants even address some of the most critical issues on the list suggested above, such as migration and environmental policy.

The final and central policy question is, of course, whether a new G2 could overcome the problems that hamstring the G7/8 (and other international bodies) so severely. The honest answer is that it could do so only if it were launched with strong political commitment on the part of the top political leaders on both sides of the Atlantic and then implemented, on an ongoing and sustained basis, by officials with the same dedication. The model is, of course, the American and European unions themselves: both have overcome enormous odds due to the compelling nature of the gains from 'deep integration' and implementation by a cadre of dedicated supporters of the concept.

Similar conditions will need to be met if a G2 is to flourish in the early part of the 21st century. The driving elements would have to be a conviction on the part of both American and European leaders that their own relationship required a firm new foundation, that they needed to protect themselves from some of their own worst proclivities (unilateralism in the US, insularity in Europe) and that they could exercise their responsibilities for global leadership only by acting together in a more concerted manner. All three make a strong case for launching the G2 initiative as soon as possible.

The G2 would of course have to work closely with other countries and groups thereof to achieve its global leadership objectives. The recent WTO Ministerial Meeting in Cancun, for example, showed that G2 agreement – while clearly a necessary condition for global progress – is no longer sufficient. In that case, the G2 needed both to make a much more forthcoming offer to liberalise its own agricultural policies and to work cooperatively with the G20, the nascent combination of key developing countries that demonstrated its veto power for the first time.

As noted at the outset, the G2 must operate at the centre of a series of concentric circles of international decision-making. The EU and the US must constantly consult with their closest allies in the next ring of countries, e.g. Russia and Japan, respectively, both to take their views fully into account and to help win their approval for essential G2 positions. The procedures and leadership of the multilateral institutions, notably the IMF and the WTO, must be involved at all stages. But effective global economic management requires leadership from the only two superpowers in that domain, the EU and the US; the G2 would thus prove to be an essential component of global governance in the early 21st century.

Adapted from a paper co-authored by C. Fred Bergsten and Caio Koch-Weser.

C. Fred Bergsten

C. Fred Bergsten was born in New York in 1941. Director of the Institute for International Economics (IIE) in Washington DC since its creation in 1981. Assistant Secretary for International Affairs of the US Treasury (1977–81); Assistant for International Economic Affairs to the National Security Council (1969–71); also worked with the Brookings Institution (1972–76), the Carnegie Endowment for International Peace (1981), and the Council on Foreign Relations (1967–68). Numerous publications on a wide range of international economic issues.

Jonathon Porritt

No-Choice Collaboration: Capital Markets in the Governance Revolution

Capital market controls on the governance of corporations and financial institutions themselves have been increasingly challenged during the 1990s. Massive volatility in emerging market debt finance; the series of major corporate scandals in America and Europe; failure of privatised utilities to deliver adequate capacity and safety; loss of customer trust in long-term savings providers; the increasing impact on corporate reputation of poor environmental and social performance – all of these challenges to the 'Anglo-American' model of capitalism have found the majority of financial institutions wanting. Perhaps the main reason is that many if not all of these issues have the characteristics of 'public goods'. It is in the interest of all to find solutions, but it pays individual institutions to free-ride, hindering any joint action! However, such is the scale of the challenge facing financial institutions that innovative new coalitions have been formed. Whether or not they succeed may well prove to be the key to determining whether or not the current model of Anglo-American capitalism will survive. It's worth looking at each of the five factors in turn.

A lot of this goes right back to the early 1990s and the explosion in foreign direct investment. Such has been the volatility of debt finance provided to the emerging economies that the World Bank now welcomes the current decline of this form of financing as positive for development prospects. From very low levels in the early 1990s, private debt flows ballooned to $90 billion by 1997, before collapsing to repayments of $25 billion in 2001. These debt repayments, plus accumulation of assets by a number of central banks, mean that the developing economies have become net suppliers of financial capital to the Organization for Economic Cooperation and Development (OECD). Capital is no longer flowing from high-income countries to economies that need it to sustain progress towards the Millennium Development Goals.

Within the developed economies, and particularly the United States, the series of major corporate scandals beginning with Enron has demonstrated a remarkable failure of governance by shareholders and other financial stakeholders. Corporations have lost a valuable economic asset in the collapse of trust that resulted from these scandals, but capital markets were hardly blameless. Bubble conditions in 1990s equity markets put pressure on corporations to report double-figure growth in earnings to sustain both their market ratings and (more disturbingly) the value of their executives' share options. Perhaps it was hardly surprising that the less scrupulous resorted to making up the numbers. More surprising was the lack of activism by equity owners and their fund managers on basic corporate governance issues.

Privatisation of previously state-run utilities has spread from developed to developing economies during the past 20 years. The injection of competition has clearly increased the efficiency with which these assets have been 'sweated'. Rates of return on capital employed have risen dramatically. However, experience in the UK and elsewhere has shown that investment in capacity and asset maintenance, as well as the wider public interest, has suffered in a number of industries. Electricity generation has suffered from a lack of sufficient capacity, causing a series of blackouts in America, Europe and New Zealand. Rail transport may have trimmed safety margins too far. Privatised water companies have sometimes found the equity finance model inconsistent with the need to maintain water quality and environmental standards, and some utilities are trying new models of governance. Corporate governance by capital markets of the privatised utilities has not worked as well as hoped.

The governance of financial institutions themselves has been called into question by widespread mis-selling of long-term savings products in the UK. Such has been the collapse of customer trust in insurers and asset managers that there is now a substantial savings gap, estimated by the Association of British Insurers at £26 billion, a shortfall that is contributing to perceptions of a looming pensions crisis. Clearly there are demographic and public finance issues underlying the pensions crisis, but the fact is that consumers are not saving enough and their lack of trust in financial institutions is a major contributory factor.

Finally, one of the by-products of the revolution in information technology has been the increasing activism of customers and NGOs in response to poor environmental and social performance by multinational corporations. Gone are the days when local communities could be uprooted with little compensation to make way for a dam, or labour employed without regard to international standards. Gone also are the days when investment banks could finance such projects and companies without risking their reputations and share price. It is true that new markets for environmental products (such as carbon emissions permits) are providing new business opportunities for financial institutions. However, it's clear that the major motivating force on governance of sustainable development issues by financial institutions has been the growing risk to reputation.

Change in response to these challenges has been slow. Capital markets are traditionally fiercely competitive and not conducive to collaborative ventures. Engagement with other stakeholders, such as NGOs, has been almost completely absent. Yet there is little payoff for financial institutions to act on their own. The Chief Investment Officer for Citigroup, Tom Jones, was recently quoted in the *Financial Times*: 'I've got to say that I've got higher priorities. I'm not a do-gooder. I want to do what I get paid for, and shareholder activism isn't what I get paid for … If we spend money to do shareholder activism, Citigroup asset management shareholders bear the expense but don't get a benefit that is distinct from other shareholders.' That last point is the key. In order to reap the benefit and spread the cost, collaboration is required. Some financial institutions are now responding with collaborative ventures that may point to the emergence of a new partnership approach.

One such venture has been the Equator Principles led by the project finance teams of major banks such as Citibank and ABN-Amro. Last June, 10 of these banks from seven countries announced the adoption of a voluntary set of guidelines developed by the banks for managing social and environmental impacts related to the financing of major development projects. The principles are being applied globally to project finance in all sectors, including mining, oil and gas, and forestry. Collaboration has been essential simply because the extra cost of compliance with these principles exposes new project finance deals to competition from non-signatories. This partnership model is very new to these highly competitive players. The business case depends on there being a resulting decline in reputational risk. It remains to be seen whether the banks come to realise that this will require extending their partnership model to include the NGOs that are the principal transmission mechanism for such risks.

Another example is the Carbon Disclosure Project, a collaboration by a number of large institutional investors and asset managers who have realised that climate change policies represent a serious risk to their investment returns. The group wrote to the 500 largest companies in the world in May 2002 and November 2003 asking for the disclosure of 'investment-relevant information concerning their greenhouse gas emissions'. The need to find new ways of addressing this particular investment risk has brought together 87 institutional investors with assets totalling $9 trillion. Information disclosure is obviously just the first step to successful governance of climate change impacts; however, the fact that investors are working together to address a global issue is promising.

The partnership approach in this part of the financial services industry has not been limited to the climate change issue. The public health crisis in emerging markets (and HIV/AIDS in particular) led to the recent formation of the Pharma Group, another coalition of large institutional investors and asset managers. As with the Carbon Disclosure Project, it focuses on getting companies to disclose information – this time, the big pharmaceutical companies on issues relating to access to patented medicines. Why is this an investment issue? The investors in this partnership believe that the pharmaceutical sector's response to the public health crisis in emerging markets could impact shareholder value in the long term. On this issue, investors have taken the further step of partnering with key NGOs in order to better inform their engagement with the companies involved. A case study (reported in the Forum for the Future/Co-operative Insurance publication *Sustainability Pays*) reveals how the combination of an informed NGO (Oxfam) and a number of major investors positively influenced GlaxoSmithKline's decision to improve access to medicines in Africa.

Forum for the Future has pioneered the partnership approach with business in the UK and is trying to extend the handful of initiatives that have begun to emerge in the financial sector. The Forum's Centre for Sustainable Investment has emphasised that financial regulators need to be brought into some of these partnerships if there is to be change across the financial system. Voluntary coalitions of financial institutions will go only as far as the business case for collective action.

The Centre's analysis of just how financial regulators can work with financial market mechanisms to improve the sustainability of market outcomes was launched by the UK prime minister at the 2002 World Summit on Sustainable Development in Johannesburg. One of the key messages of *Financing the Future: The London Principles of Sustainable Finance* (2002) was that equity and debt prices must more accurately reflect environmental and social risk. Credit rating agencies and investment bank equity analysts need to broaden their analysis and valuation of companies if this is to happen. In fact, this *is* starting to emerge with, for instance, the regular publication of corporate governance ratings by Standard and Poors, and the publication of research into the investment impact of climate change policies by major international banks such as UBS and DrKW.

Our Centre for Sustainable Investment has also been working with the United Nations Environment Programme and the African Institute for Corporate Citizenship to use the same framework as the London Principles to assess the sustainability of the African banking system. We are working with these institutions and others such as the Royal Institute of International Affairs to try to build a global coalition of international institutions to work in partnership with financial regulators.

But so far, there have only been a handful of initiatives from the private financial sector. Once the glossy reports are stripped away, there is as yet very little evidence of any widespread joint action by mainstream financial institutions. It remains to be seen whether the partnership approach is widely adopted, and what impact this may have on the long-term sustainability of the current model of Anglo-American capitalism.

Jonathon Porritt
Jonathon Porritt was born in London in 1950. Co-founder and Programme Director of Forum for the Future, London; Chairman of the UK Sustainable Development Commission; **337**

co-director of the Prince of Wales's Business and Environment Programme. Received a CBE in January 2000 for services to environmental protection. Among his recent publications: *Playing Safe: Science and the Environment.*

Ong Keng Yong

Prosper Thy Neighbour: Community Building in South East Asia

Why should there be an ASEAN Community? Partnership among the countries and people of South East Asia is an evolutionary process. The pace and depth of this evolution are influenced by national, regional and global dynamics. Partnership is a result of sustained interactions among governments, economies and societies within the region and beyond. At the core of this coalition is the Association of South East Asian Nations (ASEAN), which has played an enabling and enriching role since its establishment in 1967. ASEAN is a dynamic institution that has shown its willingness to adapt to the changing times, challenges and opportunities.

The ASEAN region consists of 10 countries of differing size and with different political systems and levels of development. Nevertheless, they share a common interest in the promotion of social and economic development and in the maintenance of regional peace and stability. The establishment of an ASEAN Community is the culmination and realisation of the vision of the founding fathers to embrace and transform all 10 countries of South East Asia into a community of nations. At the same time, the Community is the region's response to the need for a collective voice and concerted action in an increasingly interdependent and globalising world.

Beyond these manifest motivations and interests, the ASEAN Community is an expression of shared values and identity which have been shaped over the centuries by common geography, climate, culture and shared historical experience. In this sense, the Community is a faithful manifestation of the region's resolve 'to establish a firm foundation for common action in the spirit of equality and partnership' as stated in the Bangkok Declaration of 1967. The decision of the ASEAN leaders at their summit in Bali in October 2003 to advance the form and substance of the ASEAN Community with a capital 'C' is the latest milestone in the history of the organisation.

The establishment of an ASEAN Community requires partnership not only among the countries of South East Asia, but also between them and other countries with legitimate roles and interests in the region. It involves comprehensive partnership in the political, security, economic and social spheres. It is an inclusive, not exclusive, partnership that favours engagement rather than containment policies. Partnership in and with the ASEAN Community is about promoting common interests and mutual benefits in today's interdependent world.

What is the significance of such institutional evolution of one of the most successful regional organisations in the world today? What are its implications for intraregional cooperation among its members and between the ASEAN Community and its partners from outside South East Asia?

Partnership within ASEAN

ASEAN's partnership principles, enshrined in the Treaty of Amity and Cooperation in Southeast Asia, include equality, non-discrimination and mutual benefit. These principles, which have served the organisation well since its establishment, have guided the member countries in embarking on major initiatives in recent years.

The ASEAN Community has given form and direction to the long-term agenda of regional cooperation, which consists of the three parallel but related areas of security, economic and socio-cultural cooperation. This inclusive and balanced approach aims at addressing the multifaceted opportunities and challenges of regional interdependence.

The ASEAN Security Community seeks to ensure that countries in the region live at peace with one another and with the world in a just, democratic and harmonious environment. The ASEAN Economic Community promotes economic stability and competitiveness through the free flow of goods, services, investment, capital, and greater mobility of professionals and skilled labour. The ASEAN Socio-Cultural Community aims at building a community of caring societies, thereby fostering a regional identity.

ASEAN has painstakingly maintained equality in its decision-making by ensuring a fair balance between the smaller and larger countries in the region. For example, Indonesia, whose population accounts for more than 40 percent of the population of the entire region, has played a constructive and responsible role. In fact, Indonesia has placed its weight and prestige on the international stage at ASEAN's disposal. On the other hand, smaller countries have been responsive or supportive of any decision or position taken by other countries as long as they do not threaten their national interests.

The greater sense of community engendered by the accession of Cambodia, Laos, Myanmar and Vietnam to ASEAN in the 1990s has led to an enhanced sense of shared responsibility in managing regional affairs and in ensuring that regional cooperation is of mutual benefit. ASEAN leaders have adopted a 'prosper thy neighbour' policy not only for economic reasons, but also because it contributes to the building of a regional community.

Vietnam, the first of the newer member countries to have assumed the rotating chairmanship of ASEAN, did not waste time in conveying the message that ASEAN must address the gap in the levels of development between its founding members and the accession countries; special measures are being taken to accelerate their integration into the ASEAN

341

mainstream. In July 2001, the ASEAN foreign ministers issued the Hanoi Declaration on Narrowing the Development Gap. This is binding upon ASEAN to 'devote special efforts and resources to promoting the development of the newer member countries of ASEAN with priority given to infrastructure, human resource development, and information and communications technology'.

In November 2002, the ASEAN leaders approved a six-year plan to reduce the development gap among ASEAN member countries, expedite greater regional economic integration, promote equitable economic development, and help alleviate poverty in its member states. To mobilise resources for the implementation of the plan, the ASEAN Secretariat (based in Jakarta) convened a development cooperation forum which brought together international organisations, donor agencies, industrial economies, private foundations and non-governmental organisations (NGOs).

The ASEAN Free Trade Area (AFTA) is now in place among the six original signatories of the scheme: Brunei Darussalam, Indonesia, Malaysia, Philippines, Singapore and Thailand. As a demonstration of fairness and flexibility, the later member countries have been given the same time frame in which to reduce their tariffs to below five percent. Thus, Vietnam is expected to meet its commitment by 2006, Laos and Myanmar by 2008, and Cambodia by 2010. Moreover, since January 2002, the region has adopted the ASEAN Integration System of Preferences scheme, whereby preferential tariffs are offered to the newer members by the older members on a voluntary and bilateral basis.

The 'prosper thy neighbour' policy is a win–win solution in the attempt to address the uneven levels of economic development among ASEAN's members. Improving the economic situation of poorer members enables them to become business partners for the better developed countries. At the same time, by strengthening economic cohesion and competitiveness within its 10 member countries ASEAN can improve its negotiating position on issues such as market access, technology transfer and foreign investment vis-à-vis the rest of the world. Beyond the manifest material benefits, an improved economic situation will contribute to the overall political stability of the whole region, mitigating issues such as illegal migration.

Partnership beyond ASEAN

To promote economic development in the region, South East Asian countries must attract foreign investment, access the global market and encourage technology transfer from industrial economies. The region, which is of strategic importance and location, is a melting pot of various civilisations. A major part of East Asia and the Pacific Rim, its seas straddle the Indian and Pacific Oceans. All the major powers have a strategic presence in the area in one way or another, with significant interests that need both promoting and protecting. These factors have compelled ASEAN to adopt an open foreign economic policy and active external relations.

The development of external relations was one of the earliest and most active areas of ASEAN cooperation, beginning with an inter-regional cooperation initiative with the then European Economic Community (EEC) in the early 1970s. Today, ASEAN has a robust dialogue partnership with its major trading partners and other states with strategic roles in the region including Australia, Canada, China, the European Union, Japan, India, New Zealand, South Korea, the Russian Federation and the United States. The United Nations Development Programme has also been accorded the same status.

The term 'dialogue partnership' understates the actual depth and scope of activities between ASEAN and its partners. While the regular exchange of views on international political and economic issues occupies an important position in the relationship, it also includes a broad range of activities **343** in the economic, social and cultural spheres. The dialogue partnership is an innovative strategy to promote the collective interests of smaller states in relation to their major partners. At the same time, it offers the major powers a platform from which they can exercise their influence and assume their respective roles in the region. The multilateral nature of the ASEAN Regional Forum and the ASEAN Post-Ministerial Conferences bolsters the establishment of a security community in the broader Asia-Pacific region.

AFTA and other forms of economic cooperation have prepared the groundwork for ASEAN to link up with its major economic partners. The partnership with East Asia has been developing rapidly since the first summit attended by the leaders of ASEAN, China, Japan and the Republic of Korea in 1998. A proposal to establish an East Asian Free Trade Area within an East Asian Community has been articulated. East Asian leaders have agreed that such would be the long-term goal of the ASEAN Plus Three (China, Japan and the Republic of Korea) process. Present framework agreements with China, Japan and India form the basis for common economic spaces with all of these countries that it is hoped will be in place by 2012. The future ASEAN Economic Community is expected to further boost the region's economic confidence and competitiveness.

In a sense, these formal agreements merely ratify what has been happening on the ground. Over the years, intra-East Asian trade has shown increasing growth and interdependence, and is fast approaching 50 percent of the region's total trade. A common economic area in East Asia would bring about a combined market of two billion people or almost a third of humanity, a combined GDP of US$6.3 trillion or almost 20 percent of global GDP in 2002, and a total trade volume of US$2.2 trillion or about 17 percent of global trade in 2001.

Meanwhile, discussions with the EU and the US are proceeding on the Trans-regional EU-ASEAN Trade Initiative and the Enterprise for ASEAN Initiative, which offer the prospect of bilateral free trade agreements with ASEAN member countries over the long term.

Conclusion

ASEAN is aware that community building needs to involve all sectors: public, private and civil society. ASEAN cannot accomplish everything on its own, but it can serve as an enriching catalyst of activities and policies that have a multiplier effect on the ground. ASEAN will remain focus on the promotion of a favourable environment through maintaining regional peace and stability, enhancing economic integration and competitiveness and shaping a common regional identity.

The 'ASEAN way' of partnership and community building through consultations and consensus has served South East Asia well in its external relationship with other countries and regions. The principles of equality, non-discrimination and mutual benefit have been extended to multilateral and inter-regional processes. Global governance in the 21st century should draw upon these same values and principles.

Ong Keng Yong
Ong Keng Yong is Secretary-General of ASEAN (since January 2003). Has held numerous posts in the Singapore Ministry of Foreign Affairs (MFA), which he joined in 1979. Holds degrees from the University of Singapore and Georgetown University.

Olusegun Obasanjo

Nigeria: From Land of Corruption to a Model for Africa

Nigeria is important to Africa. And therefore what happens in Nigeria determines to a large extent what happens in Africa and that's why I feel particular responsibility. I say to Nigerians, God doesn't make mistakes; God looks at our small space of land and has made the people in it dynamic and energetic. He has a purpose: that they should do well for their country and do well for Africa. Our charity in Nigeria must begin at home, but it must never end there. Our charity must extend from Nigeria to West Africa and to the rest of the continent, because indeed, we have a responsibility to the world in which we live.

The story of my country, Nigeria, is fairly well known. Until 1999, corruption was practically institutionalised as the foundation of governance. Societal institutions had decayed to an unprecedented extent as opportunities were privatised by the powerful.

As could be expected, this process was accompanied by the intimidation of the judiciary, the subversion of due process, the manipulation of existing laws and regulations, the suffocation of civil society, and the containment of democratic values and institutions. Power became nothing but a means of accumulation and subversion as productive initiatives were abandoned for purely administrative and transactional activities. The legitimacy and stability of the state became compromised as citizens began to devise extra-legal and informal ways to survive.

The corruption quagmire in Nigeria was rooted in the failure and virtual collapse of governance, the contamination of democratic values, the erosion of accountability procedures and the prevalence of bad leadership. Waning public confidence in the country's political and economic institutions promoted a culture of contempt for the rule of law, leading ultimately – and unfortunately – to a societal tolerance for behaviour previously considered abominable.

Neither today nor in the future can Nigeria afford the social, political or economic costs that systemic corruption has inflicted. Reforms aimed at providing greater transparency and accountability of public institutions and government operations are still urgently needed to redress our circumstances.

Post-1999: laying the foundations for good governance and accountability

When I assumed the presidency in 1999, it was clear that the climate of corruption was one of the primary hindrances to national development. Realising that only a well-designed public sector accountability reform package could improve governance and put Nigeria on the right track, I proclaimed the campaign against corruption as a fundamental mission of the new government.

During the first term of my administration, we established a number of institutional and structural measures that signalled a new attitude to governance. These measures included:

- Open and competitive tender arrangements for government contracts.
- The establishment of a 'due process' mechanism to vet and eliminate excess 'fat' from government contracts.
- Massive anti-corruption campaigns involving all public officials as well as the president.

347

- Public sector reforms to reduce, if not completely eliminate, the opportunity for corruption, especially through the comprehensive monetisation of benefits to public officers.
- A committed focus on privatisation and auctions for government licences, leading, for example, to the liberalisation of the telecommunications sector.
- The establishment of the Independent Corrupt Practices and Other Related Crimes Commission (ICPC) and the Economic and Financial Crimes Commission (EFCC).
- The establishment in the president's office of the Policy and Programmes Monitoring Unit responsible for building a comprehensive policy database, following up all presidential decisions and monitoring programmes in ministries and parastatals.

We hope that these governance reform measures will move Nigeria ever further towards integrity over the next four years. Taking these steps has taken great courage given how institutionalised corruption had become. Laws to deal with corrupt practices already exist – what we have done is to make these laws relevant and enforceable through reforms in the justice system, the police force, prisons, and other related sectors.

So far, we have made considerable headway in introducing policies that are beginning to alter perceptions, attitudes and the ways in which public institutions work. A few examples are given below.

Enforcing anti-corruption laws

The ICPC has to date chalked up a number of successes in the enforcement of existing anti-corruption laws, and the EFCC is pursuing a vigorous campaign to arrest known fraudsters, many of whom are still being held in custody awaiting trial. The leadership of the Commission, working in partnership with the OECD-Financial Action Task Force (FATF), has demonstrated its strong commitment to tackling the financial crime, money laundering and other economic misconducts that have created difficulties for the country in the past.

The ubiquitous scam letters promising shares of proceeds of illicit activities, emanating from fraudulent Nigerians (and other nationals posing as Nigerians) are fast losing their widespread appeal. Through the efforts of the EFCC, tighter controls and enforceable sanctions have been applied in a number of cases, signalling the wholehearted commitment of the government to the containment of the corruption virus.

The work of the ICPC and EFCC is fully complemented by ongoing reforms in the system of justice administration and the police. These range from an anti-corruption campaign, recruitment and training to the provision of equipment, increased wages and allowances, and general improvement in conditions of service. It is my hope that the international community will appreciate and reward our efforts. The truth is that it is much tougher to fight corruption in a developing society than it is in the developed world.

The due process mechanism

Historically, Nigeria's poor transparency image could be ascribed to the manner in which previous governments awarded contracts. We have therefore set up the Budget Monitoring and Price Intelligence Unit (BMPIU) to review, monitor and certify such activity – this has become known as 'due process'. This is a simple mechanism that certifies for public funding only those projects that have passed the test of proper project implementation packaging. Such packaging must have adhered stringently to the international competitive bid approach in the award process. Through the instrument of certification, value for money is once again returning

349

as the fundamental premise for public expenditure. 'Due process' has been reasonably successful: some contracts which contravened the rules have been cancelled and government officials are aware that they can no longer get away with inflating contracts. Nigerians are beginning to realise that corruption is being checked by the government.

Transparency

We are well aware that public perception of opacity in the activities of the dominant oil sector of the economy accentuates the poor governance-of-resources record of government. As a result, we have become a signatory to the Extractive Industries Transparency Initiative (EITI). The administration will seek to encourage the private sector and civil society to check on the exercise of power by government by providing information about its actions, receipts and expenditures in the oil sector.

The privatisation and liberalisation of key economic sectors has been a deliberate action to entrench transparency and accountability, and to build consensus in support of reforms. For example, the sale of government-held equity in cement, petroleum marketing and banking companies in 2000 and 2001 was by open, competitive bidding. The televised auction in 2001 of digital mobile licences, carried out with the technical assistance of consultants from the United Kingdom, was hailed as one of the most transparent licence auctions in the world. The second and third phases of the privatisation and market liberalisation programme have been implemented with the assistance of the World Bank with the same degree of transparency – advertisement of all advisory services being procured, assets and shares being sold, and live televised auctions with national coverage for all divestiture transactions. It is encouraging to note that private companies and parastatals are now following this trend.

At the political level, we have embarked on a number of initiatives designed to complement our anti-corruption drive. From our emphasis on efficiency, civil service reform and service delivery to our campaigns for quality leadership at the local level, democratisation of political parties, empowerment of civil society and the transformation of institutions, we have unleashed a new energy directed at building accountability movements in the country. The local government reform initiated by the government is designed to check disobedience, waste, disorganisation, inefficiency and corruption. Poor performance combined with corruption at the local level destroys our people's faith in democratic governance and contaminates their spirit and enthusiasm for positive leadership. Poor leadership also limits opportunities for social justice tolerance and democratic development. We are currently campaigning to persuade the various state governments to adopt our federal reforms, and new initiatives are also being worked out to consolidate structures of transparency and accountability. Thus, with the reforms being made at federal, state government and local levels, it is my hope that Nigeria will emerge from the pond of despair and corruption to become an island of hope, growth and integrity.

Current challenges in the anti-corruption campaign

We still have a long way to go. The executive branch of government is setting an example, but the legislature and the judiciary must measure up to the same high standards. It is important that the people of Nigeria regain confidence in government as a whole. Moreover, we must face the challenge posed by the fiscal federalism that governs the relationship of the federation, the states and local governments. Due to the autonomy constitutionally accorded states and local governments, the federal government can do no more than exercise moral persuasion to encourage the rest of the federation to embrace transparency and accountability in government operations. This situation is reflected damningly in the general and pervading sense and perception that transparency is a sliding scale: high at the federal level, low at the state level and almost absent at the local level.

With regard to the private sector, successfully weaning companies from the old guarantees of profit from little productivity through failures and distortions in public sector operations and policies is a Herculean task. It will, in the short to medium term, result in social dislocations. However, my administration will remain resilient in promoting only those economic policies (such as privatisation and deregulation) that improve creativity and innovation by value-driven productive private sector initiatives. Such a productive private sector will be able to take advantage of the opportunities offered by a cleaner, more efficient and incentive-structured public sector, and should ultimately develop into a real engine of economic growth. Growth made possible by such a private sector is certainly the antidote to the army of underpaid, unemployed persons who constitute a willing constituency for corruption for reasons of economic survival.

With regard to the media and civil society, including professional bodies and the public at large, they remain cynical. They still suspect that government is suppressing opportunities for synergy, cooperation and collaboration for a united assault on a cancer that everyone acknowledges as a common foe to the development imperatives of our nation. Bridging the gulf between government and civil society tests the interaction skills of all parties involved. We have only just started to let our people know that it pays to celebrate successes rather than focus repeatedly on disappointments, and that everyone must develop the courage, dedication and networks to expose and fight corruption at all times and in all places.

Nigeria needs partners

Nigeria and Nigerians cannot achieve their goals alone. For, in this global war against corruption, no nation can carry on as an island unto itself. The international community must recognise the key role it should play in moving international businesses toward non-corrupt competition for markets and procurement in developing economies by implementing global standards and providing the technical and, where appropriate, the financial support that some of these economies need to adequately respond to those standards.

I note with sadness the involvement of some corporations from the developed world that have, even in recent times, been heavily involved in criminalising our business cultures, compromising our policymakers, contaminating our institutions and subverting due process. International development and financial institutions, and the OECD nations led by the United States should, by their conduct, acknowledge and respond to the politically, economically and socially costly reform measures of reform-minded governments in developing countries through well-structured and optimally designed economic support interventions. They must appreciate the serious political risks we face in fighting corruption and join us in celebrating our gains rather than complicate issues for us. Less rhetoric and more concrete support would help to reinforce anti-corruption reforms in our countries. Waging a global war on corruption is not just an idea engendered by the indefatigable efforts of Transparency International (TI) – it is non-negotiable for the peaceful coexistence of all nations of the world. Clearly, governments in the developed world must outline enforceable sanctions to be imposed on corporations and individuals who become involved in corrupt practices abroad. I am pleased to announce that Nigeria is in the leadership of the UN Convention against Corruption. The signing of the Convention must be hailed by all who have led anti-corruption campaigns within national and extra-national borders.

To conclude, I congratulate TI on the magnificent work it is doing, and I should like to urge it to add further indexes to its already famous classification of corrupt countries. TI should henceforth compile and publicise a complete list of nations that are fighting corruption and outline the measures they are employing. And perhaps even more importantly, TI should publish a list of countries, many of which are in Europe, involved in encouraging corruption and corrupt practices in other nations, and receiving and keeping stolen funds. A further three indexes – a Corruption Encouraging Index, a Corruption Perception Index, and a Corruption Reduction Effort Index – would give an overall picture of the campaign against corruption and corrupt practices nationally and globally. Only such a holistic approach will give us a real-istic picture of the task that we have set for ourselves: a zero corruption-tolerant world.

Adapted from a lecture delivered by Chief Olusegun Obasanjo on the occasion of a 10th anniversary celebration of Trans-parency International, Berlin, 7 November 2003.

Olusegun Obasanjo

Olusegun Obasanjo was born in Abeokuta, Nigeria, in 1937. President of Nigeria since 1999; became Military Ruler in 1976, voluntarily turned over his power to civilian rule in 1979 and subsequently retired from politics. Jailed by the military from 1995 to 1998 and elected president the follow-ing year.

Appendix

The Alfred Herrhausen Society for International Dialogue

Board of Trustees:
Josef Ackermann (Chairman), Frankfurt am Main
Jean-Christophe Ammann, Frankfurt am Main
Sybille Ebert-Schifferer, Rome
Wolfgang Frühwald, Bonn
Detlev Ganten, Berlin
Anthony Giddens, London
Peter Gomez, St. Gallen
Heather Grabbe, London
Tessen von Heydebreck, Frankfurt am Main
Wolfgang Ischinger, Washington D.C.
Jürgen Jeske, Frankfurt am Main
Sergej A. Karaganow, Moscow
Hans Werner Kilz, Munich
Charles A. Kupchan, Washington D.C.
Eckard Minx, Berlin
Jürgen Mlynek, Berlin
Andrej Plesu, Bucharest
Bruce M. Ramer, Los Angeles
Lynn Forester de Rothschild, London
Stephan Sattler, Munich
Christoph Schwöbel, Heidelberg
Haig Simonian, Zurich
America Vera-Zavala, Stockholm
George Weidenfeld, London

Executive Board:
Wolfgang Nowak (Spokesman), Berlin/Frankfurt am Main
Maike Tippmann, Frankfurt am Main
Norbert Walter, Frankfurt am Main

The Alfred Herrhausen Society for International Dialogue analyses the critical issues, the need for reform and trends in international civil society, and initiates debate on proactive and reactive response options. The immense and complex problems confronting today's society are blind to national borders; solutions can be sought only through cross-border dialogue.

The Alfred Herrhausen Society is a centre of independent thinking that seeks to identify traces of the future in the present, and thereby raise public awareness of the directions in which society is moving. As Deutsche Bank's socio-political think tank, the Herrhausen Society brings together people who are committed to working for the future of civil society.